Expressive Arts Interventions for School Counselors

Suzanne Degges-White, PhD, LMHC, LPC, NCC, is professor and chair of the Department of Counseling, Adult and Higher Education at Northern Illinois University in DeKalb, Illinois. She received her master's degree in community counseling and her PhD in counseling and counselor education at the University of North Carolina at Greensboro, where she also earned a graduate certificate in women's studies. She is also a licensed counselor in private practice serving children, adolescents, adults, and couples. Dr. Degges-White's research interests include development over the life span, gender issues in counseling, and the use of creative and innovative techniques in counseling. She has been the recipient of multiple grants and research awards for her work. She has published numerous articles and book chapters addressing emotional and psychological development. Dr. Degges-White is also on the editorial boards of multiple counseling journals, and she is the coeditor of the book *Integrating the Expressive Arts Into Counseling Practice* and the coauthor of *Friends Forever: How Girls and Women Forge Lasting Relationships.*

Bonnie R. Colon, MS, LMHC, NCC, NCSC, is an associate clinical professor in the Counseling and Development program in the Department of Graduate Studies in Education at Purdue University Calumet in Hammond, Indiana. She received her master's degree in counseling at Purdue University Calumet. She is a licensed/certified professional school counselor in both Indiana and Illinois and has 15 years of experience working as a high school counselor. She is postsecondary vice president of the Indiana School Counselor Association and is an active advocate for the profession of school counseling in the state of Indiana.

Expressive Arts Interventions for School Counselors

Suzanne Degges-White, PhD, LMHC, LPC, NCC
Bonnie R. Colon, MS, LMHC, NCC, NCSC

Editors

SPRINGER PUBLISHING COMPANY
NEW YORK

Springer Publishing Company, LLC
11 West 42nd Street
New York, NY 10036
www.springerpub.com

Acquisitions Editor: Nancy S. Hale
Production Editor: Shelby Peak
Composition: Amnet

ISBN: 978-0-8261-2997-0
e-book ISBN: 978-0-8261-2998-7

14 15 16 17 / 5 4 3 2 1

The author and the publisher of this Work have made every effort to use sources believed to be reliable to provide information that is accurate and compatible with the standards generally accepted at the time of publication. The author and publisher shall not be liable for any special, consequential, or exemplary damages resulting, in whole or in part, from the readers' use of, or reliance on, the information contained in this book. The publisher has no responsibility for the persistence or accuracy of URLs for external or third-party Internet websites referred to in this publication and does not guarantee that any content on such websites is, or will remain, accurate or appropriate.

Library of Congress Cataloging-in-Publication Data

Expressive arts interventions for school counselors / Suzanne Degges-White,
  PhD, Bonnie R. Colon, MS, editors.
     pages cm
  Includes bibliographical references.
  ISBN 978-0-8261-2997-0 (print: alk. paper) — ISBN 978-0-8261-2998-7 (e-book) 1. Art therapy for children. 2. Arts—Therapeutic use. 3. School children—Mental health services. 4. Student counselors. I. Degges-White, Suzanne, editor. II. Colon, Bonnie R., editor.
  RJ505.A7E97 2015
  615.8'5156083—dc23
                                                                                    2014029360

Special discounts on bulk quantities of our books are available to corporations, professional associations, pharmaceutical companies, health care organizations, and other qualifying groups. If you are interested in a custom book, including chapters from more than one of our titles, we can provide that service as well.
For details, please contact:
Special Sales Department, Springer Publishing Company, LLC
11 West 42nd Street, 15th Floor, New York, NY 10036-8002
Phone: 877-687-7476 or 212-431-4370; Fax: 212-941-7842
E-mail: sales@springerpub.com

Printed in the United States of America by McNaughton & Gunn.

*We dedicate this book
to all of the counselors who work in the schools,
in honor of the work that you do to serve the youth who are our future.*

Contents

Contributors

Christine Abrahams, EdD, NCC, LPC, ACS
K-12 School Counseling Supervisor
Hopewell Valley Regional School District
Hopewell Valley Central High School
Pennington, New Jersey

Adrienne E. Ahr, MS, LPC-Intern
Counselor/Consultant
EnvisionEd Consulting
Dallas, Texas

Susan R. Barclay, PhD, NCC, ACS, LPC
Assistant Professor
Department of Leadership Studies
College of Education
University of Central Arkansas
Conway, Arkansas

Stephanie C. Bell, MS
Doctoral Candidate
University of Mississippi
Oxford, Mississippi

Sherry A. Bosarge
Art Teacher
J. W. Alvey Elementary School, Prince
    William County Schools
Midland, Virginia

Imelda N. Bratton, PhD, LPCC, RPTS, NCC
School Counseling Program and Clinical
    Coordinator
Co-Director of Talley Family
    Counseling Center

Western Kentucky University
Bowling Green, Kentucky

Laura Bruneau, PhD
Associate Professor
Department of Counselor
    Education
Adams State University
Alamosa, Colorado

Lisa Burton, PhD, NCC, LPC, ALPS
Associate Professor
Graduate School of Education and
    Professional Development
Marshall University
South Charleston, West Virginia

Amanda N. Byrd-Desnoyers, MEd, NCC
Counselor
Trent Lott Academy, Pascagoula School
    District
Biloxi, Mississippi

Montserrat Casado-Kehoe, PhD, LMFT, RPT
Associate Professor
Department of Counseling
    Psychology
Palm Beach Atlantic University
Ocoee, Florida

Tori Charette, MEd, EdS
School Counseling Intern
University of Florida
Gainesville, Florida

Katrina Cook, PhD, LPC-S, LMFT-S, CSC
Assistant Professor
Department of Leadership and
    Counseling
Texas A&M University—San Antonio
San Antonio, Texas

Elizabeth Crawford, MSEd, LSC
School Counselor, Grades K–4
West Branch Local Schools/
    Damascus Elementary and
    Knox Elementary
Beloit, Ohio

Allison Crowe, PhD, LPC, NCC, ACS
Assistant Professor
Counselor Education
East Carolina University
Greensville, North Carolina

Penny Dahlen, EdS, LPC
Core Faculty
Walden University
Denver, Colorado

Neffisatu J. C. Dambo, MS
Doctoral Candidate
University of Central Florida
Orlando, Florida

Kanessa Miller Doss, PhD, NCC
Assistant Professor of Psychology
Troy University
Montgomery, Alabama

Kylie P. Dotson-Blake, PhD, LPC, NCC
Associate Professor
Counselor Education
East Carolina University
Greensville, North Carolina

Diane M. Dryja, MAT El Ed, MEd, NCC
Clinical Assistant Adolescent
    Programming
Psycamore
Flowood, Mississippi

Stephanie E. Eberts, PhD
Assistant Professor
Department of Counseling, Leadership,
    Adult Education and School
    Psychology
Texas State University
San Marcos, Texas

LaWanda Edwards, PhD, ALC, NCC
Associate Professor
Counselor Education
Alabama State University
Montgomery, Alabama

Lori Ellison, PhD, LPC, ALPS
Associate Professor
Department of Counseling
Marshall University
South Charleston, West Virginia

Kelly Emelianchik-Key, PhD, LPC, NCC
Assistant Professor
Counseling Department
Argosy University Atlanta
Atlanta, Georgia

Linda G. English, PhD, LPC
Professor of Counselor Education
Henderson State University
Arkadelphia, Arkansas

Amanda M. Evans, PhD, LPC, NCC
Assistant Professor, Coordinator
    Clinical Mental Health Counseling
    Program
Special Education, Rehabilitation, and
    Counseling
Auburn University
Auburn, Alabama

Kevin A. Fall, PhD, LPC
Professor/Program Coordinator
Department of Counseling,
    Leadership, Adult Education and
    School Psychology
Texas State University
San Marcos, Texas

Trey Fitch, EdD, LMHC
Associate Professor
Division of Counseling, Rehabilitation
    and Interpreter Training
Troy University Panama City
Lynn Haven, Florida

Nancy L. A. Forth, PhD, NCC, LPC
Professor of Counselor Education
Department of Educational
    Leadership and Human
    Development
University of Central Missouri
Warrensburg, Missouri

**Jennifer M. Foster, PhD,
LMHC (FL)**
Professional School Counselor
Assistant Professor
Counselor Education and Counseling
Psychology
Western Michigan University
Kalamazoo, Michigan

Benjamin P. Friedman, MEd
Doctoral Candidate
Columbia University
New York, New York

Erin N. Friedman, BA
Master's Candidate
Northern Illinois University
DeKalb, Illinois

**Magdalena M. Furniss, MA, NCC,
LAC**
Counseling Intern
Rider University
Princeton, New Jersey

Laura L. Gallo
High School Counselor
Linn-Mar High School
Doctoral Candidate
University of Iowa
Cedar Rapids, Iowa

**Marta Garrett, EdD, LPC-S, LMFT-S,
RPT-S, CCMHC, ACS**
Associate Professor of Counseling
Director of Graduate Counseling Program
University of Mary Hardin-Baylor
Belton, Texas

**Michael T. Garrett, PhD, GAPSC,
NCLSC**
Professor of Counselor Education and
College Student Affairs
Department of Clinical and Professional
Studies
University of West Georgia
Carrollton, Georgia

Joseph Graham, MA, RMHCI
Doctoral Candidate
University of Central Florida
Orlando, Florida

Jennifer H. Greene, EdS
Doctoral Candidate
University of Central Florida
Winter Park, Florida

Cynthia B. Greer, PhD
Associate Professor of Counseling/
Education
Director of the MEd Curriculum and
Instruction, Educating for Change
Program
Trinity Washington University
Washington, DC

Lindsey B. Guidry
Master's Candidate
University of Louisiana at Lafayette
Lafayette, Louisiana

Shannon Halligan, L-CAT
Private Practice
Rochester, New York

Elizabeth Hancock MS, CRC
Doctoral Candidate
Auburn University
Auburn, Alabama

Lauren R. Hasha, MS
Counseling Intern
University of Louisiana at Lafayette
Lafayette, Louisiana

**Sherrionda Heard-Crawford, PhD,
LPC**
School Counselor
Opelika City Schools
Opelika, Alabama

Bridget Tuohy Helms, MSEd, LSC
School Counselor
Hanover Community School Corporation,
Jane Ball Elementary School
Cedar Lake, Indiana

Anne Stuart Henry, MEd
Professional School Counselor
J. W. Alvey Elementary School, Prince
William County Schools
Manassas, Virginia

Katherine M. Hermann, PhD
Assistant Professor
University of Louisiana at Lafayette
Lafayette, Louisiana

Marco Hernandez, MS
Clinical Practitioner III
The Center for Health Care Services—
    Integrated Care Team
San Antonio, Texas

Rebeca Hernandez, BA
Bilingual Kindergarten Teacher
Northside Independent School District—
    Fisher Elementary
San Antonio, Texas

Tamara J. Hinojosa, PhD
Assistant Professor
Department of Leadership and
    Counseling
Texas A&M University—San Antonio
San Antonio, Texas

Allison Hrovat, MEd
Doctoral Candidate and Adjunct
    Instructor
Syracuse University
Syracuse, New York

James R. Huber, PhD, LMFT
Associate Professor of Psychology
Holy Family University
Newtown, Pennsylvania

**Edward F. Hudspeth, PhD, NCC, LPC,
    RPh, RPT-S, ACS**
Assistant Professor of Counselor
    Education
Henderson State University
Arkadelphia, Arkansas

Marie Bonner Huron, MA
Doctoral Candidate
Human Development Counseling
    Department
University of Illinois at Springfield
Springfield, Illinois

Glenda L. Hyer, EdD
Assistant Professor of Special
    Education
Henderson State University
Arkadelphia, Arkansas

Eric Jett, NCC, LPC
Counselor
Eric Jett, LLC
Tulsa, Oklahoma

Lenore Katz, MEd, LPC
Professional School Counselor
Clarke Central High School
Athens, Georgia

**Michael A. Keim, PhD, NCC,
    NCLSC**
Assistant Professor
Counselor Education and College
    Student Affairs
University of West Georgia
Carrollton, Georgia

Sarah O. Kitchens, MS
Doctoral Candidate
Auburn University
Auburn, Alabama

Sarah LaFont
Master's Candidate
Clinical Mental Health Counseling
University of Montana, Missoula
Missoula, Montana

Saron N. LaMothe, MS
Doctoral Candidate
Education—Counselor Education
University of Central Florida
Orlando, Florida

Christopher Lawrence, PhD
Assistant Professor
Northern Kentucky University
Highland Heights, Kentucky

Karen L. Lee, MA
Clinical Instructor
Human Development Counseling
    Department
University of Illinois at Springfield
Springfield, Illinois

**Elsa Soto Leggett, PhD, LPC-S,
    RPT-S, CSC**
Counselor Education Program
    Coordinator
Associate Professor in Counseling
University of Houston-Victoria at
    Sugar Land
Sugar Land, Texas

Jonathan Lent, PhD, NCC, PC, LSC
Assistant Professor
Graduate School of Education and
    Professional Development
Marshall University
Huntington, West Virginia

Sandra Logan, MS, CSC
Doctoral Fellow and Instructor
University of Florida
Gainesville, Florida

Melissa Luke, PhD
Associate Professor
Counseling and Human Services
    Department
Syracuse University
Syracuse, New York

**Hennessey Lustica, MS, CAS,
    MHC-LP**
Doctoral Candidate
Counselor Education and
    Supervision
Warner School of Education
University of Rochester
Rochester, New York

**Laurel Malloy, MEd, LPC,
    CSC**
Counselor
John Paul Stevens High School,
    Northside ISD
San Antonio, Texas

**Suneetha B. Manyam, PhD,
    LPC, NCC**
Associate Professor
Department of Counseling and Human
    Sciences
Mercer University
College of Continuing and Professional
    Studies
Atlanta, Georgia

**Jennifer L. Marshall, EdD,
    LMHC**
Associate Professor
Division of Counseling, Rehabilitation
    and Interpreter Training
Troy University Panama City
Lynn Haven, Florida

**Mary G. Mayorga, PhD, LPC-S, NCC,
    CCDS, CART**
Assistant Professor
Educational Leadership and Guidance
    Counseling Department
Texas A&M University—San Antonio
San Antonio, Texas

Clare Merlin, MEd, NCC
Doctoral Candidate
Counselor Education
The College of William & Mary
Williamsburg, Virginia

Tony Michael, MA, LPC, ACS, RPT
Assistant Professor
Department of Counseling and
    Psychology
Tennessee Tech University
Cookeville, Tennessee

Rebecca E. Michel, PhD, LCPC
Assistant Professor
Counseling
Governors State University
University Park, Illinois

Rochelle Moss, PhD, LPC
Associate Professor of Counselor
    Education
Henderson State University
Arkadelphia, Arkansas

**Suzanne D. Mudge, PhD, LPC-S,
    NCC, NCSC**
Associate Professor, Program
    Coordinator, Counseling and
    Guidance
Texas A&M University—San Antonio
San Antonio, Texas

**Charles E. Myers, PhD, LCPC, NCC,
    NCSC, ACS, RPT-S**
Assistant Professor
Department of Counseling, Adult and
    Higher Education
Northern Illinois University
DeKalb, Illinois

Lindsey M. Nichols, PhD, NCC
Assistant Professor
Department of Counselor Education
University of Montana
Missoula, Montana

Michael Paz, MS, CSC, LPC-Intern
School Counselor
Hackberry Elementary School
Little Elm, Texas

Michelle Perepiczka, PhD, LMHC, CSC, RPTS, NCC
Core Faculty
Social Work and Human Services
Walden University
New York, New York

Jake J. Protivnak, PhD, PCC-S, LSC
Department Chair, Associate Professor
Department of Counseling, Special Education and School Psychology
Youngstown State University
Youngstown, Ohio

Nicole M. Randick, MA, ATR-BC, LPC, NCC
Adjunct Faculty
Psychology
Governors State University
University Park, Illinois

Dee C. Ray, PhD, LPC-S, NCC, RPT-S
Professor, Counseling Program
Director, Child and Family Resource Clinic
University of North Texas
Denton, Texas

Lacey Ricks, PhD
Columbus State University
Columbus, Georgia

Ajita M. Robinson, MA, NCC, LCPC
Clinical Instructor in Education Specialties
Loyola University, Maryland
Bethesda, Maryland

Evelyn Esther Robinson, MA
Graduate
Trinity Washington University
Washington, DC

Hewitt B. Rogers, MEd, NCC
Mental Health Counselor
Child Advocacy and Play Therapy Institute
University of Mississippi
Oxford, Mississippi

Varunee Faii Sangganjanavanich, PhD, LPCC-S, NCC
Associate Professor, Coordinator,
Counselor Education and Supervision (PhD) Program
University of Akron
Akron, Ohio

Corie Schoeneberg, EdS, LPC, NCC, RPT-S
Adjunct Faculty
University of Central Missouri
Warrensburg, Missouri

Lisa L. Schulz, PhD, LPC-S, LPSC, NCC
Clinical Assistant Professor
Counseling and Higher Education
University of North Texas
Denton, Texas

Brandy Schumann, PhD, LPC-S, RPT-S, NCC
Clinical Assistant Professor
Department of Dispute Resolution and Counseling
Southern Methodist University
Plano, Texas

Alicia H. Schwenk, MS
Former Professional School Counselor
J.W. Alvey Elementary School, Prince William County Schools
Burke, Virginia

Atsuko Seto, PhD, NCC, LPC
Associate Professor
The College of New Jersey
Ewing, New Jersey

Genevieve Shaw, BFA
Art Teacher
Piney Branch Elementary School, Prince William County Schools
Bristow, Virginia

Diane J. Shea, PhD, LPC, NCP
Assistant Professor
Graduate Program in Counseling Psychology
Holy Family University
Newtown, Pennsylvania

Megyn Shea, PhD
Assistant Professor
School Counseling
New York Institute of Technology
New York, New York

Michelle Kelley Shuler, PhD, LPC-S, LADC-S
Assistant Professor, Program Chair
  Masters in Addiction Counseling
Northeastern State University
Tahlequah, Oklahoma

Amanda N. Siemsen
Master's Candidate
Department of Counseling, Adult and
  Higher Education
Northern Illinois University
DeKalb, Illinois

Atiya R. Smith, MS, LCPC
Doctoral Candidate
Counselor Education and Supervision
Warner School of Education
University of Rochester
Rochester, New York

Carol M. Smith, PhD
Associate Professor of Counseling
Marshall University
South Charleston, West Virginia

Kevin B. Stoltz, PhD, NCC, ACS, LPC
Associate Professor, Leadership Studies
  College of Education
University of Central Arkansas
Conway, Arkansas

Stefi Threadgill, MS
Master's Candidate
Southern Methodist University
Plano, Texas

Jenny Wagstaff, MS, LPC
Assistant Director, Campus Alcohol
  Abuse Prevention Center
Virginia Tech
Blacksburg, Virginia

Laura S. Wheat, PhD, LPC, NCC
Assistant Professor, School Counseling
  Program Coordinator
Department of Counselor Education,
  Leadership and Research
Georgia Regents University
Augusta, Georgia

Peggy P. Whiting, EdD, LPC-S
Licensed NC K–12 School Counselor
CT Professor and Program Coordinator,
  Counselor Education
North Carolina Central University
Durham, North Carolina

Barb Wilson, PhD, LPC, NCC
Middle School Counselor
West Hall Middle School
Oakwood, Georgia

Gaelynn P. Wolf Bordonaro, PhD, ATR-BC
Director, Graduate Art Therapy Program
Department of Counselor Education
Emporia State University
Emporia, Kansas

Jennifer Rhodes Wood, BA
Artistic Director/Dance Instructor
Studio E3 Dance
Hernando, Mississippi

Jacqueline J. Young, MS, LPC-Intern
Applied Behavioral Interventionist
Concept Connections
Fort Worth, Texas

Preface

Students today are perhaps the most demanding "customers" that school counselors have ever faced. The vast majority of students have grown up in homes filled with technology and on-demand entertainment. Televisions are now personal theaters that can be programmed to offer viewers whatever genre they prefer, as many times as they like, until they are satiated. Smartphones in every hand mean instant connection via text, e-mail, FaceTime, or the old standby, voice-to-voice means. We can rewind, fast forward, or "slo-mo" our lives and still stay connected with our friends and family networks, although we may be losing connection with our own selves. The increasingly short attention span of our youth is progressively more difficult to hold in the classroom and in the counseling office. Thus, we have collected over 100 interventions that invite your student clients to take a break, take a breath, and gain a new take on their lives.

We hope this book will provide useful information that will allow school counselors to stretch themselves and grow their confidence as they integrate these expressive arts interventions into their work with students.

THE SCOPE OF THIS BOOK

This book provides a wealth of contemporary and engaging interventions across multiple modalities. The book opens with a chapter addressing the value of the expressive arts as a conduit to personal growth and development. Also addressed is the integration of the arts into the school counseling milieu. The following six sections of the book each focus on a separate form of the expressive modalities. Within each section, we present the interventions based on the American School Counselor Association (ASCA) model domains: academic, career, and personal/social. The modalities that we include are the visual arts, music, movement and dance, expressive writing/poetry, drama, and a final section incorporating other modes of creative expression. The book closes with a chart that presents the various types of concerns for which students typically need assistance (such as grief and loss, self-esteem, social skills, etc.) and the interventions that may be most effective in addressing these issues.

In addition to providing the basic information necessary to put each intervention into practice, we have also included two additional areas of information.

The first addresses the suggested modifications for special populations—a brief description is provided for alterations that might be made to accommodate diverse student groups. Second, we provide suggestions for evaluating the effectiveness of each intervention. This may include suggestions for relevant check-ins down the road or the use of included pre- and postintervention assessments.

Who Would Benefit From This Book?

While this book's primary audience is school counselors or students pursuing a degree in school counseling, it is an excellent resource for anyone working with school-aged youth, including teachers, after-school program leaders, and community counselors. Although the focus of the book is geared toward school personnel, it is an excellent resource for anyone who would like to add variety and expressive activities to his or her work with youth.

Overall Value of This Book

Typically, books addressing the expressive arts are written for a specific modality, such as "Drama Therapy," "Music Therapy," and so on. This book provides a wider variety of modalities as well as easy-to-follow step-by-step instructions for each intervention. We chose to present a wide range of activities addressing a wide range of presenting issues. With over 100 interventions, we have covered a great deal of ground, but each intervention is complete in itself. There are plenty of options available based on your preferred modality—whether you are choosing an activity that is located on familiar ground or whether you are stretching yourself to try something new. There is a great deal of creative effort in the contributions to this book, and we hope that readers enjoy integrating these activities into their professional practice to provide students with creative outlets that unplug them from technology long enough to plug into their own inner worlds.

I ✷ Laying the Foundation

1 Introduction

OVERVIEW OF THE EXPRESSIVE ARTS

The use of expressive arts as a healing modality has been around for thousands of years. The arts are the language through which history and healing are transferred from person to person and culture to culture. There are cave drawings, hieroglyphics, and native dances that tell the story of a people and provide a sense of connection. We are born to express ourselves through creative outlets. In fact, singing, dancing, using crayons on paper, and play-acting as adults are all pastimes that children naturally explore, if given the freedom to do so.

Not only are the expressive arts a natural fit for youth and adults alike; they are also a passageway from the everyday to the realm of possibility. They provide infinite perspectives on how things might be in our lives—some more realistic than others. However, only when our clients begin to imagine a world different than their current state is it possible for change to take root. Until we have envisioned a different future, we cannot construct one. In addition, it is in the process, not the processing, of a client's creative expression that change and growth will occur. However, for each intervention in this book, we have provided suggestions for evaluating its effectiveness. This is for the satisfaction of the school counseling assessment needs, not for the evaluation of the client's expressive arts creations.

In relation to the evaluation suggestions, we also acknowledge that these interventions are designed to be extensions of the therapeutic work that is done by the school counselor. Each counselor must discover and refine the therapeutic practice that works best for him or her. We are merely providing creative additions to the work in which a counselor is currently engaged.

CREATIVE ARTS MODALITIES

The expressive arts encompass a wide variety of creative productivity. They provide a means through which we are able to express ourselves in ways that often go beyond where counselor–client dialogue can allow us. Multilayered self-discovery and the outward expression of the inner world are possible through the arts that talk therapy may not spawn. A brief overview of the modalities included in this book are described here to provide you with a basic foundation for understanding their origin, their use, and the organizations that support them. As with similar works, the purpose of this volume is to explore these modalities in depth. We are providing information to raise your awareness of the variety of expressive arts formats that may be used adjunctively within your existing practice. Each of the separate interventions included in this book includes clear instructions for successful implementation.

Visual Arts

The field of *visual arts* encompasses many forms of art making as well as the use of existing artistic work to allow clients to creatively express themselves without the need for verbal dialogue. One of the earliest pioneers in the use of art therapy was Margaret Naumburg, who introduced art into psychotherapy in the 1940s (Naumburg, 1950). Naumburg's success led art therapy to be included as a customary component of mental health care in treatment centers. The therapists who followed her lead were generally psychiatrists or art teachers who entered the mental health field. Today, art therapy is a highly specialized area of therapeutic practice and healing and there are numerous degree programs in art therapy, but there are ways in which nonspecialized clinicians can infuse art therapy experiences into their practices. The professional association for art therapy is the American Art Therapy Association (www.arttherapy.org).

Music Therapy

Music therapy first found its way into mental health care on a large scale in part due to the care of veterans being treated in the veterans' hospitals for war injuries (Wigram, Pedersen, & Bonde, 2002). Musicians, who were volunteers, played to entertain the infirm, but their musical gifts were found to provide curative effects for the patients. It was noted that four areas of functioning are understood to be improved through music therapy—physical, cognitive, psychological, and social functioning. Music therapy can incorporate a variety of different activities, from original composition to being led in specific activities by the therapist. As for most expressive arts therapy disciplines, there is a specific training program for those interested in being recognized as a licensed practitioner. However, school counselors are encouraged to incorporate aspects of music therapy into their work with students. The professional association for music therapy is the American Music Therapy Association (www.musictherapy.org).

Movement and Dance Therapy

In the early 1940s, in addition to art and music as therapeutic modalities, dance and movement were also developed into modes of therapeutic experience (Malchiodi, 2005). In fact, it was the modern dance movement and its spontaneous and highly expressive form of movement that provided dancers with a freeing, health-promoting experience. Then, Marian Chace, a choreographer of modern dance, introduced this form of freeing self-expression to psychiatric patients who responded favorably. It is perceived that the integration of the mind and body occur during dance and movement and it is this synchronization that provides the salubrious benefits. It is believed that therapeutic movement and dance provide a means by which complex feelings can be processed safely and effectively. The professional association for dance and movement therapy is the American Dance Therapy Association (www.adta.org).

Expressive Writing/Poetry Therapy

Many individuals find writing out their feelings—either in prose or poetry—to be safer and more easily accomplished than speaking the words aloud. Thus, the integration of narrative expression via the written word can be an excellent modality for giving students a chance to explore their inner worlds. In essence, expressive writing provides a safe way to work toward healing and coping with psychological distress. Often, therapists will provide clients with specific writing prompts, and the use of this modality, due to its inherent safety and freedom to explore, has been found to be effective in diverse settings (Baikie & Wilhelm, 2005). Whether clients are working through expected developmental events such as dealing with new schools, family transitions, or grief and loss, or working through environmental and cultural events (cataclysmic weather events, tragedies, etc.) or health and safety concerns, expressive writing has been found to be healing to clients. Beyond expressive narrative writing, poetry therapy and bibliotherapy are also beneficial to clients through the use of the written word, although these may include "prescribed reading" of works that address the issues being faced by clients. The professional association for poetry therapy is the National Association for Poetry Therapy (www.poetrytherapy.org).

Drama Therapy

In the early 1900s, Jacob Moreno pioneered the implementation of the healing properties of drama and self-expression in therapeutic settings in the form of group therapy. This medium of *drama therapy* is powerful and provides a highly experiential medium of expression. In this mode of therapy, drama therapists direct the action between clients and provide a safe space in which exploration of feelings, behaviors, and thoughts may actively take place. Clients are often encouraged to play out the parts of themselves that they typically inhibit or censor. Dramatic interventions include a wide variety of activities, including storytelling, improvisation, puppetry, enactment, and role play of significant events. The professional association for drama therapy is the National Association for Drama Therapy (http://www.nadt.org).

THE CHALLENGES OF SCHOOL COUNSELING

The roles and responsibilities of professional school counselors have undergone many changes since the profession's humble beginnings in the late 19th century. Shifts in the sociopolitical, economic, and educational climate are contributing

factors to these changes. Many of the challenges faced by today's school counselors would not even have been conceivable a generation ago. Schools today
have increasingly diverse student populations with a wide range of multifaceted
needs. Advancements in technology and virtually omnipresent access to media
in schools, homes, and businesses have created a society that demands constant entertainment and immediate gratification. Education reform has raised
accountability standards for school counselors while, at the same time, student-
to-counselor ratios in our schools have significantly increased. If they are to
effectively meet these challenges and provide a comprehensive school counseling program that addresses the needs of all students, school counselors need to
have innovative strategies and interventions available on their school counseling
"tool belts." Interventions should capture students' attention, impact them positively, and allow efficient use of time and resources. The expressive arts interventions that we have included in this book provide such innovative strategies
and interventions and also fit well within a comprehensive school counseling
program.

The ASCA National Standards for Students

In 1997, the American School Counselor Association (ASCA) first published the
ASCA National Standards for School Counseling Programs. This was one of the
first steps in providing definition and clarity to the role of the school counselor.
Since that time, the ASCA National Standards for Students and the ASCA National
Model have been developed to provide guidance and structure in the development
of comprehensive school counseling programs. Both have been revised several
times. The most current revision of the ASCA National Standards for Students
was completed in 2004 and can be found on the ASCA website at www.school-
counselor.org. According to *The ASCA National Standards for Students—One
Vision, One Voice* (American School Counselor Association, 2004), "The ASCA
National Standards identify and prioritize the specific attitudes, knowledge, and
skills that students should be able to demonstrate as a result of participating in a
school counseling program." The described attitudes, knowledge, and skills fall
into three domains: Academic Development, Career Development, and Personal/
Social Development. School counselors utilize these standards in setting goals
for working with their students in each of these domains and many of these standards can be addressed through expressive arts interventions.

Academic Development

School counselors can utilize expressive arts interventions to assist students in
meeting the standards in the academic domain. Students find expressive arts
engaging and more eagerly participate in and learn from such activities. Since
expressive arts appeal to different learning styles, such activities lend themselves well to differentiated instruction. Auditory learners can benefit from
interventions using music or poetry. Drawing, painting, or graphic design interventions will engage visual learners and drama, movement, and dance appeal to

kinesthetic learners. Students will find classroom guidance lessons that incorporate expressive arts to be more meaningful and memorable and, thus, may become more engaged and motivated in their academics.

Career Development

Expressive arts interventions can also be used in working with students in the career domain. Through the use of creative activities students can explore their interests, skills, and values to assist them in identifying potential occupations and career paths and set goals for meeting them. The opportunity to imagine a "future me" through an expressive arts intervention can have a powerful impact on a student's ability and desire to set goals and work toward that future vision.

Personal/Social Development

The use of expressive arts techniques is "natural" in facilitating student development within the personal/social domain standards. Engagement with the arts allows students to explore and understand more about themselves, their world, and those around them, thus making it possible for them to more successfully navigate through personal issues and negotiate social relationships. Since the arts transcend gender, race, religion, socioeconomic status, and other differences, they encourage the development of connections among groups of students. Working together on shared art projects and activities can improve interpersonal communication skills and promote community building.

Addressing the ASCA National Student Standards and meeting the counseling goals of enhancing student competencies in self-awareness, self-confidence, self-expression, communication, cooperation, problem solving, decision making, and so on, can all be met through the use of expressive arts interventions. Each of the interventions in this book indicates the domain standards it best addresses. However, many of the interventions can be modified or adapted to fit more than one domain. The arts provide freedom to imagine, create, experience new roles, and gain new perspectives across multiple behavioral and developmental facets. As students grow in one area, they will typically evolve across multiple areas of functioning.

The ASCA National Model

As its title states, *The ASCA National Model: A Framework for School Counseling Programs* (American School Counselor Association, 2012) provides school counselors with a framework around which to develop a comprehensive school counseling program. The Model was most recently revised in 2012 and is available on the ASCA website at www.schoolcounselor.org. The framework consists of four components: foundation, management, delivery, and accountability.

The foundation component includes The ASCA National Standards for Students. As mentioned earlier, the use of expressive arts interventions can help support and strengthen the student competencies or standards that make up the foundation of the school counseling program. The management component consists of organizational assessments and tools that help the school counselor in defining, planning for, and assessing the effectiveness of program activities. Expressive arts interventions can be incorporated into the curriculum, small group, and closing-the-gap action plans that are part of this component.

Included in the delivery component are direct student services. These services include the school counseling core curriculum, consisting of structured lesson plans that are designed to help students attain the attitudes, knowledge, and skills appropriate to their developmental level. According to Graves (1996), a curriculum that is well designed engages students through active learning, a process that involves both *action* and *reflection*. *Action* occurs through directly interacting with "people, materials, events, and ideas" (p. 4) and *reflection* occurs when students are asked to construct knowledge about those interaction experiences in a way that is relevant and meaningful. Since expressive arts activities involve both *action* and *reflection,* their inclusion in the school counseling core curriculum is both logical and appropriate. The other direct services in the delivery component are individual student planning, which includes activities to assist students in developing and meeting goals, and responsive services, which are activities to meet the immediate needs of students and include individual, small-group, and crisis counseling. Expressive arts interventions naturally fall into this component and these are the activities through which such techniques are most apt to be utilized by school counselors.

With the final component, accountability, the evaluation of interventions and the collection of data are addressed. Currently school counselors, like all educators, are being held accountable for demonstrating the effectiveness of their student interventions through evaluation and the use of analytic data. To that purpose, each of the interventions in this book includes an evaluation plan for assessing its effectiveness of use with students.

School counselors today are faced with many challenges and demands on their time. Building a comprehensive school counseling program that meets the developmental needs of all students requires knowledge, skills, and a variety of innovative counseling tools and techniques. The use of creative interventions by school counselors can help to establish an environment in which students are engaged and can explore and express themselves in new and exciting ways. Expressive arts techniques can enhance the development of student competencies and increase the overall effectiveness of the school counselor. Since artistic activities can assist students in identifying thoughts and feelings more accurately and quickly than "talk" therapy, expressive arts are a more efficient use of time.

In summary, we believe that the introduction of the expressive arts into your school counseling program will allow you to grow as a counselor and your clients to grow as individuals. During most of our education programs, we were instructed to "trust the process" as we developed personally and professionally. Integrating the expressive arts into your work will also require that you "trust the process" and will benefit your students. By allowing your students to experience immersion into the creative process, you are encouraging them to grow and develop in a way that didactic or directive instruction cannot provide. Students may spend the majority of the school day in a structured setting with little opportunity to think outside the box, but the interventions within this book will invite students to try out new behaviors, new ideas, and new perspectives through the creative process. Trust the process and enjoy the positive developments you yourself experience as you find new ways to integrate the expressive arts into your work.

REFERENCES

American School Counselor Association. (2004). *ASCA national standards for students*. Alexandria, VA: Author.

American School Counselor Association. (2012). *The ASCA national model: A framework for school counseling programs* (3rd ed.). Alexandria, VA: Author.

Baikie, K. A., & Wilhem, K. (2005). Emotional and physical health benefits of expressive writing. *Advances in Psychiatric Treatment, 11*, 338–346.

Bruneau, L., & Protivnak, J. J. (2012). Adding to the toolbox: Using creative interventions with high school students. *Journal of School Counseling, 10*(9). Retrieved from http://www.jsc.montana.edu/articles/v10n19.pdf

Graves, M. (1996). *Planning around children's interests: The teacher's idea book 2*. Ypsilanti, MI: High/Scope Press.

Horowitz, S. (2000). Healing in motion: Dance therapy meets diverse needs. *Alternative and Complementary Therapies, 6*, 72–76.

Knill, P., Barba, H., & Fuchs, M. (2004). *Minstrels of the soul: Intermodal expressive therapy* (2nd ed.). Toronto, ON: EGS Press.

Malchiodi, C. A. (2005). *Expressive therapies*. New York, NY: Guilford Press.

Naumburg, M. (1950). *An introduction to art therapy: Studies of the "free" art expression of behavior problems of children and adolescents as a means of diagnosis and therapy*. New York, NY: Teachers College Press.

Wigram, T., Pedersen, I. N., & Bonde, L. O. (2002). *A comprehensive guide to music therapy: Theory, clinical practice, research and training*. London, UK: Jessica Kingsley Publishers.

II ❖ Visual Arts

2 Visual Arts Interventions in the Academic Domain

CREATING A VISION (BOARD) WITH YOUR STUDENTS

Lisa Burton and Jonathan Lent

This intervention is designed to be utilized in individual, small-group, or large-group guidance. The use of vision boards can help students set and visualize goals. In addition, it provides a visual representation for the student of his or her goals that can be kept as a daily reminder.

Modality: Visual Creative Intervention and Expressive Arts

ASCA National Model Domain: Academic, Personal/Social, and Career, depending on focus of the lesson

Deliver via: Individual, group, or classroom guidance

Age Level: Upper elementary, middle, and high school

Indications: This is a flexible intervention that can be used in a variety of ways with students in any school setting. It can be used in individual counseling, small-group counseling, or in large-group guidance, which all meet the competencies of the American School Counselor Association (ASCA) National Model. This could be used for short-term/immediate goals or long-term life goals. This intervention could be used with students in transitional periods (5th graders moving on to 6th grade, 8th graders moving on to 9th grade, or seniors who are graduating). This could be an activity used to help these students create a vision for the transition and for their future.

In addition, the vision board can help with many different situations or issues students must deal with in today's world. Students today are facing a number of challenges and difficult situations: trust, divorce, academic concerns, gender-identity issues, social issues, depression, anxiety, and behavior concerns.

Furthermore, the vision board can be used at different times in a counseling relationship. If you are having difficulty connecting with a student, this can be a great opening activity that will open the lines of communication.

However, it could also be used at the end of a counseling relationship to remind the student of all the progress that has been made and allow the student to keep the goals visible when counseling either comes to a close or a student moves to another school.

Materials: Some type of "canvas" for creating the board, a variety of magazines, glue/glitter glue or tacks, Mod Podge, markers, scissors, and, if possible, Internet access along with a printer (for printing specific images from online). Since creativity and individualized visions are big parts of this process, remember that the "canvas" can be anything. You may choose to use blank masks, construction paper, scrapbook paper, folders, poster board, terra cotta flowerpots, different-shaped foam boards, sheet protectors to place in binders, covers of journal books, cork boards, coffee cans, and actual canvases.

Preparation: The first step in creating any vision board is to envision goals and decide whether the purpose of the vision board is to identify immediate or long-term goals or both. For short-term goals, students could set goals to include friends, school, fun, or family. For long-term goals, students may focus on areas such as career, family, accomplishments, where he or she will live, wants, or values. Begin by asking the student to list several goals that she or he has for her or his life on a blank sheet of paper. In some cases, the student may have little difficulty identifying goals. In other cases, the student may have unclear or no goals that can be identified right away. In order to help with the process of identifying goals, ask open-ended questions focusing on the areas mentioned previously. These questions might sound similar to the following: *Where would you live? Who would you help? Where would you work? What do you value?* After goals have been identified, assist the student in choosing which goals will be the focus of the vision board.

Instructions:

1. The first step, once the goals have been identified, is to begin work on the vision board. With the materials ready, describe to the student that he or she should look for images or words that represent goals that have been identified. This may take more than one meeting with the student. Remember, it is the student who chooses what goes on the vision board.

2. Once all of the images or words are identified, the student may begin cutting out the images and placing them in a creative, meaningful arrangement on the canvas. Since creativity and individualized visions are a big part of this process, remember that the "canvas" can be anything.

   In addition, there are also applications that can be used with your computer or a smartphone that will allow the student to create a virtual vision board. Students may also choose to use markers to write or draw images or words that represent goals that they were unable to find representation for. During this process, provide encouragement to your student. It is important that the student is allowed enough time to complete the arrangement on the canvas and not feel rushed. This may occur over several meetings.

3. When the student finishes the vision board it is good to have him or her share it with you. This allows you to visually see what the student wants out of life. In order for the vision board to work, the student must understand that he or she needs to focus on what is included on the board. The more the student immerses him- or herself into the board, the more it will work. It becomes a visual reminder of the student's goals and can be changed as he or she grows and evolves. During this process, you can ask questions about the board to help clarify any areas. In addition, you may prompt students to actively think about and discuss each area on the vision board.

4. The last step is important because you must take time to explain the purpose of the vision board and how it is to be used. Students must decide where to keep the vision board (e.g., home, school, their binder, their locker, or their smartphone if completed using an electronic application). It is important to emphasize that they should keep it in a prominent place so that they will see it daily. Daily viewing of the words and images will unconsciously help them to make choices throughout the day that are consistent with the goals listed. A nice way to end the session is to have the student sign and date the back of the board.

Suggested Modifications (for Special Needs Populations): This intervention does not need many modifications for special needs populations; however, you may need to spend more time explaining goals or working more closely on what or how the student creates the vision board.

Evaluation Plan: The evaluation plan for this type of intervention would be to periodically check back with the student to discuss progress made on the desired goals depicted on the vision board. Sometimes visions change; therefore, the board may need to be updated.

FOUR DIRECTIONS

Michael T. Garrett and Michael A. Keim

*M*any cultures throughout the world have some representation of the circle as a symbol reminding us of the interrelationship we share with other living beings and with our surroundings. For Native peoples, the image of concentric circles that move outward from the self is important, much like the rippling effect of still water that had a stone dropped in it. Circles of life energy surround us, exist within us, and make up the many relationships of our existence. In all, we each have a circle of self, comprised of the many facets of our own development (e.g., heart, natural surroundings, body, and mind); a circle of immediate family, extended family, tribal family, community, and

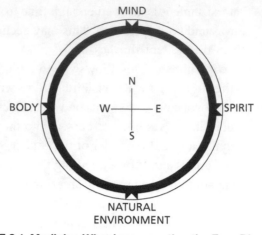

FIGURE 2.1 Medicine Wheel representing the Four Directions.

nation; a circle consisting of all our relations in the natural environment; and a circle of our universal surroundings. As we honor the power of the circle, we can also honor the power of the Greater Circle by drawing on age-old traditions of peoples who view coming together in the circle as a very special event in any context. One such people, Native people, across nations, look to some representation of the Four Winds or Four Directions for guidance, clarity, wisdom, and strength.

As a symbol of this great circle, the Medicine Wheel is a traditional Native American symbol emphasizing the cyclical nature of the world and the self, both of which are composed of four basic dimensions represented by the Four Directions—east, south, west, and north. Each Direction represents one aspect of life or the living being; all of the directions together are necessary for a harmonious and functional way of life. The cyclical nature of world and self are only possible given harmony and balance among the Four Directions— heart, natural environment, body, and mind—symbolizing the four points on a circle or the four cardinal directions of east, south, west, and north, respectively (although this varies from tribe to tribe). The Medicine Wheel shows the relationship of each aspect of life to the greater whole; it also shows the interrelation of all dimensions within the living being.

This activity supports goals that are noted in the Four Winds Development Project (1989). These include the following: (a) increase self-esteem represented by how one feels about oneself and one's ability to grow and change; (b) increase self-determination represented by one's ability to use one's volition (will) to explore and develop potentials; (c) increase body awareness represented in how one experiences one's physical presence; and (d) enhance positive self-concept represented by what one thinks about oneself and one's potentials (Four Worlds Development Project, 1989).

Modality: Music or Movement/Dance, Visual Arts, Expressive Writing/Poetry, Drama

ASCA National Model Domain: Academic Success and Personal/Social

Deliver via: Classroom guidance or group, but could also be modified for use as an individual activity/intervention. Possible classes in which to integrate this activity include science, social studies, language arts, and homeroom. It lasts approximately one class period.

Adaptations: Incorporating complementary activities based on the class curriculum can be done to help youth learn more about biology, conservation, and the natural environment (see examples from Caduto & Bruchac, 1997, listed in the following as well). Wording and method can be modified as necessary, depending on the age level and specific needs of the group/classroom.

Age Level: Elementary and middle school (K through 8)

Indications: The focus of the activity is on taking/keeping perspective, being positive, and making positive life choices, as well as understanding and respecting different strengths in different individuals. As such, it becomes important for the school counselor/facilitator to be vigilant as students identify characteristics or experiences in each direction that might benefit from normalizing, support, or reframing.

Materials: Native American legends/myths (see references below for examples) can be used and even selected based on geographic region to help stimulate thought about the topic; in addition, a compass, tape, and notecards (with process questions written on them) would be helpful.

Preparation: The activity description (in the introduction) can be read out loud to participants and/or discussed.

Instructions:
1. Consider beginning the activity with reading/telling a legend/story from Native American traditions (such as "Why the Possum's Tail is Bare," in Scheer, 1992) as an example to get students reflecting on underlying concepts related to body, mind, heart, and natural environment. One creative approach could include having the children creatively act out the animal story with roles as a way of introducing the subsequent activity focused on directions. An additional creative approach/intervention can be incorporated with younger students who might want to draw their own Medicine Wheel/Circle, for example, as a way of creatively expressing what each direction represents in their life. Use the process questions below to help facilitate dialogue. Summarize, and help students think through how they can incorporate into their lives an increased awareness about the natural world and the inner world of their continually emerging identity.
2. Create an open space if possible, and have the participants visualize a large open circle with four spots that correspond to the four cardinal directions (it may be helpful to make the circle by putting tape on the floor and labeling each of the Four Directions—east, south, west, and north). Begin by having all participants move to the center of this circle and face outward. The first

participant starts by moving to the direction of the east and answering the process question for that direction. The participant then moves on to the direction of the south and waits while the next participant moves from the center of the circle to the east and answers the same question. All of the participants proceed around the circle starting in the east (belonging), moving to the south (mastery), then to the west (independence), and finally to the north (generosity), answering the respective questions for each direction as they go and elaborating as they wish.

3. As each participant moves completely around the circle, he or she returns first to the east and then back to the center of the circle once again, symbolic of coming back into harmony and balance. Time should be given for discussion of differences and similarities among participants with an emphasis on each participant's own answers to the four questions and ways of working on anything that he or she wishes to change (i.e., improving a particular direction or area of his or her life). In addition, emphasis should be placed on the group's experience as a whole. This is also an excellent opportunity for feedback or encouragement to individual members from the group.

Processing Questions:
1. East (Sun)—**Belonging,** characterized by a sense of caring and connection with certain special others: *"Who or what are you a part of, where do you belong; where do you not belong?"*
2. South (Earth, Nature)—**Mastery,** characterized by recognition of one's abilities and a meaningful sense of achievement in life: *"What do you enjoy doing or do well; what do you not do well or struggle with?"*
3. West (Water, Body)—**Independence,** characterized by a belief in oneself through the presence of self-awareness, self-reliance, and self-discipline: *"What are your strengths and source of strength; what limits you?"*
4. North (Wind, Mind)—**Generosity,** characterized by openness to different experiences through the recognition of a (potential) unique personal contribution: "What do you have to offer/contribute to others; *what do you have to receive?"*
5. Center (Fire Within)—**Harmony and balance** of all four directions/dimensions: *"How can you bring each of these directions together in your own life to create a center that best fits you? What would that center be like for you (be specific)? What do you want to do to move to that center in your life? How can you balance your directions for your own success and for being a helper to others as well?"*

Suggested Modifications (for Special Needs Populations): None

Evaluation Plan: Presentation and evaluation of the session must appropriately match the developmental level of the audience. As such, here are some suggested approaches for each level presented:

Grades K through 2: After reading one of the Native stories mentioned above, discuss with students the overall meaning of the story. Can they think of a similar story they have heard before? Also, ask and help students to identify the elements within the story related to "mind" (i.e., thoughts), "body," "spirit" (i.e., values, creativity), and "nature." After students have drawn their Medicine Circles, have them draw parts from the story that match each of these areas listed above. Finally, ask for students to share their Medicine Circles with others.

Grades 3 through 5: After reading one of the Native stories mentioned above, ask students, *"What do you think the story means?"* After discussing the possibilities, explain that in this story the characters may have represented specific values, actions, or beliefs. Then ask, *"What do you think each of the characters represented here?"*

After moving through and completing the circle activity mentioned above, ask, *"What was this experience like for you? What were you thinking as you moved through the circle? Did those thoughts change? What was different for you as the activity ended?"* Assist students in processing their thoughts and feelings related to completion of the circle and what the activity meant to them.

Grades 6 through 8: At the beginning of the session, explain to students, *"The 'quest' is a recurring theme in all cultures around the world. In European culture, this is exemplified in the epic poem* The Odyssey *by Homer, in which the Greek warrior Odysseus and his crew are blown off course after returning from fighting in the Trojan War. They must overcome many obstacles along their way, learning to rely on each other to survive and eventually grow wiser through their trials and ultimately return home in peace."*

Then say, *"The Medicine Circle is a form of quest as well. Each individual must travel an inner path of mind, body, spirit, and harmony with the natural world while making a symbolic physical journey through the four directions. As you are traveling through this activity, keep in mind what you are experiencing, not only in thought but in the other areas that define who you are."*

After completing the lesson, have students explain what this experience was like for them—their thoughts, their physical movement, their walk with others (as in life), and the meaning that it had for them personally. This is necessary for understanding individual as well as cultural perspectives when discussing symbolism and meaning making across cultures.

REFERENCES/RESOURCES

American School Counselor Association. (2004). *ASCA student standards.* Alexandria, VA: Author.

Arneach, L. (2008). *Long-ago stories of the eastern Cherokee.* Charleston, SC: History Press.

Brendtro, L. K., Brokenleg, M., & Van Bockern, S. (2002). *Reclaiming youth at risk: Our hope for the future*. Bloomington, IN: Solution Tree.

Caduto, M. J., & Bruchac, J. (1997a). *Keepers of the animals: Native American stories and wildlife activities for children*. Golden, CO: Fulcrum.

Caduto, M. J., & Bruchac, J. (1997b). *Keepers of the Earth: Native American stories and environmental activities for children*. Golden, CO: Fulcrum.

Duncan, B. R. (Ed). (1998). *Living stories of the Cherokee*. Chapel Hill, NC: University of North Carolina Press.

Four Worlds Development Project. (1989). *The sacred tree: Reflections on Native American spirituality*. Wilmot, WI: Lotus Light.

Garrett, M. T., Brubaker, M. D., Torres-Rivera, E., West-Olaunji, C., & Conwill, W. (2008). The medicine of coming to center: Use of the Native American centering technique—Ayeli—to promote wellness and healing in group work. *Journal for Specialists in Group Work, 33,* 179–198.

Garrett, M. T., & Crutchfield, L. B. (1997). Moving full circle: A unity model of group work with children. *Journal for Specialists in Group Work, 22,* 175–188.

Garrett, M. T., & Garrett, J. T. (2002). Ayeli: Centering technique based on Cherokee spiritual traditions. *Counseling and Values, 46,*149–158.

Scheer, G. F. (1992). *Cherokee animal tales*. Oakland, CA: Council Oak Books.

IMAGINATIVE MIND MAPPING

Tamara J. Hinojosa and Suzanne D. Mudge

The purpose of this activity is to help students solidify their creative ideas and thoughts when struggling with difficult decision-making processes or when organizing academic projects (e.g., research papers, science projects). School counselors will help students develop their own fluid mind-map creations so that students can see and interact with a visual representation of their thoughts. Students are encouraged to "play" and be creative with their ideas so that they begin discovering the connections and/or gaps among them. During the session, school counselors can help students process and challenge their ideas. At the end of the session, students take their mind map home with them.

Modality: Visual

ASCA National Model Domain: Academic, Career, and Personal/Social

Deliver via: Individual or group

Age Level: Middle or high school

Indications: This activity can be used with individuals or small groups and is designed to help students acquire self-knowledge, make decisions, set goals, and/or cope with life changes/transitions.

Materials: Self-adhesive dry-erase paper, various colors of dry-erase markers, self-adhesive pictures, stickers, and any other visual aids that would enhance students' ideas.

Preparation: Prior to conducting this activity, counselors may want students to be prepared with a difficult decision or academic project they want to work on. Additionally, counselors should have all materials out and ready to go.

Instructions:

1. Introduce the activity by explaining that the focus of the session is to help the student reflect on a difficult decision and/or to get started on an academic project. Explain that the student will be creating a visual mind map using the materials provided.

2. School counselors can define what a visual mind map is or provide an example. The suggested definition is as follows: *"A visual mind map is a tool used to help us understand ideas and thought patterns we have about a certain topic. To create a visual mind map, we can use pictures, different colors, words, and other images to represent the ideas we have in our mind. We will then illustrate how all of these ideas may or may not be connected."*

3. After checking in with the student to make sure he or she understands, the counselor will then explain that the student is free to use all materials and be as creative as possible.

4. If the student struggles to get started, the counselor can use the following prompts:

   a. *"What is the main idea of your project (or decision)? It is okay if your main idea changes; you can always erase or rearrange anything on your map."*

   b. *"What other factors influence this main idea?"*

   c. *"What do you see when you think about this project (or decision)? Can you draw that on your visual map?"*

   d. *"What are you hoping will be the end result of your project (or decision)? Can you draw that out? Where would it go on your map?"*

   e. *"What colors do you think about when reflecting on your topic (or decision)?"*

5. As the student draws out her or his map, counselors can identify patterns, connections, gaps, and other important details to help the student gain new realizations.

6. Students are using self-adhesive dry-erase paper; therefore they can stick their imaginative mind map to any surface and view their map from different perspectives. For example, students who prefer to move or stand while mapping out their ideas may stick their drawings to the wall and walk around while processing their thoughts.

7. Once students have completed their maps, they can take them home with them to continue working on them or to use as they work on their decision and/or academic project.

Suggested Modifications (for Special Needs Populations): School counselors may need to provide an actual example of a mind map to help students begin their own. Also, school counselors can adjust the language and materials they use when leading this activity so that students from all developmental levels can effectively participate.

Evaluation Plan: To evaluate the effectiveness of this intervention, school counselors are encouraged to conduct a follow-up individual session with students to explore how the mind map helped them make a decision, complete their academic project, and so on.

TOTEM ACTIVITY

Michael T. Garrett and Michael A. Keim

In many Native American traditions, it is believed that each of the animals in the natural world around us holds a particular lesson for us to learn. As we learn more about the animals that are important to us, we learn more about ourselves, and the way we see ourselves. Each animal has its own "medicine" or particular way of life, and therefore possesses its own unique set of distinguishing qualities. The same is obviously true of people. For every person, there is at least one animal with which that person can identify. Understanding the lesson offered by a person's totem animal carries with it a lesson in identity and a source of pride and strength, which can be drawn upon at any time, and can help in making positive life choices.

Among indigenous peoples, a totem can be a powerful symbol representing the tribe, family/clan, or individual in the form of an animal. The totem itself is a symbol representing the animal in the form of an item, a crest, a totem pole, an emblem, a small figurine, or any other form of expression that may be important to that nation of people. According to some Native American traditions, each person is connected with one or more animals that accompany him or her through life either literally or symbolically, acting as a protector and guide. Furthermore, different animal guides come in and out of our lives at different times depending on the nature of the challenges we are facing at different points and the resulting life lessons we are learning. A person's totem or animal guide, therefore, acts as an embodiment of our true selves or of the true selves we are being challenged to emulate. The animal may not be one that we actually spend time with, but it is one that seems to emerge in our consciousness as something important with something for us to learn. The following are examples of questions for reflection that help one determine one's totem animal:

- *Have you ever felt drawn to a particular animal, bird, or insect, without being able to explain why?*
- *Which animals do you find to be extremely frightening or intriguing?*
- *When you go to the zoo, a park, wildlife area, or forest, what are you most interested in seeing?*
- *Is there a particular animal that you see frequently when you're out in nature?*
- *Does a certain kind of animal consistently appear in your life, or seem to show up at certain times, whether it be physically or symbolically?*

■ *Have you ever been bitten or attacked by an animal?*
■ *Have you ever had a recurring dream about a certain animal, or a dream that you have never been able to forget?*

The goals of this activity include the following:

■ *Increase self-esteem represented by how one feels about oneself and one's ability to grow and change (Four Worlds Development Project, 1989)*
■ *Increase self-determination represented by one's ability to use one's volition (will) to explore and develop potentials (Four Worlds Development Project, 1989)*
■ *Increase body awareness represented in how one experiences one's physical presence (Four Worlds Development Project, 1989)*
■ *Enhance positive self-concept represented by what one thinks about oneself and one's potentials (Four Worlds Development Project, 1989)*

Modality: Visual Arts, Music or Movement/Dance, Expressive Writing/Poetry, Drama

ASCA National Model Domain: Academic

Deliver via: Classroom guidance or group, but could also be used as an individual activity/intervention. Possible classes in which to integrate activity: science/earth science, social studies, language arts, and homeroom. Adaptations: Incorporating complementary activities based on the class curriculum can be done to help youth learn more about animals, biology, conservation, and the natural environment (see examples from Caduto & Bruchac, 1997, listed in the following as well).

Age Level: Elementary and middle school (K through 8)

Indications: The focus of this activity is on taking/keeping perspective, being positive, and making positive life choices, as well as respecting different strengths in different individuals. As such, it becomes important for the school counselor/facilitator to be vigilant as students identify characteristics and behaviors of animals that might be communicated or framed as negative or harmful/hurtful, and help them to reframe this as positive and helpful. For example, any predator animal that hunts other animals can be framed as an animal that is diligent, has to stay intently focused on its goal for survival, keeps itself strong, and also works hard to protect and provide for its family. This process of reframing can be incorporated into the discussion through facilitated dialogue as a way of helping other students learn to reframe as a helpful skill.

Materials: Native American animal legends/myths (see references for examples) can be used and even selected based on geographic region to help stimulate thought about the topic, particularly in terms of strengths/challenges and ways for resolving human dilemmas and building upon one's natural talents/gifts.

Preparation: The activity description can be read out loud to participants and/or discussed.

Instructions:

1. Consider beginning the activity with reading/telling an animal legend/story from Native American traditions as an example to get students reflecting on their own connection with animals and the inherent strengths in each.
2. With younger students, a creative approach/intervention can be incorporated by having them draw an animal as a way of creatively expressing this connection.
3. You may use the approach of having the children creatively act out animal roles (with props) as one or more of the animal stories/legends is read aloud as a basis for introducing the subsequent activity of choosing one's own totem.
4. Use the process questions below to help facilitate dialogue and encourage students to make a list of their responses as you read the questions.

Processing Questions:

■ *"Think of an animal (or even two) that you are most like or that is most like you. What is it?"*
■ *"What are some of that animal's qualities and behaviors?"*
■ *"What does it use as skills to survive? What are its strengths?"*
■ *"What are some things about you that are similar to this animal?"*
■ *"How can this help you in your own life in terms of making positive life decisions and dealing with challenges you are facing or may face in the future?"*

5. Summarize, and help students think through how they can incorporate into their lives an increased awareness about the natural world and the inner world of their continually emerging identity.

Suggested Modifications (for Special Needs Populations): None.

Evaluation Plan: Presentation and evaluation of the session must appropriately match the developmental level of the audience. As such, here are some suggested approaches for each level presented:

Grades K through 2: At the beginning of the session, ask students to describe various animals. *"What does the animal look like? Does it have stripes? Spots? Claws? A beak? What color is it?"*

Next, ask, *"If you could be any animal, what would you be? Tell us why."*

After finishing the lesson, ask students, *"Do you still want to be the same animal? If not, why did you change your mind?"*

Grades 3 through 5: At the beginning of the session, ask students, *"What animal do you like the most?"* Then ask, *"What do you like about it? Do you like the way it looks? What can it do?"*

After finishing the lesson, ask students, *"Now that you have learned more about these animals and what they may stand for, has anyone changed his or her mind about his or her choice of 'totems'? Why or why not?"*

Grades 6 through 8: At the beginning of the session, explain to students, *"In European culture during the Middle Ages, noble families often chose animals as symbols on coats of arms to represent them both to other nobles and on the field of battle. Similarly, Native peoples often chose animals as 'totems' to represent their families, as well."* Then ask, *"If you were to choose an animal to represent you or your family, which animal would you choose? What is unique about that animal?"*

As part of the lesson, it is important to explain that the same animal may have different meanings for various cultures. That is why it is important to understand the meaning attached to it from that cultural perspective.

After completing the lesson, have students not only explain what animal they chose to represent themselves or their families, but also what meaning that animal has for them personally. This is necessary for understanding individual as well as cultural perspectives when discussing symbolism and meaning making across cultures.

REFERENCES

American School Counselor Association. (2004). *ASCA student standards*. Alexandria, VA: Author.

Arneach, L. (2008). *Long-ago stories of the eastern Cherokee*. Charleston, SC: History Press.

Brendtro, L. K., Brokenleg, M., & Van Bockern, S. (2002). *Reclaiming youth at risk: Our hope for the future*. Bloomington, IN: Solution Tree.

Caduto, M. J., & Bruchac, J. (1997). *Keepers of the animals: Native American stories and wildlife activities for children*. Golden, CO: Fulcrum.

Caduto, M. J., & Bruchac, J. (1997). *Keepers of the Earth: Native American stories and environmental activities for children*. Golden, CO: Fulcrum.

Duncan, B. R. (Ed). (1998). *Living stories of the Cherokee*. Chapel Hill, NC: University of North Carolina Press.

Four Worlds Development Project. (1989). *The sacred tree: Reflections on Native American spirituality*. Wilmot, WI: Lotus Light.

Garrett, M. T., & Crutchfield, L. B. (1997). Moving full circle: A unity model of group work with children. *Journal for Specialists in Group Work, 22,* 175–188.

Scheer, G. F. (1992). *Cherokee animal tales*. Oakland, CA: Council Oak Books.

3 ❋ Visual Arts Interventions in the Career Domain

CAREER CARDS

Laurel Malloy and Katrina Cook

*T*his activity is designed to be used in small-group counseling, and can also be used in individual counseling or even classroom guidance. The counselor will ask the students to identify the three job-related activities in which they think they would be interested. Students will create a card to represent each activity they have identified, being sure to provide a place to write down job possibilities.

Modality: Visual

ASCA National Model Domain: Career

Deliver via: Group counseling

Age Level: Middle school and high school

Indications: This activity could be used in small-group counseling related to career choice or decision making. It could also be used in classroom guidance.

Materials: The materials for this activity include pencils, paper, three 3 × 5 index cards for each participant, markers, crayons, magazines that could be used for collage, scissors, and glue. Also, have some sample career trading cards available for the students to view (see Figures 3.1 and 3.2).

Preparation: Have some sample career trading cards available for the students to view, either some that you have created yourself as examples, or some that previous students have made and donated to the counseling office for future use. Remind students that they might change their minds many times before they finally decide what they would like their career to be. This activity will give them an opportunity to explore some careers that they may have already shown interest in, as well as some that they might not have considered before.

FIGURE 3.1 Sample career card.

FIGURE 3.2 Sample career card.

Instructions:
1. Introduce the session by saying, *"For today's activity in career exploration, you will identify possible factors that you are looking for in a job. From that information, you will identify careers that best represent your preferences."*
2. Ask the students to reflect on what activities they like or think they would like to do. Encourage the students to jot down their ideas on paper. Allow time for students to do this.
3. Show students a blank 3 × 5 card and explain that each of them is going to create three cards representing those things they would like to do in a job.
4. Then, show samples of career cards that have previously been made. Ask the students to identify an activity represented by that card. For example, for the career card depicted in Figure 3.1 that says "music," the students may respond with singing, playing an instrument, being a DJ, or any other music-related activity.
5. Then give each student three cards, and ask them to review their activity lists and choose three activities. Using the art supplies and magazines, each student will make a card representing each activity.
6. Say to the students, *"Looking at each of your cards, can you think of a job that involves that activity? In pencil, write that job on the back of the card."*
7. Each student will choose one card for sharing. Ask the following questions:
   a. What job and activity are represented by this card? How are the job and activity related?
   b. Can anyone think of any other jobs related to these activities? (Encourage students to jot down additional jobs in pencil on the back of the card.)
   c. What other activities might someone interested in those jobs do?
   d. Then ask the original student to indicate, by circling, the job he or she is most interested in getting more information on.
   e. Repeat with all students.
8. As time permits, allow the students to process the other two cards.

Suggested Modifications (for Special Needs Populations): School counselors may need to adjust the length of time for the activity depending on the number of students in the group. Also, depending on the available time, school counselors may ask students to complete only one or two cards instead of three. School counselors may need to assist some students with identifying ways to depict different activities on their cards. Having previously designed sample cards as examples can help. For students with identified learning needs, larger cards and precut pictures may be used, and students do not have to write down their activities if they prefer verbal communication. The school counselor may write down the student's choice of jobs on the back of the card if the student struggles with writing.

Evaluation Plan: To evaluate the effectiveness of this intervention, ask the students to name three job choices they would like to explore further.

ENVISIONING YOUR FUTURE

Montserrat Casado-Kehoe

*T*his activity is designed to help students explore and envision themselves in specific careers. It facilitates student understanding of what is required for a specific career and the steps needed to get there. The counselor should begin the activity by inviting students to do a guided visualization in which they will think of their future and the specific career they would like to pursue. Students will be encouraged to reflect on what they will need to do to achieve this career and create a picture of themselves performing the desired profession.

Modality: Visual Arts, Guided Imagery

ASCA National Model Domain: Career, Personal/Social

Delivery via: Individual or classroom guidance

Age Level: High school (it could be used with other age groups as well, but would need to be modified to align with students' cognitive developmental level)

Indications: It is designed to be used individually to help students envision their future and career choices.

Materials: Drawing or construction paper, crayons/markers, cutout words and images, scissors, glue stick; nature music, music player. (The student can create either a drawing or collage of their vision of the future.)

Preparation: Lay out paper, crayons/markers, cutout images/words, scrapping materials (encouraging words), scissors, and glue stick on a table. Prepare nature music to be used in a guided visualization with the student.

Instructions:

1. *Activity Introduction*

   Introduce the activity by telling each student individually to consider potential careers that he or she would like to pursue. From this discussion, encourage the student to begin to daydream and introduce a guided visualization exercise.

2. *Guided Imagery*

   A guided imagery exercise encourages the students to daydream about what they would like to do in the future. Inform them that you are going to do a breathing activity followed by some visualization that allows them to visualize their professional interests and what steps to take to pursue that career (see the example at the end of the intervention). After the students have visualized their potential careers, ask them to open their eyes and begin the art activity. The students will create drawings/collages of the career(s) they envision pursuing in the future and the various steps needed to get there. Remind students to also place themselves in the drawing/ collage.

3. *Arts Expression and Processing*
   a. After the drawings/collages have been completed, the school counselor will process the activity.
   b. The school counselor will ask questions to facilitate discussion of the potential careers students have chosen, the necessary steps to take to achieve the career, and specifics of what they will be doing:
      ■ *"Let's explore how you envisioned yourself in the future. What will you be doing?"*
      ■ *"For this specific career, what will you need to do to accomplish this dream?"*
      ■ *"What will you be doing when you have this kind of job? Can you describe what I would see if I was able to see you doing this job? What would I notice?"*
   c. The school counselor may encourage the student to continue to daydream and envision the chosen career(s) at home.

Suggested Modifications (for Special Needs Populations): School counselors may need to modify the activity when using it with younger age levels by adjusting the language used, specifically during the guided visualization. The younger the child, the more concrete the terminology the school counselor needs to use. This activity is appropriate for most students, but there are some individuals who do struggle with visualization. For those students, one may ask the student to think of scenarios rather than visualizing themselves involved in a specific career in the future. The activity could also be modified to be used in small groups or classes in which students are exploring a variety of careers.

Evaluation Plan: To evaluate the effectiveness of this intervention, the school counselor may design a preassessment and postassessment that looks at each student's considerations of careers.

Students will complete this assessment at the end of the activity to measure their understanding of the careers they have envisioned during the activity.

1. What careers have you considered at this point?
2. What steps do you need to take to pursue your most desired career?
3. List some personal characteristics that make you a good candidate for this profession.
4. On a scale from 1 to 5, with 1 one being not confident and 5 being very confident, how confident are you that you know what to do to pursue this career?
5. Is there something your school counselor can do to help you in this process?

Guided Imagery Script

Relax and settle into your seat comfortably. Let your body relax all over from the top of your head to the tips of your toes. Take a few slow, deep breaths . . . breathe in through your nose and slowly exhale fully through your mouth.

Now, as you are getting so very comfortable in your chair, I want you to imagine yourself 10 years in the future, on a workday morning, getting up and getting ready to go to your job.

As you wake up, look around the room and examine the place you live. What is it like? What kind of clothes are in your closet? Casual clothes for an outdoor job? Dress clothes for an office job? Some kind of uniform?

Now, after you've had breakfast, you head out the door to your job. How will you get there? Car? Bus? Walk? Train?

Now that you are at the job, where exactly are you working? What does your worksite look like?

Who is at the worksite with you?

What will you spend your day doing? Where do you go? Who do you see? What keeps you busy?

Now, it's the end of the day and you are heading home. What thoughts run through your mind about your day at work? What do you like best about your job? What is the most satisfying aspect?

Now, as you are feeling satisfied with the job and your life, I want you to slowly wiggle your toes and your fingers. Feel alertness travel from your fingertips and toes up into your body. Slowly open your eyes and feel yourself reluctantly returning to the room. Now, let's hold on to that image of the future Professional You and focus on giving that identity life.

HEROES: IDENTITY AND ADAPTABILITY IN THE WORLD OF WORK

Stephanie C. Bell, Kevin B. Stoltz, and Susan R. Barclay

*T*he purpose of this activity is self-exploration for career preparation. Counselors can utilize this activity to help students examine both their emerging identity and their adaptive strategies, which they will take forward to the world of work. Identity and adaptability are important constructs in career counseling and preparation (Hall, 2001; Savickas 2011; Super, Savickas, & Super, 1996), and this activity can help students learn more about how they approach life tasks, including career preparation. The activity begins with the counselor asking students to reflect on who their heroes are or were growing up. These heroes may be real people from the student's life or fictional characters from stories, books, movies, or television shows. Encouraging students to reflect and remember a meaningful hero is an important aspect of this activity. Students will use the art materials provided to draw or make a collage of their heroes. Counselors *will encourage students to include and explain their perspectives of the hero's values, behaviors, and overall approach to life. In essence, the counselor is assessing what the student gleaned from the portrayal of the hero. Additionally, students will explain how the hero uses the identified characteristics to approach life's challenges. Relationships between the student's challenges and the hero's resolutions are an important aspect of this activity. The counselor should ask what the student thinks are the strengths and weaknesses of the hero and what is most salient about the hero. The characteristics, values, and strengths that the student identifies can be thought of as the student's strivings toward those ideals (Maree, 2013; Savickas, 1998; Taber & Briddick, 2011; Taber, Hartung, Briddick, Briddick, & Rehfuss, 2011). The weaknesses can be seen as the student's vulnerabilities and challenges. Armed with these two often-opposing views, students can learn more about how they approach solving problems, what strengths they employ to overcome challenges, and how they engage in developing a personal work identity.*

Modality: Visual Art

ASCA National Model Domain: Career

Deliver Via: Group or individual counseling

Age Level: Elementary, middle, or high school (appropriate for use with any age group—modify materials and relevant discussion to align with the developmental level of students)

Indications: Groups, in individual settings, or in classroom guidance activities with a focus on self-exploration and development of adaptability with a career perspective

Materials: For 8th grade and younger: white, unlined paper; colored pencils; crayons; markers; magazines and newspapers for building a collage; scissors; glue stick; sticky notes; and stickers.

For 9th grade and above: white, unlined paper; pipe cleaners; magazines and newspapers; scissors; glue sticks; and sticky notes.

Preparation: Provide each student with a piece of the blank, unlined, white paper and the other materials listed (depending on the age group).

Instructions:

1. Begin talking with students about who their heroes are or who their heroes were when they were growing up. Explain to students that this could be anyone, a superhero from a comic book, a character from a favorite television show or book, a respected adult outside the family (e.g., teacher, clergy, neighbor), or anyone else. Try to steer the student beyond immediate family members. Ask them to think about what makes that figure heroic. Ask them, *"What were the characteristics of the hero in your eyes?"* Follow up to these exploratory, narrative-producing questions by inviting students to

define how they are like the hero and different from the hero. Additionally, asking clarifying questions about how the hero may solve problems that each student is facing would be important in helping students understand their reliance on the heroic figure.

2. To further the students' narratives, instruct students to either draw the hero they think of most often (if working with a younger age group) or use the materials provided to make a collage of things that represents their hero (if working with an older age group). Ask students to label the strengths and weaknesses of their hero, and have them identify salient characteristics of the hero with words or artistic rendition.

3. After they have finished drawing or constructing the hero, ask students to present the finished creation to you or the group (if used in a group or class-room setting). Sharing should include presenting the hero's strengths and challenges. Also, the presentation should include salient characteristics of the hero and what the student admires most about the hero.

4. Following the presentation, the counselor can help students by identifying similar strengths, challenges, and characteristics between each student and his or her hero. Relating these strengths, challenges, and characteristics to developmental tasks (e.g., making friends, learning new skills, exploring careers) that each student is facing is an important aspect of closing this activity. Future interactions with students should include reference to the hero and salient characteristics described by the student.

Suggested Modifications (for Special Needs Populations): You may need to alter the materials used for this activity depending on the age group with whom you are working and the students' developmental level and their ability to self-reflect. This activity may be helpful especially for those who enjoy hands-on activities and those who like to create things. However, students with difficulty in motor skills may have trouble with this activity, so altering the activity to use in a one-on-one discussion format with an older child, or one in which the student may direct the counselor how to draw his or her hero (with a younger child), may be appropriate.

Evaluation Plan: The goal of this activity is to increase identity and self-awareness in problem solving (adaptability). To evaluate the outcome of this activity, you can use a simple pretest/posttest design adjusted for the developmental level of the student. If you want to evaluate this activity, we suggest developmentally appropriate modifications to the process used by Rehfuss (2009) in *The Future Career Autobiography* (FCA). Before the activity, have students write a paragraph detailing their abilities, skills, and future work goal. Retain this paragraph and perform the activity. After the activity, have students write a new paragraph detailing their abilities, skills, and future work. Compare the narrative of the two paragraphs, looking for a deeper understanding of self and how that may be translated into career and planning tasks.

An additional measure would include having students complete the simple assessment listed below, both before and after the activity. There should be a more complete listing of characteristics and strengths after the activity. You may note more realistic assessment of challenges and use of problem-solving strategies after the activity.

Students may complete this assessment before and after finishing the "Heroes" career activity. Counselors might alter this assessment depending on the age and developmental level of the child or the group with which the activity is implemented.

1. List five important characteristics you possess:
   (a)
   (b)
   (c)
   (d)
   (e)

2. List three important strengths you use when you experience challenges in your life:
   (a)
   (b)
   (c)

3. What is one aspect of your life that you want to improve?

4. Of the characteristics and strengths you listed, which will help you make the improvement you wrote about above?

5. This activity helped me understand more about myself and how I can apply myself in a future career.

   Strongly agree   Agree   Somewhat agree   Disagree   Strongly disagree

REFERENCES

Hall, D. T. (2002). *Careers in and out of organizations*. London, UK: Sage.

Maree, J. G. (2013). Practical implementation of career construction as shown through case studies. In J. G. Maree (Ed.), *Counselling for career construction: Connecting life themes to construct life portraits: Turning pain into hope* (pp. 81–111). Rotterdam, Netherlands: Sense.

Rehfuss, M. C. (2009). The future career autobiography: A narrative measure of career intervention effectiveness. *Career Development Quarterly, 58*(1), 82–90.

Savickas, M. L. (1998). Career style assessment and counseling. In T. J. Sweeney (Ed.), *Adlerian counseling: A practitioner's approach* (4th ed., pp. 329–359). Bristol, PA: Accelerated Development.

Savickas, M. L. (2011). *Career counseling.* Washington, DC: American Psychological Association.

Super, D. E., Savickas, M. L., & Super, C. M. (1996). The life-span, life-space approach to careers. In D. Brown & L. Brooks (Eds.), *Career choice and development* (3rd ed., pp. 121–178). San Francisco, CA: Jossey-Bass.

Taber, B. J., & Briddick, W. C. (2011). Adlerian-based career counseling in an age of protean careers. *Journal of Individual Psychology, 67,* 107–121.

Taber, B. J., Hartung, P. J., Briddick, H., Briddick, W. C., & Rehfuss, M. C. (2011). Career style interview: A contextualized approach to career counseling. *Career Development Quarterly, 59,* 274–287. doi:10.1002/j.2161-0045.2011.tb00069.x

---

I'M THE SCHOOL COUNSELOR. WHAT DO I DO?

Edward F. Hudspeth and Linda G. English

This activity is designed to allow young students to get to know their school counselor and what he or she does. It facilitates awareness and trust between students and the counselor. The counselor should begin the activity by asking the students what a school counselor is and what he or she does. Students will work individually on their visual depictions.

Modality: Visual Arts

ASCA National Model Domain: Career

Deliver via: Classroom guidance

Age Level: Elementary (This may be utilized with any age group. Modify the activity and the processing questions to align with the students' developmental level).

Indications: This could be used as an ice breaker at the beginning of a school year to introduce the counselor. The activity allows the counselor to tell students about his or her role and about some of the things he or she may be doing as classroom guidance counselor during the year.

Materials: Coloring pencils, crayons, or markers; a blank face image

Preparation: Have art media out and available to all students. Make sure each student has a blank face handout (see Figure 3.3). The counselor should complete a face, with all the parts that will be discussed, prior to beginning the activity.

Instructions: Introduce the activity by asking, *"What is a school counselor?"* and *"What does he or she do?"* If there are responses, acknowledge those who respond. Next say, *"I'm the school counselor. Let me tell you what I do."*

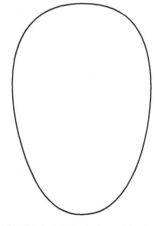

FIGURE 3.3 Blank face handout.

Activity: Invitation 1: The counselor starts by saying, *"On your desk is a face. All we need to do is fill it in. Let's start with our ears. Can you draw your ears?"* As the students draw the ears say,

Script 1: *"Do you know what is the best thing a person can do for another person? The best thing we can do is listen. Yes, I said listen.*

"By listening, we are saying to the other person, 'You're so important to me.'

"By listening, you show you care about them. Everyone wants to know that he or she is heard and understood by other people.

"If you want to show your friends, or parents, or teachers that you care, listen so carefully and closely that you can say what they have said to you back to them. This may surprise them so much that they may fall down!

"If you want to be listened to, come see me. That's what I do. Counselors listen. They are all ears!"

Invitation 2: *"Now that we have ears, I think we need some eyes. Can you draw your eyes?"* As the students draw the eyes say,

Script 2: *"Do you know another thing we can do to show another person that we care? We can look at them when we are talking.*

"By looking at them, we are saying to the other person, 'You're so important to me.'

"By looking at them, you're saying, 'I'm paying attention to you and I see that you are happy or mad or sad or scared.'

"If you want to show your friends, or parents, or teachers that you care, look at them when you are talking to them or when they are talking to you. This may surprise them so much that they may smile or jump up and down!

"If you want someone to see that you are happy or mad or sad or scared, come to me. That's what I do. Counselors pay attention. Counselors have big, big eyes!"

Invitation 3: *"Now that we have ears for listening and eyes for seeing, I think we need a mouth. Can you draw your mouth?"* As the students draw the mouth say,

Script 3: *"We said that we use our ears for listening and eyes for seeing and we know this tells others that we care. What else can we do to tell others that we care? We can talk to them.*

"By talking to them, we are saying to the other person, 'You're so important to me.'

"By talking to them, you can say things that make them feel better.

"If you want to show your friends, or parents, or teachers that you care, talk to them. Say something nice. Say something funny. This may surprise them so much that they may laugh their heads off!

"If you want someone to talk to, come see me. That's what I do. Counselors talk about things that make you happy and things that make you sad. Counselors talk about a lot of things. Counselors have bunches and bunches of things to say—so much that it might just fill up the ocean!"

Final Invitation: *"So, we have ears for hearing. We have eyes for seeing. We have a mouth for talking. What's left? I think it's a nose. Can you draw your nose?"* As the students draw a nose say,

Final Script: *"I think your face is finished. It has all of the things you need to show people how important they are and to show that you care. Your face has the same things as my face."* (Counselor holds up a face that he or she has completed before the activity.) *"So, I want to tell you how important you are and that I care."*

Suggested Modifications (for Special Needs Populations): The words utilized in the scripts may need to be modified for different ages/developmental levels. This activity is useful with younger students, particularly kindergarten through 2nd grade. Students who have difficulty with fine or gross motor skills may need assistance, from the counselor or a classmate, when drawing the parts of the face.

Evaluation Plan: To evaluate the effectiveness of this intervention, you may use the attached survey as a pre- and postassessment. The primary goal of the activity is to familiarize students with the school counselor and what he or she does.

Students will complete this assessment as a pre- and postassessment of their understanding of the concepts addressed during the activity and awareness brought about by the activity. For younger students, this may be done verbally.

1. What are three things a school counselor does?
    (a)
    (b)
    (c)

2. True or false: The school counselor listens.
3. True or false: The school counselor sees how I feel.
4. True or false: The school counselor is good at talking about things.

MY FAMILY'S CAREERS: USING PLAY GENOGRAMS TO EXPLORE CAREER

Stephanie E. Eberts

*T*his activity is designed to be utilized in a variety of settings: individual settings and small or large groups. It facilitates students' understanding of their families' career histories and how those careers can influence their own career identity development. This activity combines ideas from two activities: Play Genograms (Gil, 1994) and Career Genograms or "Career-O-grams" (Thorngren & Feit, 2001). Students will use play miniatures, drawings, or magazine cutouts to explore the careers of their family members and their own career aspirations.

Modality: Visual Arts

ASCA National Model Domain: Career

Deliver via: Individual, small group, or classroom guidance

Age Level: Elementary, middle, or high school (appropriate for any age group with modifications made for each developmental level)

Indications: This intervention can be used to help students to build a greater understanding of their family career history and learn about their families' influences on personal lines of career inquiry.

Materials: Blank paper (construction paper or white paper), markers/crayons, glue, scissors, play miniatures, or magazines

Preparation: Ensure that the students ask family members what their jobs are prior to coming to the session, group, or class. Prepare the room by setting out all of the miniatures or magazines so that the student(s) can see all of them. The paper, markers, and glue should also be put out in the places where the students will be working.

Instructions:
1. Introduce the activity by asking the students to discuss a job they would like to have when they are finished with school, and how they figured out that this job interested them.
2. Tell the group or individual that they are going to explore how their families' careers have influenced their career aspirations by creating a visual representation of their families' careers.
3. Direct the students to get a piece paper. On that piece of paper the students should write their names and the names of the people who live in their homes (they can use the names that they call them such as Mom or Uncle Tim, etc.) or the people they feel are their family. Most families fall into the

category of "nontraditional" and this language allows for students to identify their families in ways that feel most comfortable for them. In traditional genograms there is a distinct format for how people lay out their family, but in this activity, students can feel free to arrange their family members as they wish. This activity seeks to explore the career influences in a student's life rather than give the counselor an understanding of the family structure. The counselor could ask the students to put themselves in the middle with other family members around them if that would be helpful to the students.

4. Once the names of the family members are on the paper, direct students to find a miniature or a magazine picture that represents or symbolizes the career of each of the family members that they have put on their papers. The students may also draw a picture if they cannot find a miniature or picture that works. The idea of a symbol for a career might be hard for a younger child to process, so it would be important to have miniatures that represent more concrete versions of careers. If the counselor does not have a wide selection of miniatures, then the students should draw a picture or cut out pictures from magazines.

5. The students should also pick a miniature, draw a picture, or cut out a picture of the career that they hope to have one day.

6. The students will then place the miniatures or magazine cutouts that they have selected over the name of the family member (see Figures 3.4 and 3.5).

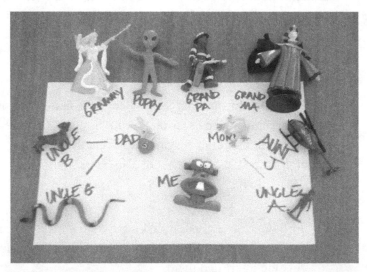

FIGURE 3.4 In this photo, the student has picked a variety of miniatures to represent the careers of family members. The miniatures represent the following careers: A snake for Uncle G, who works in sales; a dog for Uncle B, who is a veterinarian; a fairy for Grammy, who was a preschool teacher; an alien for Poppy, because the student did not know what he did for a living; a fire fighter for Grandpa, because he was a fireman; a teacher for Grandma, because she stayed at home but taught everyone in the family important lessons; a helicopter for Aunt J, because she was in the military; a policeman for Uncle A, because he was a police officer; a frog for Mom, because she works in the garden; a heart lock for Dad, because he is a counselor; and a purple funny creature for me, because the student wants to be a cartoonist.

FIGURE 3.5 This photo is an example of a student who used magazine cutouts to create her family picture. The cutouts represent the following careers: A picture of a coffee cup for Brother, who works in a coffee shop; a jacket for Uncle A, who works at a dry cleaner; a woman walking a dog for the student, who wants to be a veterinarian; college banners for Mom, who works at a college; and a house for Grandma, who takes care of the home.

7. After the family career picture has been created, use the following questions to process the picture:
   a. *"What do you notice about your picture?"*
   b. *"How have your family members influenced your choice of career?"*
   c. *"What do all of you family members' careers have in common? Differences?"*
   d. *"Do you want to have a career like any of your family members? Why or why not?"*
   e. *"What do your family members say about what you want to do after you finish school?"*
   f. *"What kind of education or training did your family members get in order to have their jobs?"*
   g. *"What kind of training or education do you need in order to get the job you want?"*
   h. *"What can you do right now to make sure you are prepared to do your future job?"*
   i. *"What are a few new things that you learned about yourself or your family members?"*
8. If the students used miniatures to create their pictures, photograph each picture so that there is a record of their creation. In order to best see the miniatures, they will need to be laid down (see Figure 3.4).
9. Finally, ask the students to share their pictures or photos of their pictures with their families.

10. As a follow-up activity, the students can begin to research the careers they have selected. They should be instructed to find out such things as what training is needed for the selected career, how many years of training, where the training is offered, what the training would cost, and how the students' current schoolwork could influence whether or not they could get that training. For example, if a student identifies that she wants to be a veterinarian, she would need to know how many years of education are needed to pursue that career, the average cost of that education, and what the requirements are for getting into those educational settings.

Suggested Modifications (for Special Needs Populations): Modifications should be made based on developmental abilities of the students. Students who are cognitively operating from a concrete perspective may not be able to think of a symbol that represents a career. They may need to have miniatures or magazine cutouts that are more of a concrete representation of the job rather than a symbol of the job. In Figure 3.4, the miniatures range from a firefighter (Grandpa) and police officer (Uncle A), which are more concrete, to a heart lock (Dad) and a frog (Mom), which are more symbolic. Some school counselors may be working with classes in which some of the students will be thinking more abstractly, thus being able to conceptualize the idea of finding a symbol, while other students in the same group need more concrete examples. It would be beneficial to have as wide a variety of miniatures or different types of magazines as possible to accommodate the needs of the majority of students.

If the school counselor does not have a large selection of miniatures or enough magazines to represent what he or she needs for the group or individual with whom she or he is working, it is possible to create this sort of picture on a computer. Students who have difficulty with fine motor skills, such as cutting, may find this method of representing their families' careers more accessible.

Evaluation Plan:
The counselor can evaluate the students' learning by using the attached assessments. The first assessment can be given directly after the intervention. The follow-up assessment should be given several months after the intervention.

Initial Assessment
1. Name one thing that you learned about your family that you did not know before you started this activity.
2. List two short-term goals that will help you to achieve your future career. Create a plan to reach those goals.
   Goal #1:
   Plan:
   Goal #2:
   Plan:
3. Name one way your family can help you to achieve your goals.

Follow-Up Assessment

1. Have you been able to achieve any goals?
2. What has helped you to achieve your goals? Or, what has gotten in the way of you achieving your goals?

REFERENCES

Gil, E. (1994). *Play in family therapy.* New York, NY: Guilford Press.

Thorngren, J., & Feit, S. (2001). The Career-O-Gram: A postmodern career intervention. *Career Development Quarterly, 49,* 291–303.

PROMOTING CAREER ASPIRATION THROUGH MOVIE CHARACTERS

Varunee Faii Sangganjanavanich

The purpose of this intervention is to facilitate the development of career aspiration of high school students through the use of movie characters. This intervention is a way to make promotion of career development relevant to the developmental level and culture of adolescents. This intervention is conducted in a small-group format (six to eight students) where students discuss their favorite movie characters and link them to their career aspiration. A group environment not only makes this intervention interactive, but also inspiring and meaningful.

Modality: Visual Art using Cinematic Inspiration

ASCA National Model Domain: Career

Deliver via: Group

Age Level: High school

Indications: High school can be a turning point for many adolescents. Too often, high school students lack knowledge about themselves (e.g., personality, interest), resulting in career indecision. This intervention can be implemented with all students, with a wide range of academic and career potential, as every student can benefit from discussion about career aspirations. For students struggling with their career development trajectory (e.g., lack of self-knowledge and understanding), this activity can help them explore and discover meaningful parts of themselves (e.g., personality, inspiration, preference) and build the foundation of career aspiration.

Materials: One poster board, poster-size papers, different kinds of recycled craft materials (e.g., color paper, ribbons, buttons, etc.), multiple color crayons, glue, scissors, and pins/invisible tape. The quantity of the materials depends on the number of students in a group. Diversity of recycled craft materials and color crayons is important as this provides more selection for students.

Preparation: On one side of the room, all materials, except a poster board and pins/invisible tape, should be placed on the table where all students can easily access them. There should be multiple sheets of poster-size paper, different kinds of recycled craft materials, color crayons, glue, and pins/invisible tape for all students to use. The counselors may place chairs and tables for students or students are free to sit on the floor to create their posters. On the other side of the room, seats should be placed in a U shape with the poster board located in the open end to complete an oval-shaped circle.

Instructions:

1. Approximately 1 week prior to this activity, the counselor should ask students to think about a favorite movie character who inspires them. The students are instructed to find out specific and detailed information on the chosen character in the following areas:
   - A picture/photo of the character
   - A general description of the character (e.g., name, role, function, personality, occupation)
   - Personal inspiration from the character (i.e., how does this character inspire you personally?)
   - Identification with the character (i.e., how do you identify with this character?)
   - Influence on a future career (i.e., how does this character influence your future career/career choice?)

   It is recommended that the counselor type up these questions on a sheet of paper for the students to take home. These questions (e.g., sequence and detail) will also serve as the structure of student presentations during the activity time. It is also important that the counselor briefly describe the activity to the students by saying, *"I would like you to think about one of your favorite movie characters who inspires you. Once you choose the character, you will search for the information on that character—be as detailed as you can be. Then, we will come back next week and each of you will create a poster of your favorite movie character and will present that to the group. You will have 20 minutes to create a poster based on the information you prepare and will have 10 minutes to present the information on the poster to the group."*

2. **In-Session Poster Construction**. Once the students enter the activity time, they are asked to utilize the art materials provided to create a description of the chosen character on a poster-size paper within 20 minutes based on the information prepared a week prior to this activity. While the students are working on their posters, the counselor may choose to circle around the room to observe their work.

3. **In-Session Presentation**. After students finish creating their posters, the counselor asks all students to bring their posters and to get seated in the U-shaped circle. The counselor invites students to share their posters with

the group by saying, *"So, everyone has 10 minutes to tell the group about your favorite movie character and how the character inspires you and your future career. Please follow the presentation instructions you received last week. Who would like to share first?"* There is no limitation concerning who should share first, and sharing should be on a volunteer basis. When a student finishes describing the favorite movie character, it is important that the counselor briefly summarize to the group before moving to the next presentation, for instance, "Shannon said she loved Chuck Noland from the movie *Cast Away*. She is inspired by his courage and persistence—something that Shannon values. More important, she admires that Chuck did not give up even when facing adverse situations, like being cast away, which is similar to what Shannon is going through—trying to get good grades in science classes and being persistent with her job shadowing at the factory because she wants to be a mechanical engineer."

Once all students complete their presentations, the counselor may begin to process the activity by asking, *"It is very obvious to me that everyone put a lot of thought into these presentations. I learned so much about you—who and what inspires you. I enjoyed learning about your career dreams and choices you are contemplating. I am wondering whether anybody would like to share any thoughts that emerged during the activity?"* This provides an opportunity for students to share their thoughts and to interact with each other.

Suggested Modifications (for Special Needs Populations): When working with students with disabilities, this activity can be modified. For example, school counselors may ask a student who is blind or has visual impairment to think about a novel character he or she knows from audiobooks and to narrate their stories rather than create a poster. For students who experience extreme social anxiety or severely low self-esteem, school counselors may consider reducing the number of group members or conducting this activity in an individual or triadic format. In addition, it is also important for the counselors to attend to cultural differences among students that may emerge during the activity (e.g., different views on human personality, occupational prestige, and values).

Evaluation Plan: The purpose of this intervention is to facilitate the development of career aspiration of high school students through the use of movie characters. To evaluate the effectiveness of this intervention, school counselors may utilize multiple assessment methods. First, during the poster construction, the counselor may observe how students are able to articulate the information and put it in the poster (e.g., whether they lack the information required or struggle putting the information together). Second, during the presentation, the counselor may evaluate to what extent a student is able to articulate and describe the chosen characters as well as to address all domains listed in the instructions of the activity (e.g., personal inspiration, influence on a future career). Third, while processing the activity, the counselor may observe reactions (e.g., thoughts and feelings), both verbal and nonverbal, of the students.

TRYING A STEM HAT ON FOR SIZE

Michelle Perepiczka and Megyn Shea

*T*his activity is designed to introduce STEM (science, technology, engineering, math) careers by using expressive arts to symbolize the knowledge gained about a STEM-related career. Students will have the opportunity to "try on" a STEM career by creating a hat that is decorated with icons associated with that career. Students will have the opportunity to learn about the career they choose as well as learn about the chosen careers of their peers through group process toward the end of the session. The activity will be evaluated by using pointed questions to assess the level of knowledge prior to and after the session.

Modality: Visual Art

ASCA National Model Domain: Career

Deliver via: Classroom guidance

Appropriate Age Groups: Elementary – 4th to 6th grades

Note: Students may need assistance with the vocabulary related to the exercise

Indications: The goal of the activity is to increase awareness of STEM careers, specifically, to increase student ability to identify multiple STEM careers and become familiar with one particular career. The rationale is to expose elementary school students to STEM careers as a motivator to engage in science and math, as well as to increase awareness of underrepresented populations in STEM careers.

Materials Required: Magazines, scissors, construction paper, tape, glue, markers, list of provided STEM careers, and provided posttest worksheet

Preparation Needed: Precut the construction paper into strips at least 6 inches long that can be rounded into a crown. Print off the list of STEM careers and cut the individual careers into slips that will be passed out to students. (Be sure to make enough copies for all students. Some students may have the same career depending on the group size.) Print off the posttest writing form for each student.

Instructions:
1. Start the session by asking the class the following pretest questions. Allow the group to answer the questions to the best of their ability before continuing.

    a. What does STEM stand for?

    b. What are some careers that fall under science, technology, engineering and math?

2. Explain that STEM stands for science, technology, engineering, and math.

3. Link STEM to work students are currently doing in class.

4. Explain STEM career opportunities.

5. Highlight how STEM careers are available to women and minorities.

6. Show a video further explaining STEM and showing examples of careers, available at http://www.youtube.com/watch?v=UZBSsPiOE2Y

7. Ask the students to choose one of the prepared slips of paper that has a STEM career written on it as well as information about that career. Instruct the students to create a visual representation of the selected career on the construction paper provided. Students may choose to use markers or look for pictures in the provided magazines to decorate their crown. At the end of the time period, you will use the tape to connect the sides of the construction paper to make a crown. Students may wear the crowns during the processing period for all to see.

8. Processing the activity can be done in multiple ways. The school counselor may adapt the process to best fit the needs of the class.

    a. *Processing I (in pairs)*: The school counselor will ask the students to choose a partner in the class and take a few minutes to explain to their partners the career they chose. Students may continue to switch as time allows.

    b. *Processing II (volunteers as a group)*: The school counselor will ask for one volunteer from each STEM category to share the career he or she chose and read what is provided on the career slip.

    c. *Processing III (full group)*: The school counselor will initiate a class discussion about the careers that students chose and why they did or did not like them.

9. End the session by having the students complete the written posttest.

Suggested Modifications (for Special Needs Populations): Students who struggle with fine motor skills may need assistance with cutting or drawing. Students with reading challenges may need help reading their career slip. These students may benefit from the school counselor or a peer providing support. School counselors are encouraged to utilize the vocabulary appropriate for the class's developmental level.

Evaluation Plan: School counselors are encouraged to use the initial discussion as a pretest screening tool to determine the level of baseline knowledge of STEM and STEM careers. The school counselor may utilize the posttest handout to assess the impact of the session on student knowledge and awareness of STEM careers.

Career List for the Students

Please make a copy for your students and cut these into individual strips.

....

Name: Marine engineer and naval architect

Description of duties: Design, build, and maintain ships from aircraft carriers to submarines, from sailboats to tankers.

Schooling: Bachelor's degree (4-year college)

Salary: $79,920 per year

....

Name: Architect

Description of duties: Plan and design buildings and other structures.

Schooling: Bachelor's degree (4-year college)

Salary: $72,550

....

Name: Software developer

Description of duties: Software developers are the creative minds behind computer programs.

Schooling: Bachelor's degree (4-year college)

Salary: $90,530 per year

....

Name: Financial analyst

Description of duties: Help businesses and individuals make money decisions.

Schooling: Bachelor's degree (4-year college)

Salary: $74,350 per year

....

Name: Physicist and astronomer

Description of duties: Study the universe.

Schooling: Doctoral degree

Salary: $105,430 per year

....

Name: Zoologist

Description of duties: Study the characteristics and habitats of animals.

Schooling: Bachelor's degree (4-year college)

Salary: $57,430 per year

....

....

Name: Computer support specialist

Description of duties: Provide help to people using computer software or equipment.

Schooling: Some college, no degree

Salary: $46,260 per year

....

Name: Environmental science and protection technician

Description of duties: Monitor the environment and investigate sources of pollution.

Schooling: Associate's degree (2-year college)

Salary: $41,380 per year

....

Name: Atmospheric scientist

Description of duties: Study weather, climate, and other aspects of the atmosphere.

Schooling: Bachelor's degree (4-year college)

Salary: $87,780 per year

....

Posttest

Name: _____

1. What does STEM stand for?
2. What is the name of your chosen career?
3. Describe the type of duties in your chosen career.
4. List the careers you heard about today.

REFERENCE

Bureau of Labor Statistics. (2012). *Occupational outlook handbook, 2012–13 edition*. Washington, DC: U.S. Department of Labor. Retrieved from http://www.bls.gov/ooh

---

THE WHEEL OF WORK

Melissa Luke and Allison Hrovat

This intervention uses the expressive arts medium of the mandala (Malchiodi, 2006) to explore students' personal self-concept, skills, values, and interests. Consistent with career theory in schools (Pope, 2009), this intervention additionally connects these personal attributes to the required work behaviors, advantages/ disadvantages, and occupational outlook for the students' chosen career.

Modality: Visual Arts

ASCA National Model Domain: Career

Deliver via: Classroom guidance

Age Level: Middle school

Indications: This intervention is appropriate for middle school-aged students who are developmentally at a point of considering initial career exploration. This intervention is equally appropriate for students who have an identified career of interest as well as those who lack certainty.

Materials: The basic materials required for this intervention include enough copies of the templates (see Figures 3.6 and 3.7) for each student with a few extras (suggestion: copy on cardstock and cut out in advance) and a writing

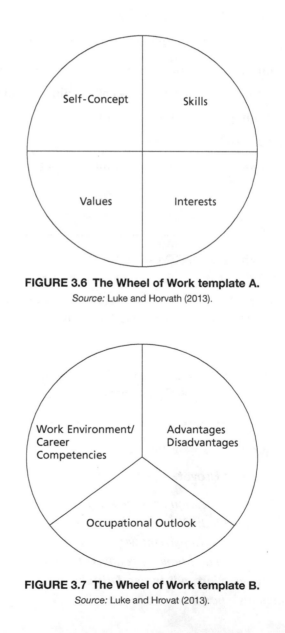

FIGURE 3.6 The Wheel of Work template A.

Source: Luke and Horvath (2013).

FIGURE 3.7 The Wheel of Work template B.

Source: Luke and Hrovat (2013).

utensil for each student. Beyond these basic materials, additional visual arts supplies will enhance students' options for expression. This list may include colored pencils, crayons, stickers, stamps, collage materials, printed copies of clip art images depicting career and personal attributes, and so on. Enough copies of a "coin" template are needed so that each student can complete one as part of the evaluation of the classroom guidance intervention. To create the "coin," the counselor should cut out a 3" circle on card stock for each student. On one side, print the word "Overlap" and on the other, print the word "Mismatch." These will be used in the evaluation phase of the intervention.

Preparations: As with any expressive therapy intervention, it is important that the school counselor try this ahead of time, both to experience the activity and to identify any other materials or directives he or she might deem necessary. Additionally, the school counselor should make an extra wheel that is half done, for demonstration purposes. The school counselor should print copies of the template, cut them into circles, and collect other visual arts supplies. This could include finding and cutting images from magazines for the students to choose from and/or printing clip art images that depict career and personal attributes. The school counselor may choose to print the additional list of words that students might choose to use on their collages (school counselors are encouraged to add to this list based on their knowledge of their students). Additionally, the school counselor should have access to a job outlook software system or an Internet search engine and can either have that resource available in the classroom or come prepared with common career choices printed for the students to review.

Instructions:
1. The school counselor introduces the activity by saying, *"We all have different parts of ourselves. Some parts are easier to see or recognize than other parts. For example, you can see here that I have an elbow, but you might not be able to see that I love scary movies. For the next 15 minutes or so, you are going to have an opportunity to create a wheel that represents some of the important parts of yourself that are not visible to the eye."*
2. The school counselor explains the four parts of the wheel: Self-concept, Skills, Values, and Interests. He or she elicits students' explanations of each of the four areas on the wheel, offering clarification of the definitions using the following examples as guidelines: Self-concept is a collection of beliefs about yourself and your identity and generally embodies the answer to the question, "Who am I?" Skills are learned abilities to carry out tasks in various contexts. Values are personal, familial, and cultural beliefs that provide an internal reference from which to act and/or judge what is good, beneficial, or constructive. Interests are the things that capture your attention and engagement.
3. The school counselor shows an example of his or her own wheel. The wheel should have some areas that are already completed and the school counselor can then complete the other area(s) as a model while students are watching.

4. *"Using the supplies available, I would like you to visually show something about each of these 'parts' of yourself: who are you (self-concept), what is important to you (values), what are you interested in (interest), and what are some things that you do well (skills)? Remember that this is an opportunity to reflect on how you see yourself and not necessarily how others see you. It is important to think about these 'parts' of yourself in all areas of life: school, home, extracurricular activities, religious communities, and so on, because you may find similarities and differences across contexts."*

5. The school counselor introduces students to the materials available and alerts students of the time limit for this part of the activity (10 to 12 minutes).

6. While the students work on their wheels, the school counselor circulates around the room and provides process observations, reflects students' experiences, probes for deeper meaning, and asks and answers questions as needed. The school counselor offers a 2-minute warning and then calls students' attention back to the large group.

   The school counselor asks for individuals to share some of their observations about the activity, themselves, and one another. The school counselor uses group-work skills across systems levels to draw out individual students, link their experiences to one another, and thematically connect their comments as a whole (Luke, 2014).

   The school counselor then introduces the concept of career, explaining that career theories (Pope, 2009) have long suggested that a person's self-concept, interests, values, and skills are related to his or her chosen *vocation* and *avocation*. (The school counselor intentionally teaches the definition of these terms as work or occupation and hobby or pastime, respectively.) The school counselor explains that *"just like all people are made up of various parts (illustrated through the past activity), careers have different parts to them as well. Similar to the way that people have some parts that are more visible than others, so too are the parts of careers."*

   The school counselor asks students to turn over their wheels so that they can see that the wheel is divided into three parts: namely, the work environment and career-related competencies, the advantages/disadvantages, and the occupational outlook.

7. Using his or her wheel as an example, the school counselor invites students to explain what may be meant by each of the three areas and offers definitions as follows: Work environment is the typical setting or context in which one typically finds the career. Career-related competencies include academic knowledge, specialty training and skills, and professional expertise necessary to perform the career. Advantages/disadvantages are the personal evaluation of benefits and drawbacks to pursuing the career. Occupational outlook addresses the expected job growth, salary compensation, and so on.

8. The school counselor instructs students to use the next 10 to 15 minutes to complete the requested information about a career (e.g., phlebotomist) or career category (e.g., medical field) that interests them at this point in their development.

9. As the students engage in this step, the school counselor circles the room and supports students' in their acquisition of the needed information. Depending on the needs of the group, the school counselor may be more task focused or able to provide students with observations about the process (e.g., *"I see that this is something you want to think about,"* or *"I'm noticing that like the student next to you, you are having an easier time identifying the advantages of the career than you are the disadvantages,"* or, *"Wow, that is surprising to you that there is so much involved to prepare for the career."*)

The school counselor gives a 2-minute warning before calling the students back to the large group. The school counselor indicates that he or she knows that not everyone has finished, and that parallels the process of career development, because the exploration, acquisition, and transitions related to a career can be considered an ongoing process. He or she suggests that students can redress their wheel at another point.

The school counselor invites students to identify something that they learned or to share an aspect of their experience of the second activity. After a few students do so, the school counselor suggests that another student who has yet to share connect this to the first activity that was focused on the "person." The school counselor directs students to think about what is similar and different, as well as how the personal and career might connect.

10. In closing, the school counselor asks students to reflect on the points/places where what they depicted on the personal side of the wheel matches up with what they identified on the career side. The school counselor can use the metaphor of "two sides of the same coin" as he or she shares an example of how the material on his or her personal side correlates with the career, as well as an illustration of where it might not.

The school counselor distributes the "coin" on which students complete their evaluation. One side of the coin asks students to identify an area of overlap between their personal–career wheel and the other side of the coin asks students to note an area of disconnect. The school counselor collects these before students leave.

Suggested Modifications (for Special Needs Populations):

a. If time is limited, the activity can be divided over 2 days. The school counselor can also assign students to work in groups for the second part of the wheel, where each group is assigned a specific career or career cluster. Although this is less individualized, it is a bit faster and can provide the group an opportunity to learn about a wider variety of careers.

b. For students who may have a hard time with abstract thinking, the school counselor can use an oversized plastic needle and thick yarn to demonstrate that like a "lacing or sewing card, there are points of intersection between who we are as a person, and our selected career."

c. "While no person-career is ever a 'perfect fit,' some might be a better match than others."

Evaluation Plan: The school counselor introduces the "coin" on which the words "Overlap" and "Mismatch" have been printed prior to the intervention, and asks students to complete both sides. (The coin symbolizes the tangible compensation that is often provided in exchange for one's work.) Side one has a place where students identify an area of overlap or connection between their personal and career wheel, and the second side of the coin asks students to note one place where their personal and career wheel do not quite match up.

REFERENCES

Luke, M. (2014). Effective group leadership interventions. In J. L. Delucia-Waack, C. L. Kalonder, & M. T. Riva (Eds.), *Handbook of group counseling and psychotherapy* (2nd ed., pp. 107–119). Thousands Oak, CA: Sage.

Malchiodi, C. (2006). *The art therapy sourcebook.* New York, NY: McGraw-Hill.

Pope, M. (2009). Jesse Buttrick Davis (1871–1955): Pioneer of vocational guidance in the schools. *Career Development Quarterly, 57,* 278–288.

APPENDIX

Wealth	Thoughtful	Physics	Teaching
!"##$%&'"(	Friendly	ATHLETICS	Business
fame	Loyal	Photography	Medicine
Family	Good with Hands	Painting	Restaurants
Success	Cooperative	Drawing	Retail
Stability	Persuasive	Videography	Sales
Pride	!""#$%&'()*)+$	Web Design	Construction
Joy	Brave	Social Media	Advertising
Challenge	Adventurous	History	Journalism
Adventure	Passionate	Politics	Architecture
Intelligent	focused	Psychology	Acting
CARING	Math	Auto Shop	Pharmacist
Athletic	Reading	Cosmetology	Doctor
Creative	Writing	Culinary Arts	Nurse
Outgoing	Public Speaking	Religion	Computers
Studious	Biology	Physical Labor	VETERINARIAN
Ambitious	Chemistry	Working with Children	SPORTS
Energetic			Law Enforcement
MUSIC			Fashion
Travel			LAWYER
			Helping Others
			REALTOR
			Entertainment

YOUR TRUE NORTH: THE LIFE YOU LEARN FROM AND THE LIFE YOU LIVE

Michelle Kelley Shuler and Katrina Cook

The counselor will describe the geographic difference between true north and magnetic north to the students, leading to an explanation regarding difference between "truth" and "attraction." Students will be given a copy of a compass that visually represents true north and magnetic north. Students will identify and contemplate images that represent true north and magnetic north to them. They will then place an image of a compass on a poster board, indicating true north and magnetic north. They will then select images from magazines, drawings, words, and so on, to represent these two concepts and place them on the poster board depending on whether they represent true north or magnetic north.

Modality: Visual

ASCA National Model Domain: Career

Deliver via: Classroom guidance, small-group counseling, or individual counseling

Age Level: High school

Indications: This activity is appropriate for students exploring career options, experiencing academic difficulties, or with personal/social challenges.

Materials: This activity requires a copy of a compass (Figure 3.8), poster board, markers, magazines with visual or written images, and glue. Students may also choose to incorporate pictures they have downloaded from the Internet, personal photos, drawings, or poems.

Preparations: Make all the materials accessible to each participating student. It is possible that not all the students will be able to complete and share their collages in the allotted time. If this is the case, the counselor should keep the collages in a safe place and return them to the students during the next meeting.

Instructions:

1. **Focus/Anticipatory Expectations Set**

    The counselor will begin the session by explaining the concepts of *true north* and *magnetic north* and the purpose of the activity to the students. Counselors may use the following script:

    > *"True north is the direction along the earth's surface toward the geographic North Pole. True north usually differs from magnetic north. Magnetic north moves over time due to magnetic changes in the Earth's core.*

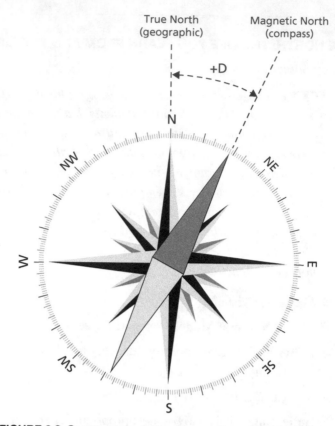

FIGURE 3.8 Compass depicting true north and magnetic north.

"The intention of this exercise is to honor your true inner guide and point awareness to what draws one toward 'true north' and what draws one toward 'magnetic north,' to recognize differences between 'truth' and 'attraction' and to allow yourself time to identify your true path and honor its home.

"Imagine true north points you in the direction of your true path. True north is considered to be your inner guide and generates the path most representative of your authentic self.

"Now imagine your magnetic north pulls you just astray from your true north. Maybe just 15 degrees left or right of center, but definitely off the path. Imagine your magnetic north is representative of those things that you are 'drawn' to or those things that have some kind of power to distract you.

"You may or may not be conscious of your attraction to these things. It is also true that these things may or may not represent something about yourself you like or enjoy. However, being 'bad' for you is not a prerequisite."

2. The Exercise

"For this exercise use the compass I've provided for each of you. Notice where true north and magnetic north are represented. Use this to help create an image in your mind of your true path and the path you are sometimes drawn toward.

"Find a quiet space and time when you can spend some time alone reflecting on this idea. Then I want you to close your eyes and imagine images or words that represent your true north. As these images and words come to you, write them down on the left side of the page adjacent to true north. Spend some time contemplating this so that you have a good idea of what these images/words may be.

"Then, spend some time contemplating your magnetic north. As these images and words come to you, write them down on the right side of the page adjacent to magnetic north. Spend some time contemplating this so that you have a good idea of what these images/words may be.

"You will use the images, words, and so on, to create a collage representing your true north and magnetic north. Use a poster board and place an image of a compass in the middle of the poster board. Draw a line marking true north and magnetic north from the compass to the edge of the poster board. Gather images or items to represent the things that came to you during the contemplative portion of exercise. Place the true north images around the true north line and the magnetic north images close to the magnetic north line.

"Take your time with this assignment. Remember there is no right or wrong, only the words, images, feelings, and meaning you associate with each."

3. Creating the Collage

After all students have completed their collages, ask them to share what the images mean to them with the rest of the students (or with the counselor if this was used in an individual counseling session).

Suggested Modifications (for Special Needs Populations): Assist students with the activity as needed.

Evaluation Plan: The students will complete collages and their explanation of the collages will demonstrate whether or not the activity objectives have been met.

4 ✺ Visual Arts Interventions in the Personal/Social Domain

ANGER SWITCH

Jennifer H. Greene and Saron N. LaMothe

*T*his activity can be utilized in a small group, as classroom guidance, or in individual counseling. The purpose is to identify and describe anger triggers and, conversely, identify and describe ways to calm down. It involves conceptualizing anger as a switch, such as a light switch. When flipped one way, we feel angry; when flipped the other, we are calm.

Modality: Visual Arts – Drawing

ASCA National Model Domain: Personal/Social

Deliver via: Group counseling, classroom guidance, individual

Age Level: Elementary (ideal with 3rd to 5th grade)

Indications: Works very well as a part of a group focused on anger control

Materials: Paper for everyone in the group, pencils, markers, crayons, colored pencils, whiteboard, and whiteboard markers (for a classroom guidance lesson).

Preparation: Have paper and other materials ready on the table for the group or be prepared to pass them out to the class after demonstrating on the board.

Instructions
1. If this is a first group meeting, ask the group what emotion tends to get them into trouble the most often. Typically they immediately respond with anger.
2. Ask them what makes them angry (i.e. *what pushes their anger buttons*). Is it someone touching their things? Is it someone telling them what to do? Others not letting them play?
3. Have the students divide their paper in two by drawing a line down the middle. If this is a classroom guidance lesson, demonstrate on a whiteboard or large piece of paper.

4. Draw a light switch or toggle switch in the middle of the paper and describe how a switch can be turned on and off. Just like there are things that make us angry, there are things that help us to calm down.

5. Ask the students what things help them calm down or stay calm. Be prepared to help with suggestions, especially in an anger-control group. Some suggestions could be taking deep breaths or counting backwards (be prepared to teach this in an anger-control group and give time to practice).

6. Allow the students time to list on one half of the paper the things that make them angry and on the other half the things that help them calm down.

7. Allow them time to decorate the sheet of paper, including both the angry side and the calm side. With a small group, work on a sheet with them as the group shares. With a classroom guidance lesson, this is a chance to check in with each student about what they learned during the lesson.

Suggested Modifications (for Special Needs Populations): With special needs learners and English Language Learning (ELL) students, use more visual aids. It is beneficial to work on an example with the group or class first and then to provide extra assistance as needed.

Evaluation Plan: At the end of the lesson, determine whether each person in the group/class is able to name several things that make them angry and also several ways to calm down.

CREATIVE EXPRESSION OF HEALING

Lori Ellison and Carol M. Smith

*I*n this intervention, students create an object or artifact that expresses the process of healing from a past crisis, loss, or traumatic experience. Participants are encouraged to use symbolism rather than words in order to access the meanings and emotions attached to the experience.

Modality: Visual Arts, Music, Movement/Dance, Art, Video, Crafts

ASCA National Model Domain: Personal/Social

Deliver via: Individual or group

Age Level: Elementary, middle, or high school

Indications: This intervention is indicated whenever a student has experienced a loss, psychological trauma, or personal crisis. This intervention can also be used when a negative event (e.g., a fellow student's death, natural disaster, etc.) has affected groups of students or an entire school. Unless counselors are on hand to provide immediate support, it is most appropriate to use older events, from which students have some emotional distance, rather than using events that are raw, unfolding, or close at hand.

Materials: Paper, paint, crayons, colored pens/pencils, glue, scissors, yarn, clay, fabric, video and/or audio recording equipment, and any additional gathered objects that can be used in the intervention.

Preparation: Because participants are free to create whatever object or artifact appeals to them, using their own hands, to create something that expresses their sense of healing and hopefulness after a negative experience, no preparation beyond providing the materials is needed. The creation can be a single object or a series of objects, to represent progression.

Instructions: Read through the following instructions completely *before* starting the project.

1. To benefit most from this assignment, be mindful. Track your feelings, thoughts, and insights along the way in a journal if that helps.
2. Recall a crisis from your past. It should be meaningful but "past-tense." You should have already experienced measurable healing from it. Please do not choose an experience that is current, raw, or unfinished.
3. This works best if you create an *unwritten* (wordless, no text) *project* that expresses your own healing process. Use this creative project to express what the healing process looks like for you, whether the process is complete or ongoing.
4. Use any medium (paper, clay, yarn, video, music, paint, fabric, etc.) to express your healing in a symbolic way that works for you (e.g., drawing, painting, sculpture, knitting, sewing, diorama, video, carving, pottery, still-life photography, music, dance, etc.). Use color or textures intentionally. You may create a "series" or a "single work" to illustrate your healing process. Do what works for you and what "feels" right. Please create something yourself, with your own hands, using your own creativity, imagination, and resourcefulness.
5. To enhance the process, think about what you have created and express what you are thinking about in writing. Discuss the project with a group or a person you trust.

Suggested Modifications (for Special Needs Populations): Modify, as appropriate, for those who have special concerns, such as color blindness, movement restrictions, and so on. The creative expression is chosen by each participant, and can be done with help, if needed.

Evaluation: Because products of creative expression are evaluated in simply an appreciative manner, counselors can support each student and help him or her process the meanings, insights, and significance of the project.

CULTURE SHOCK

Stefi Threadgill and Brandy Schumann

Culture is made up of various dimensions that are interdependent and are likely to cluster, making them mutually reinforcing and creating a "felt experience of being" (Diller, 2011, p. 71). A person's culture has many influencers, including media, peers, family, and society. This activity increases awareness of the impact of the environment on identity formation, self-esteem, and behavior. The activity also provides awareness that cultural norms and ideals change over time and vary among different groups.

Expressive arts techniques promote discovery, which leads to curiosity and awareness and invites new ways of being (Knill, Levine, & Levine, 2005). A strong, integrated sense of self generates positive self-esteem and self-regulation (Oaklander, 2007). An inauthentic sense of self creates disintegration and polarity, which negatively shape an individual's self-concept and how one can experience him- or herself and his or her world. Parts of self that are denied result in unexpressed emotions that create an incomplete gestalt or fragmented sense of self. Increased self-awareness promotes authenticity and accuracy, which creates an opportunity for change. This activity can increase awareness that personhood is holistic and is not defined purely by culture. It also promotes the awareness that perception of self occurs in the context of environment. It also encourages healthy contact, including identifying and promoting healthy boundaries of self and others. Using this activity, individuals gain awareness of how others experience them. This can lead to a more accurate self-concept and empower one to focus on more authentic qualities. Through the I/Thou relationship of the group and the here-and-now immediacy of the experience, the individual is able to gain awareness through the process of the activity. This promotes re-integration of a holistic and authentic self. Additionally, a group setting provides social support, normalization, and increased opportunity to understand that perception is subjective (Berg, Landreth, & Fall, 2013).

Modality: Visual Arts

ASCA National Model Domain: Personal/Social

Deliver via: Group counseling

Age Level: Elementary, middle, or high school

Indications: Individuals struggling with social skills, self-esteem, eating disorders, and addiction may benefit. Refugees may also benefit.

Materials: Human cutouts (i.e., paper doll), house/school/world cutouts, magazines, glue stick, paper, and scissors.

Preparation: Have all of the materials easily available for all students.

Instructions:

1. Ask the students to create a collage of images and messages you receive from your culture on a human cutout.
2. After providing time for students to create their visual image, ask students to place their human cutout on the house/school/world image.
3. Process the activity using questions such as, *"Describe your collage. Describe your school culture, community culture, and family culture? How are they the same? Different? What have you learned about relationships? Conflict? Love? Gender roles? Career? How do you define health (beauty, love)? What did you learn about the world? What messages are congruent with your personal beliefs? Incongruent? What messages have been the most influential?"*

Eating Disorders Substrate

Imagine that you are the editor of a publication. You have the power to decide what images and messages are printed in the publication. What messages do you want to offer to your readers?

Addictions Substrate

Create a collage of images and messages you receive about drug use (your choice of addictive substance and its impact on your health).

Refugee Population Substrate

Create a collage of images that represent the culture of your homeland on one side and your current culture on the other. What differences and similarities do you notice? What aspects of each culture inform who you are?

Self-Esteem and Social Skills Substrate

Create a collage of images that you receive in your culture about how a person should be.

Evaluation Plan: This intervention can be used in a pre/post fashion over time to gain a qualitative measurement of growth and provide a concrete display of change or perception shift for the student.

REFERENCES

Berg, R. C., Landreth, G. L., & Fall, K. A. (2013). *Group counseling: Concepts and procedures.* (5th ed.). New York, NY: Routledge.

Diller, J. V. (2011). *Cultural diversity: A primer for the human services.* (4th ed.). Belmont, CA: Brooks/Cole.

Knill, P. J., Levine, E. G., & Levine, S. K. (2005). *Principles and practice of expressive arts therapy: Toward a therapeutic aesthetics.* London, UK: Jessica Kingsley Publishers.

Oaklander, V. (2007). *Hidden treasure: A map to the child's inner self.* London, UK: Karnac Books Ltd.

DECREASING MENTAL ILLNESS STIGMA WITH VISUAL ART AND WRITING

Allison Crowe and Kylie P. Dotson-Blake

This activity aims to decrease stigma toward mental illness and seeking help for mental health concerns using a visual art reflection activity. Students are introduced to the topic of mental illness stigma and then encouraged to reflect on how mental illness has impacted them in their own lives or the lives of others. Students complete the activity and learn about the concept of stigma, as well as mental illness and the role that stigma has related to this. The ultimate aim is to decrease mental illness stigma and normalize help seeking for mental health concerns.

Modality: Visual Art and Writing

ASCA Domain: Personal/Social

Deliver via: Individual, group, or classroom guidance

Age Group: Middle or high school

Indications: This activity could be used with students who are currently experiencing mental health concerns, or as prevention for any student who might experience mental health concerns in the future.

Materials: Paper, colored pencils or markers

Preparation: No particular preparation needed

Instructions:

1. Introduce the topic of mental illness and define it: *"A mental illness is a medical condition that disrupts a person's thinking, feeling, mood, ability to relate to others, and daily functioning. Mental illnesses are medical conditions that often result in a diminished capacity for coping with the ordinary demands of life"* (National Alliance on Mental Illness, 2013).

2. Introduce the concept of stigma and explain how it impacts mental illness: *"Stigma is a mark of disgrace or discredit. It includes stereotypes, negative attitudes, and labels. There are different types of stigma. Self-stigma, when the person with mental illness stereotypes, judges, and labels him- or herself; associative stigma, when friends and family experience the stigma of having someone close to them with a mental illness; or public stigma—the general public labeling or stereotyping of the person who is diagnosed"* (Crowe, 2013).

3. Pass out paper, colored pencils, or markers to the students.

4. Give the following directive: *"Think of a personal event or experience you have had related to mental illness (this can be a recent experience or one from the past). This can be something that happened to you, or someone you know, or in the larger society related to mental illness."*

5. Next, ask the students to draw an image of the experience on their paper using the colored pencils or markers.

6. After students have created the image, ask them to write words or phrases that describe some of the attitudes about the event or experience at the bottom of the paper. For example, if a student drew a picture of his older sister alone in her bedroom because she was experiencing feelings of depression, words and phrases might include: *What's wrong with her? How can I help? Why is she so sad?*

7. Next, ask students to give a title to the image. For example, *Sarah Is Depressed*. Write the title at the top of the paper.

8. If using as classroom guidance, instruct students to get into small groups of three to four per group and share their images with each other. If using the activity in a group or in individual counseling, ask each person to share.

9. Next, discuss themes, differences, and similarities in the images.

10. If using as classroom guidance or as a large group, discuss how these images, situations, and so on, related to mental illness relate to help seeking and contribute to mental illness stigma. Encourage sharing among the group about this, and offer examples of this in the larger society as well.

11. Finally, wrap up by using the following reflection questions:

    ■ *"What did we learn today about mental illness and stigma?"*
    ■ *"What did you learn about yourself and others related to this?"*
    ■ *"In your opinion, what needs to happen in the larger society to de-stigmatize mental illness?"*

Suggested Modifications (for Special Needs Populations): The activity can be modified by omitting the drawing portion for any students who would rather discuss verbally.

Evaluation Plan: To evaluate whether students learned about mental illness stigma, a pre- and postassessment could be given that asked students about their knowledge of mental illness and mental illness stigma. The definitions provided earlier for each term can be used for this evaluation.

REFERENCES

Crowe, A. (2013). Mental illness stigma: Early lessons. *Counseling Today, 56,* 24–25.
National Alliance on Mental Illness. (2013). *What is mental illness?* Retrieved on December 16, 2013, from http://www.nami.org/Template.cfm?Section=By_Illness

---

DOODLE ART—JUST FOR FUN?

Bridget Tuohy Helms

The purpose of teaching Doodle Art is to give students an alternate means of coping during times of stress. The use of Doodle Art can help calm students who face a variety of stressors, including anxiety and/or depression. The counselor should start the lesson by explaining to the students that Doodle Art is one of many ways that may help student's to feel more calm, to relax, to decrease nervousness (anxiety), or in times of sadness (depression). The counselor should explain that Doodle Art may be soothing to some and not to others; that there is not a one-size-fits-all coping mechanism that will fit everyone's needs. The only way to see if this will help an individual is to simply try it. Students will be taught individually or within a group setting to learn the basics of Doodle Art.

Modality: Visual Drawing

ASCA National Model Domain: Personal/Social

Deliver via: Individual or group counseling

Age Level: Elementary, middle, or high school (Appropriate for use with any age group—modify the processing questions to align with the students' developmental level.)

Indications: This activity can be used with individuals or small groups to help students cope with a variety of stressors, including anxiety and depression, or to aide students in finding a method to relax.

Materials: Paper and pencils; colored pencils, crayons, markers may also be used.

Preparation: Each student will start with paper and writing instruments.

Instructions: To reiterate, the counselor should start the lesson by explaining to the students that Doodle Art is one of many ways that may help students to feel more calm, to relax, to decrease nervousness (anxiety), or in times of sadness (depression). The counselor should explain that Doodle Art may be soothing to some and not to others; that there is not a one-size-fits-all coping mechanism that will fit everyone's needs. The only way to see if this will help an individual is to simply try doodling.

FIGURE 4.1 Doodle Art Step 1.

1. Illustrate the process by beginning with a blank sheet of standard-size plain paper (Figure 4.1). Draw four dots near the corners of the page and show the example to student(s).
2. The school counselor will then explain that the four dots need to be connected in a "frame." Encourage student(s) to feel free to use creativity in connecting dots. Again, the counselor will show the example to student(s) (Figure 4.2).
3. The school counselor will then show student(s) that the frame needs to be divided into smaller "frames" by using two to three lines to subdivide the frame (Figure 4.3). Again, encourage student(s) to be creative.

FIGURE 4.2 Doodle Art Step 2.

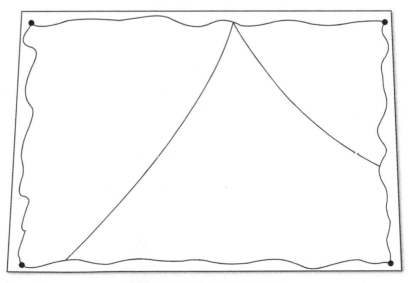

FIGURE 4.3 Doodle Art Step 3.

4. Now that the frame is set, the school counselor will explain that each section is its own little frame (Figure 4.4). Have student(s) choose one frame to start with. Continue on to subsequent frames as time allows.

5. Provide student(s) with a variety of patterns that they can use within their selected frame. Patterns can be simple or complex. (Patterns can be found in doodling-specific books or by conducting a search on the Internet.) The idea is for student(s) to feel at ease, freeing the mind of intrusive thoughts and/or feelings.

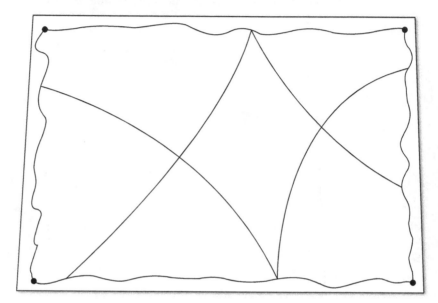

FIGURE 4.4 Doodle Art Step 4.

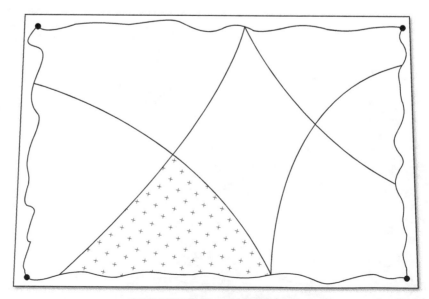

FIGURE 4.5 Doodle Art Step 5.

6. Explain to student(s) that Doodle Art can be used for a few minutes to hours; that the student can complete one frame and, if feeling better, it can be put away until the student chooses to work on it again. There is no reason to feel rushed to complete the whole page within any time frame.

Prompts for Facilitation During the Activity

- ▨ *"When could you see yourself using this?"*
- ▨ *"How would this activity help you manage your feelings?"*
- ▨ *"Do you enjoy this activity?"*

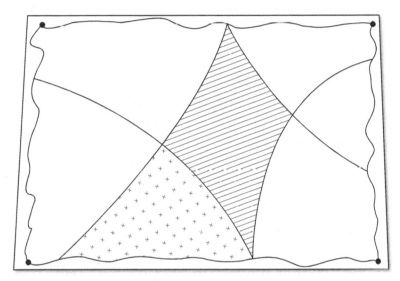

FIGURE 4.6 Doodle Art Step 6.

FIGURE 4.7 Doodle Art final product.

- ■ *"What are you thinking of as you complete this activity?"*
- ■ *"Do you notice that you feel calmer or less sad?"*
- ■ *"How do you see yourself using this activity outside of this lesson/ group?"*

Suggested Modifications (for Special Needs Populations): School counselors may need to modify the language used in facilitating the questions during the lesson and in the follow-up session to the students' developmental levels. This activity is appropriate for use with most student groups and will be particularly helpful with students who experience anxiety and/or depression. Students who have difficulty with fine motor skills may find this activity difficult and frustrating. In this situation, the student should be encouraged to work with pieces of paper and writing utensils that are larger than average or the student could also use paint and a large paintbrush.

Evaluation Plan: To evaluate the effectiveness of this intervention, you may use the attached assessment tool.

Student(s) will be verbally assessed for understanding. Student(s) will be asked a series of questions to ascertain initial understanding of what feelings are currently being experienced and how those feelings are being managed. Use questions during the lesson to facilitate learning and thought processes (questions found above). Follow up within a set timeframe (1 to 2 weeks) to determine whether Doodle Art is an appropriate and useful coping technique for student(s).

Initial Session
1. What ways are you currently using to cope with nervousness and/or sadness?
2. How is your current coping method working?
3. How is your current coping method not working?
4. What would you like to see change?

Follow-Up Session
1. How have you used Doodle Art since learning about it?
2. When using Doodle Art, what changes did you notice in your mood?
3. How did you feel before, during, and after using Doodle Art?
4. Do you feel learning Doodle Art was helpful in managing your feelings?
5. How do you feel you will use Doodle Art in the future?

REFERENCES

Bartholomew, S. S. (2010). *Totally tangled*. Fort Worth, TX: Design Originals.

Bartholomew, S. S. (2011). *Yoga for your brain: Zentangle workout*. Fort Worth, TX: Design Originals.

Corfee, S. (2011). *Creative doodling & beyond*. Irvine, CA: Walter Foster Publishing.

McNeill, S. (2010). *Zentangle basics*. Fort Worth, TX: Design Originals.

McNeill, S. (2011). *Zentangle 5: 40 more tangles and fabulous jewelry*. Fort Worth, TX: Design Originals.

ERASE AND REPLACE

Tony Michael and Hewitt B. Rogers

*A*lthough this activity was initially created for individual counseling, the exercise can also be adapted to a small-group counseling setting. The activity provides an opportunity for students to visualize different negative thoughts that they believe to be true or have heard about themselves, and replace those judgments with more constructive and affirmative thoughts. In particular, the exercise promotes healthy self-esteem and offers an opportunity for students to have negative and self-defeating thoughts challenged in a nonthreatening or intrusive manner. This activity promotes personal and interpersonal functioning through cognitive and verbal processing. School counselors and students have the opportunity to process and discuss negative and self-defeating thoughts that may be contributing to the need for therapeutic intervention; this activity provides an avenue to formulate alternative responses, which can foster the growth of constructive and optimistic thoughts.

Modality: Visual and tactile

ASCA National Model Domain: Personal/Social

Deliver via: Individual or group counseling

Age Level: Middle or high school: The exercise can be utilized with students who have reached a developmental level at which they can potentially comprehend and process cognitive distortions.

Indications: Although this activity was created for indoor use, it can also be performed outside if the school setting permits. Likewise, this exercise can work with individuals and small groups. The activity addresses potential cognitive insecurities or fallacies that a child might possess. In a group setting, students can build friendships by gaining support from peers through an atmosphere of safety and respect.

Materials: Dry erase markers, eraser, and dry erase board.

Preparation: Have the dry erase markers and large dry erase board ready for the student when the child gets to the session. Ideally, having markers in a variety of colors and a large dry erase board works best, as the materials will provide an avenue for the child to freely express his or her thoughts and feelings without creative restraint.

Instructions:
1. When the student arrives to the room for the session, introduce and describe the activity. Explain to the child that self-defeating thoughts, feelings, and behaviors have a negative impact on an individual's life. Through this discussion, encourage the student to identify any harmful thoughts, feelings, and behaviors he or she has experienced.
2. After identifying the self-defeating thoughts, invite the student to draw an outline of his or her own body on a dry erase board.

3. After drawing the outline, the student is directed to write down any negative attributions or self-defeating phrases that came to his or her mind. Bear in mind that these statements might originate from internal or external factors. In addition, some students may benefit from drawing the self-defeating words on the parts of the body that are most impacted by the negative beliefs, if relevant. Remind students that colors might be used to represent different emotions attached to the words, and emphasize the value of individual artistic expression in the activity.

4. After the words are placed on the board, the school counselor should have the student articulate whether he or she is aware of where the core of the negative self-attributions originate.

5. This activity invites you to assist students in dispelling maladaptive core thoughts and encourage their replacement with a self-enhancing belief system. Educate students to recognize that the modification of a maladaptive core belief will benefit both the self and interpersonal relationships. In particular, you should discuss the negative self-defeating thoughts, feelings, and behaviors and promote a healthy conceptualization of the student. Challenge unhealthy and irrational beliefs and promote a healthy self-worth. This may include telling the student that although an individual may have said a negative statement about him or her, it does not mean it is truth. Due to the potential complexity of the student's thoughts, feelings, and behaviors, this part of the exercise may take more than one session.

6. After identifying and discussing the self-defeating thoughts, feelings, and behaviors associated with the words in the outline of the body, encourage the student to erase the negative associations with an eraser. Process with the student the feelings of erasing away the negative beliefs.

7. Following the erasing of the self-defeating thoughts, feelings, and behaviors, ask the student to refill the body outline with positive and uplifting words or phrases. Assist the student as needed and encourage the child to think of words that he or she values. Counselors should allow students to use words that they aspire to be. These words can assist children in being goal oriented and provide an avenue for further discussions in the counseling process.

Suggested Modifications (for Special Needs Populations): This activity is particularly helpful for students who respond well to drawing and writing. Like other activities, school counselors may need to modify the language to suit the students' developmental levels. In addition, students who have difficulty with fine motor skills may be encouraged to have the counselor draw or write the body and words for them.

This exercise can also be modified for school counselors who have the opportunity to go outside with a child. In this situation, the activity can be done using chalk, a sponge, and a bucket of water. In this adaptation instead of erasing the negative words, statements can be washed away and replaced with constructive expressions.

Evaluation Plan: School counselors should evaluate the student's self-efficacy skills, decision-making skills, and engagement in school before, during, and after the exercise. By using this activity with students with whom you are familiar, observation and communication about these developments are facilitated.

EXPRESSION ON THE SPECTRUM

Adrienne E. Ahr, Jacqueline J. Young, and Lisa L. Schulz

*P*resented are three distinct activities focused on increasing the emotional, physical, and social awareness of students exhibiting characteristics of autism. The impairments associated with autism are intrusive and affect a child's development, including communication skills, abnormal behaviors, and deficits in social interactions (Dempsey & Foreman, 2001). Group dynamic allows the student's brain chemistry to change by connecting to peers in a therapeutic way (Badenoch, 2008). Due to the varied functional levels of students, screening participants is suggested. If screening members, you may use the evaluative measures included in this intervention to determine if the group is appropriate for the student. Each activity has a varying degree of structure and emotional exploration that may be used individually or in sequential order, progressing from the least structured presented in activity one to most structured in activity three.

Modality: Visual Arts and Movement/Dance

ASCA National Model Domain: Personal/Social

Deliver via: Group counseling

Age Level: Designed for children who exhibit characteristics of autism spectrum disorder (ASD) and social communication disorder (SCD), with developmental ages ranging between 4 and 12 years old.

Indications: May be used with small groups focused on increasing empathy, body awareness, and social awareness through reflections associated with movement and choice within the group activity.

Activity One: Dance and Paint With Feet

Materials: Provide 4′ × 10′ white or yellow butcher paper, two to four pans or buckets to fill with paint that the students can step into, washable paint (one primary color is suggested per activity due to the overstimulating effect of using bright and/or multiple colors), masking tape, water and cloth or wet wipes to clean feet, a device to play music. Choose music you believe the students will enjoy and feel comfortable moving to. Consider children's classics such as Disney or Sesame Street. You may also consider music without words such as classical or jazz. Music can increase group cohesion (Katagiri, 2009). You may change the music but be aware of the change in mood that may result. If you choose not to include music, encourage students to move to their own rhythm.

Preparation: Choose a room with tile flooring for easy cleaning. Lay out the piece of butcher paper, place it in the center of the room or in an area where students can sit on all sides of it, and secure with masking tape. Put one color of paint into pans for feet to step into and place pans at each end of the paper. Prepare the music selection. Have cleaning supplies available. Before they enter the room, have students take off their shoes and socks.

Instructions: Have students sit around the butcher paper. Tell students they will step into the paint and then step on the paper as the music plays. Tell students they can choose how to move their feet on the paper. Tell them that the activity will begin when the music starts and end when the music stops. You may choose to model this for students. It may benefit you to model behaviors and run the group with a cofacilitator to increase student understanding on how to connect to peers and increase student-to-counselor ratio, depending on students' behaviors.

1. Start music.
2. Tell the students they can begin.
3. Make statements about the movements they are making. Examples: You are shaking your leg. You are smiling at him.
4. After 10 minutes, turn off the music and tell students to sit down, leaving their feet on the paper.
5. Process the activity with questions and general statements:
    a. How did you move your feet? Who else moved like you? How did others move differently from you?
    b. Reflect on similarities in feet and body movements, who danced together, and who struggled to dance.
    c. Discuss any difficulty using paint: Has anyone else done something they did not like or feel before? Is there anything you don't like to touch or foods you don't want to eat?
6. Illicit a statement from students concerning their experience by stating one thing they liked or disliked about the activity.
7. Have students clean their feet and assist when needed.
8. Have students put on their shoes and end session.

Activity Two: Dance and Paint With Hands

Materials: Supply 4´ × 10´ white or yellow butcher paper with shapes drawn on the paper in black paint or marker (see Appendix), two pans or paper plates that the student's hands can fit into to fill with paint, washable paint, masking tape, water and cloth or wet wipes to clean hands, and a device to play music.

Preparation: Choose a room with a tile floor or a large table for easy cleaning. Lay out the butcher paper on the floor or table in the center of the room or an area where students can sit on all sides and secure with masking tape. Put paint into pans/plates for hands to go into and place on the edge of the paper. Prepare music selection. (Refer to Activity One for suggestions). Have cleaning supplies available.

Instructions: Have students sit around the butcher paper. Tell students they will put their hands into the paint and then put them on the paper as the music plays. Tell students they can choose how to move their hands on the paper, and they may choose to fill in the shapes or create their own. Indicate that the activity will begin when the music starts and end when the music stops. You may choose to model this for students.

1. Start music.
2. Tell the students they can begin.
3. Make statements about the movements they are making and what shapes they are using and creating. (Refer to Activity One for examples.)
4. After 10 minutes, turn off the music and have students clean their hands, assisting when needed.
5. Have students return and sit around the paper.
6. Process the activity with questions and general statements: *"How did the picture change? Name something you saw someone else do. Do you like how it changed? Say something about the art you made together. Name something you like or don't like. How do your hands want to move?"*

   Compare hands, shapes used, and movements: *"Did you move to other shapes or stay at one? What feelings came up during the activity?"*
7. Elicit a statement from students concerning their experience. Have students pick their favorite shape/drawing on the picture.
8. End session.

Activity Three: Dance and Paint Your Feelings

Materials: Provide 4′ × 10′ white or yellow butcher paper with basic round faces painted or drawn on it with four expressions on a continuum from happy to sad. Consider other continua of feelings, such as anger and fear, depending on student needs. Consider applying more than one of each expression for easy access, two pans/plates for paint, paint brushes, washable paint, masking tape, a bowl or cup for dirty brushes, water and cloth or wet wipes for cleaning, a device to play music, and one handheld mirror.

Preparation: Choose a room with a tile floor or large table for easy cleaning. Lay out the butcher paper on the floor, on a table in the center of the room, or in an area where students can sit on all sides of it, and secure with masking tape. Put paint into pans/plates and set on the edge of the paper. Prepare music selection. Keep mirror in reach for use during group process. Have cleaning supplies available.

Instructions: Have students sit around the paper. Tell students they will put their brushes into the paint and then put them on the paper as the music plays. Tell students they can choose how to move their brushes on the paper; they may choose to fill in the faces or create their own. Indicate that the activity will begin when the music starts and end when the music stops. You may want to model this for students.

1. Start music.
2. Tell the students they can begin.
3. Make statements about the movements they are making and what faces they are painting and creating. (Refer to Activity One for examples.)
4. After 10 minutes, turn off the music and tell students to sit down, putting their brushes in the clean-up cup/bowl.
5. Discuss the activity with process questions and general statements. Compare feelings and faces chosen. Ask: *"Do you have the same feeling as someone else? Show me how you are feeling in the mirror."* (Counselor holds the mirror up to the group.) *"Has anyone else felt that way before? Is there a feeling that does not feel good? What did X's face look like when you said that?"* (Use mirror.) *"What movements show how you feel right now?"* State similarities and differences, interactions, choices, movements, and facial expressions.
6. Illicit a statement from students concerning their experience. Have students summarize what they learned through the activity.
7. Have students clean themselves off and assist when needed.
8. End session.

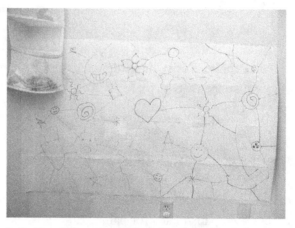

FIGURE 4.8 Activity Two (Shapes) and Activity Three (Faces), butcher paper layout before activity begins.

FIGURE 4.9 Results of Activities Two and Three.

Suggested Modifications (for Special Needs Populations):

Materials: Use Crayola Slick Sticks, chalk, shaving cream, colored glue sticks, stamps, stickers, or markers instead of paint. Use a dry erase board with dry erase markers for Activities Two and Three instead of paper and paint. Consider changing the volume of the music or brightness of the room to decrease the likelihood of overstimulation.

Format: Each activity may be repeated in order to increase impact of growth and learning (Sowden, Perkins, & Clegg, 2011). Activities One through Three may be utilized multiple times or individually to achieve the desired developmental level of empathy and social and body awareness.

Student Needs: If students have sensory sensitivities, they may wear gloves or shoes during activities. If students choose not to participate, you may reflect on how it was difficult for them to participate and ask if any other students remember a time when they did not want to participate in an activity. If students have walking disabilities, they may use braces, a wheel chair, and so on, instead of hands and feet. They may use sponges they can roll over in a wheel chair or allow wheel chair wheels in paint and roll over paper. Consider gestures and facial expressions as appropriate responses from nonverbal students.

Evaluation Plan: Included are two measures. The first, the Counselor Evaluation for Students, is designed for counselors to utilize during group activities to evaluate empathy and social and body awareness. The counselor will evaluate the student on three interactions during the group activity. For example, if the counselor observes the student turning and smiling to a peer who is talking to him or her, the counselor would place a Y in the box for number one.

1. Responds to peer verbally/nonverbally.

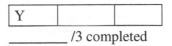

If the counselor observes the same student not responding to a peer talking to him or her on two different occasions during the same activity, the counselor would place an N in the next two boxes for item number one, and indicate that 1 out of 3 interactions were completed.

1. Responds to peer verbally/nonverbally.

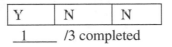

- The first measure is recommended for use as a pre- and posttest conducted whether the three activities are repeated or used in sequential order.
- The second measure, Teacher Evaluation of Student, can be administered by teachers and/or parents as a pre- and posttest. Both measures may be used for screening purposes.

Counselor Evaluation for Students

Counselor rates each group member with either a Y indicating yes in observed interaction or N indicating no for interaction not observed.

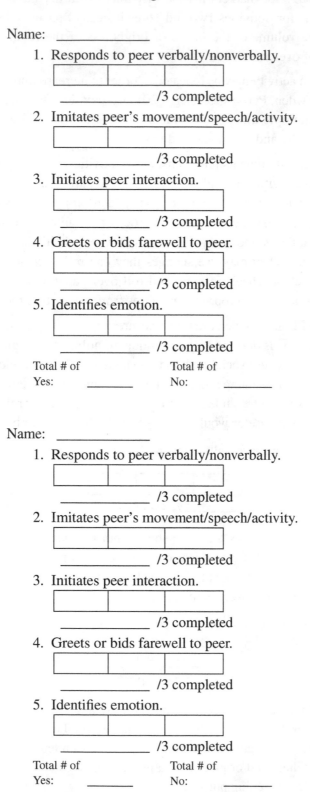

Name: _____

    1. Responds to peer verbally/nonverbally.

    _____ /3 completed

    2. Imitates peer's movement/speech/activity.

    _____ /3 completed

    3. Initiates peer interaction.

    _____ /3 completed

    4. Greets or bids farewell to peer.

    _____ /3 completed

    5. Identifies emotion.

    _____ /3 completed

Total # of   Total # of
Yes: _____   No: _____

Name: _____

    1. Responds to peer verbally/nonverbally.

    _____ /3 completed

    2. Imitates peer's movement/speech/activity.

    _____ /3 completed

    3. Initiates peer interaction.

    _____ /3 completed

    4. Greets or bids farewell to peer.

    _____ /3 completed

    5. Identifies emotion.

    _____ /3 completed

Total # of   Total # of
Yes: _____   No: _____

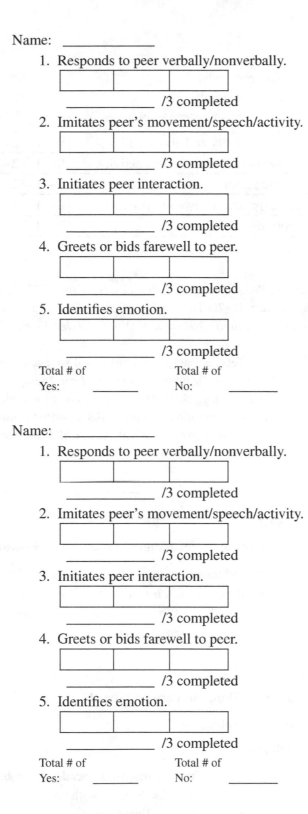

Name: _____

1. Responds to peer verbally/nonverbally.

_____ /3 completed

2. Imitates peer's movement/speech/activity.

_____ /3 completed

3. Initiates peer interaction.

_____ /3 completed

4. Greets or bids farewell to peer.

_____ /3 completed

5. Identifies emotion.

_____ /3 completed

Total # of
Yes: _____

Total # of
No: _____

Name: _____

1. Responds to peer verbally/nonverbally.

_____ /3 completed

2. Imitates peer's movement/speech/activity.

_____ /3 completed

3. Initiates peer interaction.

_____ /3 completed

4. Greets or bids farewell to peer.

_____ /3 completed

5. Identifies emotion.

_____ /3 completed

Total # of
Yes: _____

Total # of
No: _____

Teacher Evaluation of Student

Please circle the number that you believe best represents the current student skill level on the following behaviors.

Rating Scale

0   if the skill is never observed.
1   if skill is shown irregularly.
2   if skill is shown consistently.
3   if the skill is shown at a mastery level.

1. Responds to peer verbally and nonverbally.	0 – 1 – 2 – 3
2. Imitates peer's expression/movement/activity.	0 – 1 – 2 – 3
3. Initiates peer interaction.	0 – 1 – 2 – 3
4. Greets peer or expresses farewell to peer.	0 – 1 – 2 – 3
5. Identifies emotion of self or other.	0 – 1 – 2 – 3

REFERENCES

Badenoch, B. (2008). *Being a brain-wise therapist.* New York, NY: W. W. Norton.

Dempsey, I., & Foreman, P. (2001). A review of educational approaches for individuals with autism. *International Journal of Disability, Development and Education, 48*(1), 103–116.

Katagiri, J. (2009). The effects of background music and song texts on the emotional understanding of children with autism. *Journal of Music Therapy, 46*(1), 15.

Sowden, H., Perkins, M., & Clegg, J. (2011). Contexts and communication strategies in naturalist behavioral intervention: A framework for understanding how practitioners facilitate communication in children with ASD. *Child Language Teaching and Therapy, 27*(1), 21–38.

FEELING FRUSTRATED AND SAD

Anne Stuart Henry, Alicia H. Schwenk, Genevieve Shaw, and Sherry A. Bosarge

This activity is designed for use with small groups and is ideally conducted by a counselor in collaboration with an art teacher. The activity emphasizes dealing with feelings of frustration, anger, and sadness and promotes positive self-expression through art.

Modality: Visual Arts

ASCA National Model Domain: Personal/Social

Deliver via: Group counseling

Age Level: 4th/5th grade

Indications: Group candidates may demonstrate academic or behavioral concerns. However, these activities can also be used with any small group focusing on coping (divorce/separation, chronic illness, grief).

Materials: White construction paper, scissors, glue, Smart Board

Preparation: Before the group session begins, leave some of the white paper whole, and cut some of it into long strips of varying width.

On the day of this activity, get into a circle for discussion. Tell students that today's topic is feeling angry and sad. Both anger and sadness are normal emotions. Ask students to list some signs of anger, and then write on the Smart Board. Repeat the process with signs of sadness. Discuss how everyone feels angry and sad sometimes.

Instructions:

1. Ask students to define "frustration." Tell students, *"Frustration is when you have a hard time reaching your goal and you feel blocked. When you get frustrated over something, it can lead to anger or sadness."*
2. Ask students to name a time recently when they have felt frustrated (go around the circle). Ask, *"Did it lead to anger or sadness?"*
3. Tell students that you are going to read a story about feelings. Ask students to listen for the kinds of feelings the characters are experiencing.
4. Use the Smart Board to display the "When Friends Fight: Attack of the Rival Friend" story on the PBS Kids "It's My Life" website at http://pbskids .org/itsmylife/friends/friendsfight/fable3.html
5. Ask students to discuss some of the feelings the characters may be experiencing.
6. Ask students to name some of the healthy ways to let out or express our normal feelings of frustration, feeling left out, and so on.
7. Pick up a strip of paper and talk about how a feeling can be reflected by what we do to the paper as artists.
8. Encourage students to recall a specific time they were left out or excluded and describe how they felt.
9. Take the strip of white paper and demonstrate feelings by twisting, crumpling, folding, or tearing the paper.
10. Use the tab method (folding the ends of the paper and gluing them to a base sheet of paper) to model the activity for students.
11. Tell students that through spatial placement (distancing) and repeating design elements in groups of strips, an artist can physically create and emotionally express what it means to be left out.
12. Students may also cut the base paper of their project to better suit its shape and intention.
13. Once students have finished gluing, facilitate a discussion on what each specific sculpture represents.
14. Ask closing questions:
    a. *"How did you feel during this activity?"*
    b. *"Did anyone feel frustrated or have a hard time reaching her or his goal?"*
    c. *"If so, how did you deal with it?"*

Suggested Modifications (for Special Needs Populations): School counselors may need to modify vocabulary to meet all student needs during discussions. Counselors and art teachers can provide individual assistance to students who need extra help with specific projects. Students who have difficulty writing may either complete artists' statements on the computer, or may dictate answers to group leaders. Additionally, assessments may be conducted orally if necessary.

Evaluation Plan: Ask students to define "frustration." Ask students to list healthy ways of coping with frustration and expressing feelings of anger and sadness.

REFERENCE

Castleworks, Inc. (2005). *When friends fight: Attack of the rival friend.* Retrieved from http://pbskids.org/itsmylife/friends/friendsfight/fable3.html

---

FREEZE FRAME

Katherine M. Hermann and Christopher Lawrence

*E*lementary and middle school students often find it difficult to identify the range of feelings they experience in daily life. Therefore, to facilitate the understanding of nonverbal expressions and associated feelings, the "Freeze Frame" activity uses facial expression and recognition to help students practice feelings identification, expand feeling vocabulary, and explore nonverbal messages. These important interpersonal and intrapersonal skills can help facilitate students' self-understanding and comfort with emotional discussions, which can be valuable to the counseling process and normal development.

Modality: Photography

ASCA National Model Domain: Personal/Social

Deliver via: Classroom guidance, counseling groups

Age Level: Elementary and middle school

Indications: This activity is well suited for both elementary- and middle school-age students. The exercise can be used with students who have difficulty identifying or exploring a range of feelings, such as those with anger-control problems. Since this activity can be used in classroom guidance or group therapy, specific processing questions can be refined to focus the activity to the client population.

Materials: Digital camera or a smartphone with camera capabilities, chalkboard, Microsoft PowerPoint or comparable software for developing a photo slideshow, and an overhead projector or computer monitor large enough to display a presentation to students.

Preparation: You will need to be able to access and be familiar with the required technology (camera, computer, and projector). In addition, if you plan to complete the entire activity in one session, a cofacilitator, teaching assistant, or other available helper will need to be arranged. Since this activity requires students to be creative and a little silly, addressing the process with a lighthearted, nonjudgmental spirit is paramount for a successful outcome and positive experience.

Instructions:
1. Facilitate a discussion of feelings and feeling words by exploring "mad," "sad," "glad," and "scared" and the different intensities of these feelings. During this process, ask students to generate and write a list of feeling words on a whiteboard, chalkboard, or flip chart. Have the cofacilitator or teaching assistant copy the list onto a piece of paper.
2. While the lead therapist discusses the students' experiences with these feelings (e.g., *"When was the last time your experienced one of these feelings?"*), the cofacilitator escorts each student out of the room individually and asks them to select a word from the list.
3. The coinstructor then photographs the student making a face reflecting the word he or she selected, a "feeling face." Record the feeling each student presents and remove the feeling from the list to avoid duplicates. Before the student returns to the group, remind the student not to tell anyone in the class about his or her "feeling face."
4. After each student has the opportunity to be photographed (while classroom guidance material is presented on reflection of feelings), the coinstructor creates a PowerPoint presentation using the photographs of the students. A simple format is pasting the picture of a student on one slide, followed by a slide with the feeling word.
5. At the end of the guidance lesson, the feeling faces PowerPoint presentation is presented. After each "feeling face" is displayed, students are asked to identifying the feeling represented by each photograph before the feeling listed on the subsequent slide is displayed.
6. To process the experience, students may be asked to provide more information about the identifying components of each emotion. *"You all seem to think this person is angry. How can you tell? What signs do you see?"* (Eyes narrowed, jaw clenched.) *"What could be some other signs someone is angry?"* (Fists clenched, red cheeks, getting really loud/quiet.) *"What are some ways your friends/family might recognize you're angry?"*
7. You may ask students to discuss feelings that could be mistaken for one another (e.g., *"Which feelings are close together?"*). This could be based on thematic similarity ("excited" and "happy" may be similar) or based on the signs students identify (*"Someone who's embarrassed may have his or her head down. Someone who's sad may have his or her head down, too. How might we tell the difference?"*).

Suggested Modifications: Depending on the grade level of the students, you may be required to provide additional prompting to aid in the generation of feeling words. Scenarios can be helpful in such matters. For example: *"If you were* *to come home, walk in the front door, turn on the lights, and all your friends were to jump up and say 'Happy birthday!' how might you feel?"* (Surprised.) *"If you've got a big test in third period, and you're sitting in second period watching the clock get closer and closer to test time, how might you feel?"* (Nervous/anxious.)

For smaller groups, students may get a chance to model multiple feeling faces. For larger groups, instructors may need to add emotion words to the list (to ensure each student has a chance to contribute a feeling face).

If the counselor does not have assistance, students can take the photographs as they come to class (without the use of the predeveloped feeling list) or during a brief in-class activity, and the presentation can be developed after the session and used as an introduction to a follow-up session.

You may begin the subsequent session with a refresher, using photos of yourself making different feeling faces, then asking the students to identify the feelings being demonstrated.

Evaluation Plan: To evaluate this session, the counselor can focus on the processing of the "feeling faces" presentation. This discussion provides an opportunity to discover feelings that need to be explored in greater detail in future sessions, indicate areas of confusion, or highlight individual students who may benefit from additional services.

FRIENDS AND FAMILY

Amanda N. Byrd-Desnoyers

*F*amily diagrams can help both the therapist and the client explore family information (Vera Institute of Justice, 2005, p. 16). The three interventions that follow are inspired by the use of genograms and sociograms. Genograms, which are pictorial representations of a client's family tree, can be useful in therapy when the client's main concern is family issues; they allow a way for the client to discuss family relationships without being quizzed (Young, 2009, p. 231). Sociograms are a "graphic display of interpersonal relationships within a group" (Reynolds & Fletcher-Janzen, 2006). Each of these tools examines the strength of the relationship as well as cohesiveness; however, this aspect is not included in the interventions that follow. By using the frameworks for a foundation, the activities that follow can allow the client to lead the session and provide information to the counselor and themselves in a creative way.*

Adolescents may not be ready to vocalize their family relationships with a counselor. By concentrating on a tangible activity such as creating the family diagram, the adolescent's discomfort level may be reduced and his or her likelihood to share feelings may be increased (Altshuler, 1999). By deviating from a traditional genogram or sociogram approach, the child is able to direct the flow and include individuals whom he or she deems as family, whether through marital or blood relationships or not. This helps the clinician create a way of conceptualizing family patterns and relationships within the student's terms (Milewski-Hertlein, 2001). As Duba states, the client can be helped because "the use of genograms often brings clients to greater insight, awareness, and understanding about their own interpersonal patterns, as well as the communication patterns between themselves and others" (Duba, 2009, p. 16).

Furthermore, the activities described can be altered so that the client describes his or her peer relationships. As much as family is important, an adolescent's peer relationships have equal importance. Often, an adolescent's peers can have as much influence as his or her parents (Hashimoto, Onuoha, Isaka, & Higuchi, 2011). Development of positive peer relationships is critical to overall social and cognitive development (Merrell, 2003, p. 146).

Modality: Visual

ASCA National Model Domain: Personal/Social

Deliver via: Individual

Age Level: Elementary, middle, or high school

Indications: This activity is useful for students struggling with relationships, family, friends, divorce, marriage/remarriage, siblings, and death/loss.

Materials: For My Famous Family or My Famous Classmates (Friends), glue, markers, poster board, and pictures of famous people or cartoon characters. For My Natural Family, a basket or bag to hold items, and scissors to take cuttings of items.

Preparation: For convenience and time savings, utilize pop-culture websites to find images of popular characters and famous people.

Instructions:

My Famous Family
1. Talk with the adolescent about how family helps shape the individual. Explain that examining family relationships can help identify sources of joy and distress. Introduce the family diagram concept and explain how creating this diagram can help the counselor and client better work together.
2. Ask the student to create a family diagram using the cartoon characters and celebrities. If a computer with a printer is available to the student, the student can search for his or her own images to use or images that have been preselected.
3. Debrief and process the diagram. Some examples of debriefing questions could be: *"Who is that character and who does it represent? Whom did you place first and what made you put that character first? What made you choose this character? This character is spaced close/far apart from you. You are placed here; tell me more. Did you change anything or would you change anything?"* (McIntyer, 2003; Suler, n.d.)

My Famous Classmates

This activity can be done to help identify relationship issues within the school setting.

1. Introduce the concept of a school relationship diagram (sociogram).
2. Tell students you want them to use cartoon characters or celebrities' images to help answer some questions that will help you to have insight into the client's relationships at school.
3. The following questions can help elicit information.
   a. *"Who are your three best friends?"*
   b. *"Which three people at school do you most admire?"*
   c. *"Which two teachers are your favorites?"*
   d. *"Which three people do you wish you could hang out with after school?"*
   e. *"Which three people would you like to be friends with but are not?"*
   f. *"With whom do you prefer to sit in class?"*
   g. *"With whom do you prefer to eat lunch?"*
   h. *"If you had to work with a teacher one-on-one, which teacher would you choose?"*
   i. *"If you had to sit by someone on the bus who would it be?"*
   j. *"Who would you not want to work on a project with?"*
   k. *"Whom do you avoid in school?"*
   l. *"Whom do you not want to sit with at lunch?"*
   m. *"Who are the three students with whom you most like to spend your free time?"*
   n. *"Who are the three students with whom you least like to spend your free time?"*

   (Bannerjee, n.d.; Horace Mann-Lincoln Institute of School Experimentation, 1957)
4. Debrief and process the diagram.

My Natural Family

This activity is conducted almost identically to the My Famous Family activity described previously. However, rather than pictures of cartoon characters and celebrities, items from nature are used.

Procedure:

1. Take the student for a walk around the campus and talk with the adolescent about how family helps shape the individual. Explain that examining family relationships can help identify sources of joy and distress. Introduce the family diagram concept and explain how creating this diagram can help the counselor and client work together better.
2. As you are walking, ask the student to collect items from nature or found on the ground to represent his or her family members.

3. Debrief and process the diagram. Some examples of debriefing questions could be: *"Who is that item? What made you choose this item? This item is spaced close/far apart from you. You are placed here; tell me more."*

Suggested Modifications (for Special Needs Populations): Modifications to language in presenting these activities may be needed.

Evaluation Plan: Evaluation occurs during the final step of debriefing and processing each intervention.

REFERENCES

Altshuler, S. (1999). Constructing genograms with children in care: Implications for casework practice. *Child Welfare, 78*(6), 777–790.

Duba, J. D. (2009). Introducing the "Basic Needs Genogram" in reality therapy-based marriage and family counseling. *International Journal of Reality Therapy, 28*(2), 15–19.

Elkin, E. (2005). *Adolescent portable therapy: A practical guide for service providers.* New York, NY: Vera Institute of Justice.

Hashimoto, S., Onuoha, F. N., Isaka, M., & Higuchi, N. (2011). The effect of adolescents' image of parents on children's self-image and mental health. *Child & Adolescent Mental Health, 16*(4), 186–192.

Horace Mann-Lincoln Institute of School Experimentation. (1957). How to construct a sociogram. New York, NY: Bureau of Publications, Teachers College, Columbia University. Retrieved from http://babel.hathitrust.org/cgi/pt?id=mdp.39015022206562;seq=8;view=1up

Merrell, K. W. (2003). *Behavioral, social, and emotional assessment of children and adolescents.* Florence, KY: Routledge.

Milewski-Hertlein, K. A. (2001). The use of a socially constructed genogram in clinical practice. *American Journal of Family Therapy, 29*(1), 23–38.

Reynolds, C., & Fletcher-Janzen, E. (2006). Sociograms. In *Encyclopedia of special education: A reference for the education of children, adolescents, and adults with disabilities and other exceptional individuals.* Retrieved from http://0-www.credoreference.com.umiss.lib.olemiss.edu/entry.do?id=9299350

Suler, J. (.n.d). Family sociograms. Retrieved from http://users.rider.edu/~suler/sociogram.html

Vera Institute of Justice. (2005). *Adolescent portable therapy: A practical guide for service providers.* Retrieved from http://www.vera.org/files/272_529.pdf

Young, M. E. (2009). *Learning the art of helping: Building blocks and techniques* (4th ed.). Upper Saddle River, NJ: Prentice Hall.

GROUP PUZZLE DRAWING

Anne Stuart Henry, Alicia H. Schwenk, Genevieve Shaw, and Sherry A. Bosarge

This activity is designed for use with small groups and is ideally conducted by a counselor in collaboration with an art teacher. The activity emphasizes teamwork and positive self-expression through art. Students will work together as a team to create artwork.

Modality: Visual Arts

ASCA National Model Domain: Personal/Social

Deliver via: Group counseling

Age Level: 4th/5th grade

Indications: Group candidates may demonstrate academic or behavioral concerns. However, these activities can also be used with any small group focusing on coping (divorce/separation, chronic illness, grief).

Materials: White drawing paper, oil pastels.

Preparation:

Before the day of this activity, draw a large complete picture using an image of your choice. For example, you could draw a sun, a school mascot, or another positive image. Use one large sheet of paper and then cut it into enough pieces for each group member to get a piece.

On the day of this activity, arrange students into a circle for discussion. Ask students to share examples of a time they felt sad, frustrated, or lonely. Ask what helped them when they were having these feelings.

Ask students to name people they can reach out to when they are experiencing these feelings. Mention fellow group members if they have not already done so. Ask how these people can help them.

Instructions:

1. Say to students, *"Many times we feel like we are the only ones who feel this way. In your head you might know that you are not alone, but in your heart it feels like you are. Even though you feel like you are alone, this group shows there are people like you who care about you. Sometimes in life you will face circumstances that will be difficult to handle on your own. It is important to ask for help from a caring group of people during those difficult times."*

2. Tell students that they each have their own unique personalities and strengths that they bring to this group. Model for students and share that counselors are good listeners. People know that they can talk to counselors when they are upset. Ask students to share some characteristics that make them a valuable member of this group.

3. Tell students that when everyone contributes his or her strengths, they can work together to create something beautiful. They may see things clearer when others are there to help.

4. Tell students that they will be given a picture to color. They may not know what the picture is when they get it. This is similar to life. Sometimes we have problems, and we are not sure what to do.

5. Give each student oil pastels of similar color, so the picture has some continuity when it comes together. For the example of the sun image, each student may use a red, yellow, and orange pastels.

6. Encourage students to blend colors to achieve contrast.
7. Remind students that they are using their own strengths to make a unique picture.
8. When all of the pieces are complete, ask students to bring the pieces together to create a whole. Students will need to decide where their piece fits in the puzzle.
9. Say to students, "*This demonstrates that there are times in your own lives when it is important to come together as a team. The strengths and talents of everyone in the group help problems seem less complex. All of the pieces of this picture are unique, just like you, but they make a beautiful complete picture.*"
10. Ask closing questions:
    a. "*What similarities do you notice in the individual pieces?*"
    b. "*What similar feelings have you all had in life?*"
    c. "*What did it feel like to hear you are a valuable member of the group?*"

Suggested Modifications (for Special Needs Populations): School counselors may need to modify vocabulary to meet all students' needs during discussions. Counselors and art teachers can provide individual assistance to students who need extra help with specific projects. Students who have difficulty writing may either complete artists' statements on the computer, or may dictate answers to group leaders. Additionally, assessments may be conducted orally if necessary.

Evaluation Plan: Ask students to talk about what it was like to work together as a team. Ask each student to talk about a talent or an area of strength that he or she brought to the group picture.

I AM THANKFUL FOR . . .

Imelda N. Bratton

*T*he following is an art activity designed for use with students in individual or small-group counseling who struggle with body image issues or eating disorders. This activity is intended to help students associate positive images and thoughts with food. The counselor introduces the activity by asking students to reflect on the positive aspects of food and how food helps people survive. Students will focus on positive images of food and how food is necessary for people to be healthy. This activity can be especially helpful before times such as Thanksgiving and Christmas, or during summer when there is a high emphasis on food or the exposure of body parts (such as swimsuits or shorts).

Modality: Art

ASCA National Model Domain: Personal/social

Deliver via: Individual or group counseling

Age Level: Elementary, middle, or high school (This activity could be used with any age group. The questions and prompts can be easily modified to be developmentally appropriate for students' abilities.)

Indications: This activity could be used with individuals (or small groups) who have issues with body image or self-esteem, or those with eating disorders.

Materials: Paper or note cards; any art material available, such as crayons, colored pencils, markers, oil/acrylic/finger paints; scrap fabric pieces; magazines; glue; variety of colored paper; markers, and so on; envelopes in which to place the finished product (optional step); and postage to mail the finished product (optional step).

Preparation: Provide one piece of paper or notecard to each student. Place all art material where it is easily accessed. A table or hard surface to work on is suggested.

Instructions:

1. Introduce the activity by letting the students know they are going to think about food and their bodies. Acknowledge that sometimes images that are not helpful are easier to think about, but have students try to ignore those images or thoughts while they are working during the session. Suggest that they give themselves permission to only think about the positive thoughts during their work and try to stop the negative thoughts.

2. Invite students to reflect on a positive influence that food or their bodies have had during their lives. Let the students know that they may have to think back to their childhood for a time when they experienced a positive influence, before they had any worries about food or their bodies. Ask them to think of their thoughts, feelings, and what they experienced through their senses. As they are thinking about those experiences, have them think about what it felt like to have positive thoughts about food and their bodies.

3. Ask the students to identify any symbols, images, colors, words, places, or things that they connect to their positive bodily influence or experience. Tell the students that when they are ready, they may use the art materials to represent their thoughts or feelings on the paper provided. They may choose to draw, color, cut, glue, or write about their positive experience. Provide quiet time for students to work on the project.

4. When students are done, they may choose to share what they are comfortable with to group members.

5. Explore any items you think are important that the students have shared. Try to find similarities and differences among group members to help them realize they are not alone in their thoughts. Discuss how often the Thanksgiving and Christmas holidays or summertime (as appropriate) can add to the negative images that people have about food or their bodies. Media such as advertisements and Photoshopped images can also be adverse to students' self-esteem or body image. Let the students know that many people struggle with these issues.

6. Move the discussion into self-care and how it is important to remember the positive influences of food on the body. Ask them to consider how their bodies need food and what healthy food can do for their bodies. Suggest displaying their final product at home to help them when those unhelpful images are difficult to ignore. The student can even take a digital picture with his or her phone to keep the project easily accessible.

Optional: Have students place the finished product in an envelope, then address and seal the envelope. Mail the envelope for the students so they will receive it in at the address provided.

Suggested Modifications (for Special Needs Populations): This activity can be modified to meet the specific need of the school counselor and developmental levels of students. This activity is appropriate for use with most student groups and especially helpful for students who enjoy creative activities. Students who have limited fine motor skills can use magazine images instead of drawing their own images.

Evaluation Plan: As this intervention addresses long-term attitude change regarding food consumption, it may be effective to ask students to keep a 1-week food/feeling diary and to share these at a follow-up meeting.

I HAVE "TWO EYES, A NOSE, AND A MOUTH"

Marco Hernandez and Rebeca Hernandez

The counselor/teacher will read the book Two Eyes, A Nose, and A Mouth *by Roberta Grobell Intrater. Students will listen to the story and be encouraged to verbally identify differences and similarities they were able to extrapolate from listening to the story as well as from viewing the pictures in this illustrated book. After the story is read, the counselor will model how to draw a face so that the students can do the same after the demonstration. They will share their drawings with other peers and will then pick a place on the wall where they will be able to tape it up for everyone to see.*

Modality: Visual Arts

ASCA National Model Domain: Personal/Social

Deliver via: Classroom guidance or group

Age Level: 1st grade

Indications: To assist young students in identifying differences among individuals

Materials: *Two Eyes, A Nose, and A Mouth* by Roberta Grobell Intrater, blank pieces of paper, coloring supplies and precut pieces of aluminum foil (12 in. × 10 in.). If modifications are needed for special populations it would be advised to bring in or premake blank name tags with different types of facial features

drawn on them. This will allow students to pick which facial feature they identify with without having to draw it themselves.

Preparation: Have all materials ready as students arrive; ask students to sit in
the center of the room on the carpet or in chairs in a circle.

Instructions:
1. Read the book in rhythmic fashion/tone, emphasizing the parts of the face
   shown in the book and inviting the children to repeat the parts of the face
   as illustrated in the book. Pause on pages as needed to ensure that all the
   students have an opportunity to see the pictures in the illustrated book.
2. After reading the book, ask the students to get into groups (equal, if possible, depending on number of students/clients) and provide them with blank
   pieces of paper, coloring supplies, and a piece of aluminum foil.
3. Use a piece of aluminum foil as a mirror to view your face and model to
   the student how to use this method to look at characteristics of one's face.
   Demonstrate to the students how they would draw their own faces based on
   the image on the aluminum foil. The students/clients will then be asked to
   do the same with their own materials.
4. After the students have had time to draw their self-portraits, ask them to
   pick a place on the classroom or therapy room wall on which they would
   like to post their art.

Suggested Modifications (for Special Needs Populations): Student aids or
counseling cofacilitators may assist the counselor/teacher in reading the story to
individual students/clients who may have difficulty understanding the reading
in the setting described previously. Students will also be assisted in drawing (if
able) or making use of premade blank tags in order to facilitate their participation. Assistance holding up the foil to the face will also be provided as needed.

Evaluation Plan: Follow-up questions and interaction among the students/clients
can be encouraged. The following questions are examples of what could be asked
to stimulate sharing among the students/clients: *"What did you see in your mirror? Did you see anything that you had not noticed? What did you notice?"*

IF ANIMALS WENT TO SCHOOL: MAKING CONNECTIONS

Nicole M. Randick and Rebecca E. Michel

*This group activity is designed to help students gain awareness of their
thoughts, feelings, and behaviors. Pictures of animals are used as a
vehicle to facilitate communication, learn about different feelings, and
increase connection among group members. We know how it feels to go
through our own daily routine (e.g., waking up, getting dressed, eating
breakfast, going to school), but it is not always easy to know what others are*

thinking and feeling. Recognizing the integration of one's thoughts, feelings, and actions will help students explore their daily actions, ultimately becoming more aware of themselves and others. The artwork created in this activity will help students evaluate different perspectives, empower students to think critically, and foster cooperation among group members.

Modality: Visual Arts

ASCA National Model Domain: Personal/Social

Deliver via: Group counseling

Age Level: Elementary through 6th grade

Indications: This activity is designed for small groups to emphasize self- and other-awareness, sharing with others, and friendship. Specifically, this activity may be used to help students explore and name a variety of feelings; facilitate a deeper understanding about the nature of feelings, and how different feelings might lead to different ways of behaving; recognizing, accepting, and appreciating individual differences (diversity); and to explore the nature of friendships. Through the use of images, group members can safely and effectively explore their thoughts and feelings.

Materials: Glue sticks, colored paper, markers, crayons, colored pencils, pre-cut images of animals (optional: encourage the students to cut out the animal images).

Preparation: The counselor cuts animal images from magazines, books, or websites and has them available for students to use. For each animal, the counselor makes a list of different qualities and characteristics the animals may represent (see Table 4.1). This list can be used to help facilitate a discussion of how animals might feel, think, and act if they went to school.

Instructions:
1. Invite a small group of students to meet in a classroom setting or around a round table with enough chairs for each participant.
2. Begin by facilitating a discussion about *feelings*. To begin, each member of the group is asked to name a feeling. Then, the group members are invited to share how and when they might feel this feeling. Group members are encouraged to give examples of when they might feel these feelings in school (e.g., excited at recess or sad after earning a poor grade). The counselor should point out when students have shared feelings, or when opposite feelings are felt during the same school event. Finally, the counselor explains that each person is unique and may experience different feelings throughout the day.
3. Next, the counselor asks the students questions about their daily routine before, during, and after school. This reinforces student awareness of thoughts, feelings, and behaviors. The following questions can be used to help facilitate this discussion: *"What did you do when you woke up this morning? What were you thinking? How were you feeling? What did you*

TABLE 4.1 Examples of Animal Characteristics

Animal	Possible Characteristic
Lion	Powerful or Strong
Dog	Loyal or Faithful
Horse	Hard Working
Bee	Busy
Fox	Sly or Cunning
Owl	Wise
Beaver	Busy
Dolphin	Playful
Cat	Curious
Elephant	Smart
Mule	Stubborn
Chicken	Scared or Timid
Ox	Big and Strong
Lamb/Sheep	Quiet and Nice
Panther	Fast
Pig	Greedy
Rabbit	Fast

eat for breakfast? What were you thinking? How were you feeling? How did you get to school? What were you thinking? How were you feeling? Pick one activity you did in school today. What were you thinking? How were you feeling? How do our thoughts impact our feelings throughout the day?"

4. The counselor next instructs the students to take their time and look through the different animals to choose an animal they relate with. The image of the animal serves as a metaphor and will help extend the knowledge learned from the earlier discussion about feelings. Each animal will have a different set of characteristics that makes it unique, just like each student.

5. Once they choose an image of an animal they should paste it on their paper.

6. Then the counselor asks the students to describe their animals. The counselor can ask follow-up questions to learn more about the animal. For example, a student may explain that a lion represents being powerful. When explored through the lion metaphor, students can talk about *how* a lion is powerful, *when* the lion is powerful, and *what purpose* does the feeling of being powerful have for the lion.

7. The counselor will then invite the students to use the provided art materials to draw a task the animal would do if the animal were in school (e.g., learning math, playing sports in gym class, playing with friends at recess). The image of the animal is used as a starting point for the drawing. By giving this directive related to the school setting, the students are able to link their image to a specific event in their lives (i.e., school). It is important for the counselor

to foster encouragement by letting students know that each picture created is unique and special, representing their unique thoughts and feelings.

8. After students finish their drawings the counselor initiates a discussion about how animals would act if they were in school. This conversation reinforces the unique differences of all students. The following questions can guide the discussion, depending on the needs of the group members.

Special Qualities

- ■ *"What special qualities do your animals have?"* (Note: Each student is given a turn to explain what animal was chosen and what qualities or characteristics his or her animal represents. The counselor can use the list created before the lesson to help facilitate this discussion.)
- ■ *"What qualities from the animals would you like to see in yourselves?"*
- ■ *"How can we celebrate each other's unique qualities?"*

Tasks

- ■ *"What task is your animal doing?"*
- ■ *"What might make it easier for the animal to do the task?"*
- ■ *"Imagine that we had to do the same task as the animal. What might make it easier for us to do the task?"*
- ■ *"How might we prepare to learn new things in school?"*

Thinking and Feeling

- ■ *"What do you think the animals are thinking or feeling?"*
- ■ *"When an animal thinks something, how does this impact how the animal feels?"*
- ■ *"Do we all think and feel the same in every situation?"*
- ■ *"How can we understand how others might feel and think differently than we do?"*

Friendship

- ■ *"Which of these animals do you think would be friends?"*
- ■ *"What makes a good friend?"*
- ■ *"Can two animals who look different become friends (e.g., a tiger and a sheep)?"*
- ■ *"How can we become friends with others who are different than us?"*

Suggested Modifications (for Special Needs Populations): The difficulty of this activity can be modified to match students' developmental level. Feeling charts and labels can be used to help students identify with different feelings. The art materials can be modified for those with fine motor limitations by using larger crayons, markers, and paper. For sensory learners, the animals can be created out of clay and the counselor can have pictures of a variety of school settings (e.g., classroom, hallway, library) created using a variety of textures (e.g., felt fabric). This activity is optimally experienced in a group, as the artwork created helps provide students a vehicle for sharing and connecting with other group members. However, students requiring individual assistance may benefit from completing this activity during an individual session with the counselor.

Evaluation Plan: The following survey can be used as a pre-/postassessment.

Pretest / Posttest (Circle One)

Student Initials: _____

1. True or False: What we think impacts what we feel.
2. Write down the feelings you feel during the school day.
   1.   4.
   2.   5.
   3.   6.
3. If you had a hard time doing a task at school, what could you do?
4. True or False: All students have special qualities and abilities.
5. List the qualities of a good friend.
   1.   4.
   2.   5.
   3.   6.

MANDALAS AND MINDFULNESS: IDENTIFYING THE REAL ME

Nicole M. Randick and Rebecca E. Michel

This activity integrates the therapeutic use of expressive arts to increase self-awareness and promote connections with others. The perceptions we have about ourselves and others influence our thoughts and behaviors. Negative perceptions can lead to negative thoughts and behaviors, while positive perceptions can lead to positive thoughts and behaviors. The development of a positive self-concept allows students to appreciate their strengths, develop healthy thoughts, and practice prosocial behaviors. This exercise encourages students to use symbols to mindfully explore their unique qualities. The symbols represent key elements of the student's identity (passions, values, roles, strengths). As group members share their symbols with others, students learn to recognize, accept, and appreciate unique qualities of others. It also provides a bridge to recognize the similarities and differences among group members. This increased self-awareness and other-awareness provides group members with a sense of belonging and connection. The mandala image provides a sense of structure and containment to alleviate anxiety one may have during the activity. Facilitating this activity in a group setting allows for mutual sharing, encouragement, and allows group members to practice mindfulness.

ASCA National Model Domain: Personal/Social

Deliver via: Group

Age Level: Middle or high school

Indications: This group activity is especially useful for students who have a low self-concept or who struggle to get along or connect with others. This activity can also be used as an initial group counseling session to allow students to get to know one another, encourage group connections, and establish a tone of acceptance of individual similarities and differences.

Materials: Play therapy miniatures (e.g., small craft buttons) and the Mandala worksheet (see Figure 4.10); optional materials include magazine cutouts, glue stick, colored pencils, markers, and crayons.

Preparation: This activity can be facilitated in a classroom setting or around a table with enough chairs to accommodate every group member. If facilitated in a classroom setting, desks can be prearranged in a circle. The counselor sets out the art and/or play materials on a table.

Instructions:
1. Before the group begins, arrange desks in a circular pattern to foster equality, connection, and cohesiveness among all members of the group. It is

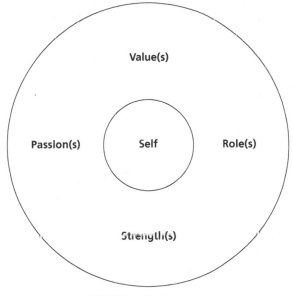

FIGURE 4.10 Mandalas.

important to foster positive group dynamics by developing an encouraging and safe environment to allow students to share and communicate with respect. The group should begin by having students develop the rules, goals, and objectives for their group sessions. Encouraging participation from the beginning facilitates ownership and a sense of belonging.

2. To begin the activity, give each group member a Mandala worksheet (see Figure 4.10). Then explain the mandala using the passage that follows:

> *"A mandala is a balanced, circular design. The name comes from a word in the classical Indian language of Sanskrit meaning 'circle.' We see this image in our daily lives; the sun, moon, Earth, and time, are some examples. Another example can be seen here, in the circle of friends we created with our desks. When a circle is created it can represent wholeness and togetherness. Not only are we all part of this group circle, each of us has our own personal mandala. The mandala image creates unity and helps us to safely explore and celebrate our unique qualities, as well as the unique qualities of others. This activity will help us become more mindful and aware of ourselves and others."*

3. Next, facilitate a discussion about the meaning of the words on the Mandala worksheet (i.e., self, values, passions, strengths, roles). This discussion allows students to self-reflect on different parts of their lives. The information discussed is used as an initial inquiry about each student's unique characteristics. The following definitions can be read and followed up by the reflection questions. Students are invited to provide examples for each definition and answer the reflection questions.

   A. *Passion*: A strong feeling about an aspect of your life. Something you are excited about, interested in, or love to do.
      i. *"What are you passionate about?"*

   B. *Value*: Something you believe in that shapes how you think, feel, and act. Values can be personal or emerge from cultural beliefs and traditions.
      i. *"What do you value?"*

   C. *Role*: Your function or position within a group that highlights your characteristics and connects your behaviors within certain situations.
      i. *"What role(s) do you take on in your family?"*
      ii. *"What role(s) do you take on in school?"*
      iii. *"What role(s) do you take on with friends?"*

   D. *Strength*: An attribute, characteristic, or quality that allows you to overcome life challenges.
      i. *"What are your strengths?"*

4. Students are next invited to go up to the table and choose an item that symbolizes or represents them personally. Students are asked, *"If you were to introduce yourself without words, what item would you choose to introduce yourself?"* Once they choose an item, it is placed in the middle of the

mandala. The students then choose an item that symbolizes each word on the mandala: passion(s), value(s), role(s), and strength(s). These items are placed on the corresponding words on the mandala. More than one item can be chosen to represent each characteristic. Ample time should be provided for students to choose and place their items. Encourage students to be mindful of their thoughts and feelings throughout the experience.

5. Be mindful of the process students take as they choose and place their items. The mandala image and the symbols chosen for each characteristic can provide a deeper meaning and insightful representation of each student. The items that are chosen, the way students choose them, and how they are placed on the mandala, can provide additional information about each student. Observe this process and note anyone who may be struggling, not sharing the items, taking his or her time choosing, and so forth. The way students interact when choosing their items provides additional information about how they interact with themselves, others, and the world.

6. Optional: If time permits, students can use art materials (e.g., magazine cutouts, glue, colored pencils) to add other symbols or images in each area of the mandala.

7. Once students have finished choosing items for their mandala, they are asked to walk in a circle and look at the other students' mandalas.

8. Each student returns to his or her seat and takes turns describing his or her mandala while other members of the group listen. The process is respectful and provides an experience of sharing and acknowledging the similarities and differences among group members.

9. Once all students have shared, process the mandala project with the students. The following questions can be used as a guide:
   a. *"How did you choose items to represent different parts of yourself?"*
   b. *"What did you notice about the symbols chosen to represent your most important characteristics?"*
   c. *"Try to remember what item you laid down first (after you chose the middle symbol). How did you decide which item to place first? How important is this characteristic in your life?"*
   d. *"What thoughts or feelings did you have as you completed this activity?"*
   e. *"What did you learn from visually seeing a representation of yourself?"*
   f. *"Were there any surprising similarities or differences among group members?"*
   g. *"What did you learn about yourself as being part of this group?"*
   h. *"What else did you learn today about yourself or others?"*

Suggested Modifications (for Special Needs Populations): This activity can be modified in a number of ways to meet specific student needs. The counselor can provide definitions and examples of the words within the mandala (i.e., self, passion[s], strength[s], role[s], and values) to fit the developmental and intellectual levels of the students. Additionally, the reflection questions and pre-/

posttest can be modified as necessary. For English-language learners, the words on the Mandala worksheet can be written in both English and the students' native language. Additionally, the session can be facilitated in both languages. Students with visual impairments can be given various objects of different shapes and sizes to touch and add to their mandala.

Evaluation Plan: The following pre-/posttest can be used to evaluate this activity.

Part One: For the questions, use the following scale:

1 = strongly disagree, 2 = disagree, 3 = neutral, 4 = agree, 5 = strongly agree

1. I can identify several of my own unique qualities.   _____
2. I feel comfortable being my true self in this group.   _____
3. I recognize the different roles I take on in my life.   _____
4. I understand how my values impact how others see me. _____

Part Two: Read the definition. Then choose the word that describes the definition.

1. An attribute, characteristic, or quality that allows you to overcome life challenges. _____
2. Your function or position within a group that highlights your characteristics and connects your behaviors within certain situations. _____
3. Something you believe in that shapes how you think, feel, and act. _____
4. A strong feeling about an aspect of your life. Something you are excited about, interested in, or love to do. _____
   A. Passion
   B. Strength
   C. Idea
   D. Value
   E. Role
   F. Function
   G. Identity
   H. Skill
   I. Character
   J. Image

MEMORY MAKING

Evelyn Esther Robinson

This activity enables adolescents to understand, express, and cope with grief by using expressive arts and serves as a coping mechanism that addresses grief by memorializing a loved one. Students design and create a memory book or memory collage.

Modality: Visual Art and Expressive Writing/Poetry

ASCA National Model Domain: Personal/Social

Deliver via: Group counseling or individual counseling

Age Level: Middle school (the activity is designed for middle school students but can be modified to use with any age and demographic group)

Indications: This intervention is targeted at individuals who have experienced a death of a relative or friend within the past year. This intervention can be completed in one group session or extended over multiple sessions.

Materials: Arts and crafts materials such as construction paper, cardstock, markers, colored pencils, lined and unlined paper, glue, yarn, popsicle sticks, scissors, tape, colored pens, sheet protectors, binders, old magazines and newspapers, and Finish the Sentence activity sheet (preprinted for each student).

Preparation: Facilitators should prescreen a small group of students who would benefit from a group that is focused on handling and coping with emotions and feelings surrounding the death of a loved one. Students can be referred to the group or individual sessions by their parents and/or teachers or as suggested by the school counselor. School counselors and teachers should work together to facilitate this group or individual session. Facilitators should have a clear understanding of what it means to grieve and how children grieve in order to be prepared to help children with handling and coping with emotions. Facilitators should provide students with an introduction to the group topic and allow them to complete the Finish the Sentence activity to understand where they are in their grieving process:

Finish the Sentence Activity

The thing that makes me feel the saddest is . . .

If I could talk to the person who died, I would ask . . .

Since the death my family doesn't . . .

My best memory with my lost loved one is . . .

If I could change things, I would . . .

One thing that I liked to do with the person who died was . . .

When the person died, I . . .

Since the death, my friends . . .

After the death, school . . .

When I am alone . . .

After the death, I no longer . . .

To help guide students during designing and creating the memory book or memory collage, provide students with a list of words that are commonly associated with grieving and memorializing. These words may include: *angry, sad, missing you, thinking of you, depressed, tearful, strange,* and *not the same.*

Instructions:

1. Begin the session by explaining its purpose, which is creating a memory book or a memory collage of a loved one they have lost.

2. Invite students to share the identity of their chosen person with the group, but respect those who prefer to remain silent.

3. Provide students with the Finish the Sentence activity to allow them the opportunity to explore their feelings and thoughts about losing a loved one. Once the activity is complete, explore with the students their understanding of death and loss.

4. Students can discuss the activity within the group and then collectively come up with thoughts and ideas about how they can memorialize their loved one in a collage or in a memory book. Provide students with different ideas for their memory books or collages. These ideas can be written on the board so that students can see them when they begin to create their projects. Some ideas for the memory books and collages are:

    a. Encourage students to write a poem, a letter, or journal entry for the beginning of their memory book or as the basis of their memory collage.

    b. Students can also construct an in-memory page and dedicate their book to their loved one.

    c. Students can also be introduced to designing an I Will Miss You page for their memory book, saying goodbye to their loved one and noting the things they will miss about that person. Students can choose what they want to place on the page—it could be a letter or a poem or a story of how they are saying goodbye and will keep the loved one's memory alive; it could be a picture that they draw; or it could just be a final word.

5. After brainstorming, invite students to collect items from the arts and crafts table to use in their projects. In addition to cutting out images and words, encourage them to draw or write their own words or pictures that they think of when they think of their loved one. Students are encouraged to use what is written on the board as a guide to create their projects, if needed. Students can either complete the activity in one session or it can be spread out over multiple meetings.

6. After the projects are completed, have students place the finished product inside sheet a protector and place it inside a binder. Invite students to decorate their binders before taking them with them.

7. Process the activity using the following questions:

    a. *"What did you enjoy about this activity?"*

    b. *"What did you notice about your feelings around death and losing someone you love that you hadn't noticed before?"*

    c. *"What was difficult about this activity?"*

    d. *"What did you learn about yourself while you were doing this activity?"*

    e. *"Did this activity help you to memorialize your loved one and understand your feelings?"*

  f. *"What would you do differently next time?"*
  g. *"What would have made the group better?"*

Suggested Modifications (for Special Needs Populations): Additional hands-on assistance may be needed by students with underdeveloped fine motor skills.

Evaluation Plan: To evaluate the effectiveness of the intervention, use students' responses to the processing questions to determine their progress.

MIRROR, MIRROR ON THE WALL

Stefi Threadgill and Brandy Schumann

*T*his activity is designed to be facilitated in group counseling. It increases students' awareness of how their sense of self impacts their perception. *A strong, integrated sense of self generates positive self-esteem and self-regulation (Oaklander, 2007). An inaccurate perception of self creates disintegration and polarity, which negatively shape an individual's self-concept and how one experiences him- or herself and his or her world. Parts of self that are denied result in unexpressed emotions that create an incomplete gestalt, or fragmented sense of self. Increased self-awareness promotes authenticity and accuracy, which creates an opportunity for change. This activity can increase awareness that personhood is holistic and is not defined only by physical appearance. It also promotes the awareness that perception of self occurs in the context of the environment. Using this activity, individuals gain awareness of how others experience them. This can lead to a more accurate self-concept and empower one to focus on more authentic qualities. Through the I–Thou relationship of the group and the here-and-now immediacy of the experience, the individual is able to gain awareness through the process of the activity. This promotes reintegration of a holistic and authentic self. Additionally, a group setting provides social support, normalization, and increased opportunity to understand that perception is subjective (Berg, Landreth, & Fall, 2013).*

Modality: Visual Arts—Collage

ASCA National Model Domain: Personal/Social

Deliver via: Group counseling

Age Level: Elementary, middle, or high school

Indications: Could be used with individuals with eating disorders, body dysmorphic disorder, or individuals who struggle with maintaining a healthy self-esteem.

Materials: Art supplies and magazines.

Instructions:

1. Invite students to create a collage that represents what they see when they look in the mirror. Encourage students to use symbols, words, photographs, magazine clippings, or colors to express characteristics, internal or external, that they use to describe themselves.

2. Ask student to choose a partner. Instruct each partner to create a second collage that represents what he or she sees when looking at his or her partner. When the collage is completed, ask the pairs to share the finished products with one another.

3. Invite the students to compare the collages they created of themselves with the collages created by their partners. Students should then share their reflections with their partner. Processing questions include: *"What did you learn about how you see yourself, in comparison to how others see you? How did you feel when you compared the two pictures? What did you learn about yourself today? Growing up, where and what did you learn about beauty?"*

Portrait Substrate

A modification, based on the Dove Real Beauty Sketches (Miller & Letessier, 2013), can be achieved by utilizing a local artist or student artist for a weekend group therapy workshop. The artist, separated by a curtain or partition, draws a portrait of the person as the client describes him- or herself. Another portrait is drawn, according to another group member's description of that person. The drawings are revealed and compared in the session. Each member could schedule individual appointments with the artist prior to the session if time is a consideration.

Evaluation Plan: To evaluate the degree of distorted self-perception counselors may use the comparison of peer and self-collages or sketches as a measure of distortion.

REFERENCES

Berg, R. C., Landreth, G. L, & Fall, K. A. (2013). *Group counseling: Concepts and procedures* (5th ed.). New York, NY: Routledge.

Miller, J. (Producer), & Letessier, C. (Director). (2013). *Dove real beauty sketches* [Short film]. United States: Paranoid US.

Oaklander, V. (2007). *Hidden treasure: A map to the child's inner self.* London, UK: Kamac Books.

THE MYTH OF THE PHOENIX

Anne Stuart Henry, Alicia H. Schwenk, Genevieve Shaw, and Sherry A. Bosarge

*T*his activity is designed for use with small groups and is ideally conducted by a counselor in collaboration with an art teacher. The activity emphasizes overcoming obstacles and positive self-expression through art.

Modality: Visual Arts

ASCA National Model Domain: Personal/Social

Deliver via: Group counseling

Age Level: 4th/5th grade

Indications: Group candidates may demonstrate academic or behavioral concerns. However, this activity can also be used with any small group focusing on coping (divorce/separation, chronic illness, grief).

Materials: Pretest; Smart Board; crumpled construction paper; white, black, and gray paint; colorful metallic paint; brushes; *Harry Potter and the Chamber of Secrets* DVD.

Preparation: A day before the activity is to take place, take each piece of construction paper and splatter it with white, black, and gray paint. Crumple each paper and then let it dry.

Instructions:

1. Ask if students know the myth of the phoenix. Explain the mythology of the phoenix: *"A phoenix is a bird in ancient Greek and Egyptian mythology. After its long life, it catches fire and then rises from the ashes over and over. It's considered a very beautiful and strong creature."*
2. Show a brief segment of *Harry Potter and the Chamber of Secrets* to give students a visual image of the phoenix bursting into flames and rising from the ashes.
3. Tell students that they, too, can be like a phoenix. They can overcome their obstacles by turning their tough times into something beautiful.
4. Give the students a crumpled piece of brown construction paper.
5. When the students unfold the paper, they discover that it is splattered and smeared in paint.
6. Explain to the students that this paper symbolizes the ashes. Ask them to think about the "ashes" or obstacles in their lives.
7. Ask the students to imagine what magnificent bird would arise from their ashes. Students then paint their versions of the phoenix with metallic paints.
8. This is an excellent time to encourage students to examine color choices and draw parallels to their emotions through the use of symbolic colors.
9. Ask closing questions:
   a. *"What tough times were you thinking of when you created your picture?"*
   b. *"When you put paint on the crumpled paper, what did the phoenix represent to you?"*
   c. *"How are you like a phoenix?"*

Suggested Modifications (for Special Needs Populations): School counselors may need to modify vocabulary to meet all student needs during discussions. Counselors and art teachers can provide individual assistance to students who need extra help with specific projects. Students who have difficulty writing may either complete artists' statements on the computer, or may dictate answers to group leaders. Additionally, assessments may be conducted orally if necessary.

Evaluation Plan: Ask each student to describe one way in which he or she can overcome an obstacle in his or her life and turn it into something beautiful.

REFERENCE

1492 Pictures, Heyday Films, MIRACLE Productions, Warner Bros. (Producers), & Columbus, C. (Director). (2002). *Harry Potter and the chamber of secrets* [DVD]. United States, United Kingdom, & Germany: Warner Bros.

OUR MULTICULTURAL STARS AND SELVES

Clare Merlin and Lenore Katz

*T*his activity asks students to describe their own multicultural selves by decorating paper stars. When students are then asked to tear off certain aspects of their stars, they are drawn to reflect on what it feels like to have parts of their own selves removed, ignored, or cut off. In processing these feelings, school counselors can improve student attitudes, multicultural awareness, and understandings of privilege in our society.

Modality: Visual Arts

ASCA National Model Domain: Personal/Social

Deliver via: Group or classroom guidance

Age Level: Suitable for 6th- through 12th-grade students

Indications: Appropriate for classroom guidance lessons to improve student multicultural awareness or small groups focused on friendship or bullying

Materials: One piece of colored construction paper for every student; scissors for every student; crayons, markers, or colored pencils for every student

Preparation: Collect colored construction paper, scissors, crayons, markers, and colored pencils for students' use.

Instructions:
1. Distribute one piece of colored construction paper to every student in the room.
2. Students are asked to draw a large five-pointed star shape on their paper, then to cut the star out. Each student will end up drawing and cutting out a slightly different shaped star than his or her classmates' stars.
3. Students each write their name on one point of the star.
4. Next, the school counselor prompts students to write one identifying characteristic on each point of the star. These characteristics should be:

   a. Their first language
   b. The color of their hair
   c. Their race
   d. Their gender

5. In the center of their star, students are prompted to write one word or phrase that describes something special about themselves that they like or are proud of. For example, "I am a good student" or "I am kind to others."

6. Students then decorate their stars using crayons, markers, or colored pencils. The school counselor encourages students to make their stars as decorative and beautiful as possible.

7. When all stars are decorated, ask students to pick up their stars and tear off relevant points on their star if the conditions below apply to them. Use the following prompts with patience as students react and take their time tearing off star points. The conditions are:
   a. If the students' name ends in anything other than "ie" or "y," tear off the point with their name on it.
   b. If the first language listed on their star is anything other than English, tear off the point with their language on it.
   c. If the hair color listed on their star is anything other than blonde, tear off the point with their hair color on it.
   d. If the race listed on their star is anything other than White, tear off the point with their race on it.
   e. If the gender listed on their star is anything other than male, tear off the point with their gender on it.

8. After students are finished tearing relevant points off the stars, facilitate a discussion about this experience. Suggested questions:
   a. *"How did you feel after you had completed decorating your star?"*
   b. *"What do the characteristics you wrote on your star mean to you?"*
   c. *"If you had to rip a point off your star, how did you feel when you did so?"*
   d. *"What did you think when I asked you to rip off one point of your star?"*
   e. *"How did you feel when you saw others ripping points off their stars when you were not?"*
   f. *"How do you feel about your star now?"*

   It is important that you accept and validate students' feelings about the potentially painful nature of ripping off parts of their selves. You may also point out to students that even when all points are removed, their stars still retain the core statement about what makes them special.

9. Open a discussion about how this activity resembles how we sometimes treat others when we bully or discriminate in our school and in society. Suggested questions:
   a. *"Have you ever felt this way before? If so, when? What caused those feelings in that circumstance?"*
   b. *"How does this activity resemble how we sometimes treat one another?"*
   c. *"When we are bullied about our religion/ethnicity/language and so forth,*

> *does it feel like parts of our selves have been torn off? What about when we are discriminated against?"*
>
> d. *"When we bully other students because of their characteristics, how do you think it feels to them?"*
> e. *"When we discriminate against other students because of their characteristics, how do you think it feels to them?"*
> f. *"How does this activity resemble how society views certain individuals?"*
> g. *"What are some ways the society "rips off star points" of certain individuals?"*
> h. *"How can we help prevent star points from being torn off? What can we do to reattach star points?"*

Draw students' attention to how their feelings in this activity can relate to the feelings of individuals who are bullied or discriminated against. Emphasize to students what those of us with privilege can do to correct systemic wrongs against those without privilege. Students may also benefit from hearing explanations of why these characteristics were selected. For instance, research shows that students with more "American" names get more positive attention in schools.

Suggested Modifications (for Special Needs Populations): Modify this lesson based on the ability and the age of students. When working with younger students, ask students to write any number of important characteristics on their star, then instruct all students to remove one or two points together. Discussion questions for students can also be modified for student age and ability. You may need to ask more specific and directive questions to younger students and those with lower academic abilities, and more ambiguous, challenging questions for older students and those with higher abilities. You may want to focus on bullying and exclusion with younger students, and dialoging about privilege and discrimination with older students.

Evaluation Plan: The following pre- and posttest can be used to evaluate student awareness of this activity. Students will be asked to complete this assessment as a pretest and a posttest of their understanding of the concepts addressed during the activity Our Multicultural Stars and Selves.

On a scale of 1 to 5, with 1 meaning not important at all and 5 meaning very important, how important are the following behaviors?

Helping other students.	1	2	3	4	5
Helping students who are different from me.	1	2	3	4	5
Being kind to other students.	1	2	3	4	5
Being kind to students who are different from me.	1	2	3	4	5
Not bullying other students.	1	2	3	4	5
Not bullying students who are different from me.	1	2	3	4	5
Not leaving people out.	1	2	3	4	5

Not discriminating against people.   1   2   3   4   5

Not discriminating against people who are
    different from me.   1   2   3   4   5

PROGRESSIVE PAINTINGS

Diane J. Shea and James R. Huber

This is an experiential activity in which students begin a watercolor painting but after a set amount of time, they must pass the painting off to other students to complete and/or alter the original. It focuses on communication and group integration.

Modality: Visual Art

ASCA National Model Domain: Personal/Social Domain

Deliver via: Group counseling

Age Level: Middle or high school

Indications: Can be used to facilitate personal/group learning regarding building trust, risk taking, being aware of feelings, team building, flexibility, coping with change, and social skills.

Materials: Watercolor paints, brushes, art paper, water to rinse the brushes

Preparations: The room should be arranged so that students sit around a table and have easy access to materials.

Instructions:
1. Explain to students that this is an experiential exercise and they should pay attention to their feelings throughout the activity.
2. Give each of the students a piece of art paper, watercolors, and a brush.
3. Tell the students that they are to begin painting anything that they want.
4. After 5 minutes tell the students that they are to pass their painting to the person on their right. Each student now has another student's painting.
5. Tell the students that they are to continue painting on their partner's painting without asking any questions.
6. After 5 minutes, repeat the process of students passing their paining to the person on their right.
7. Continue this process until each student gets his or her original painting back.
8. Process with the students what it felt like to pass off their original painting and what it felt like to see the final version. Is this what they originally had in mind when they began the painting? What lessons can be learned from this?

Suggested Modifications: Depending on the allotted time and size of the group, time should be adjusted between exchanges.

Evaluation Plan: Gather perception data based on age group and purpose of exercise. For example, for a middle school friendship group:

1. How valuable was this exercise in terms of understanding how you might feel about things changing?

   Not at all _____ A little _____ Somewhat valuable _____ Valuable _____ Very valuable _____

2. What did you learn about yourself in this exercise?

PUZZLED

Nicole M. Randick and Rebecca E. Michel

*T*his group activity uses puzzle pieces to help students establish rapport and group cohesiveness through contributing to a group art project. Through the art process, members of the group are given the opportunity to express themselves as individuals as well as participate as a member of a team. A sense of individualism is sustained as members contribute a piece of their individuality through the creation of their own puzzle pieces. A sense of belonging is promoted as each member of the group uses his or her individual puzzle piece to help facilitate putting the puzzle together.

Modality: Visual Arts

ASCA National Model Domain: Personal/Social

Deliver via: Group, classroom guidance

Age Level: Middle or high school

Indications: This activity would be appropriate in a group focused on social skills, self-esteem, diversity, or friendship. It would also be helpful in a classroom or group that required additional group cohesiveness.

Materials: Two sheets of 3´ × 4´ or larger poster board, scissors, glue, markers, crayons, colored pencils, magazines (enough materials for the size of the group)

Preparation: Before the group begins, the group facilitator draws and cuts one sheet of poster board into as many puzzle pieces as there are group members. For example, if there are 12 group members, there would be 12 puzzle pieces. Each puzzle piece is then traced onto the remaining poster board (this will be helpful when putting the puzzle back together). All art materials are displayed on a table. The facilitator should also brainstorm several theme options for the puzzle that would be appropriate for the particular group or class. General themes (such as friendship or school) can be used for start-up groups. More specific, topic-based themes (such as coping with loss or forgiveness) can be used to build on previously learned material.

Instructions:

1. Each member of the group is given a piece of the puzzle to design.
2. The group facilitator explains that each member will be creating his or her own unique puzzle piece that represents something about him- or herself. It is important that each member contributes to the group puzzle.
3. The group facilitator provides options for the puzzle theme, and the group members decide on the theme.
4. Students are next encouraged to walk up to the table and obtain the art materials needed to create their puzzle piece. The facilitator makes note of how students act while working together to share the materials. Valuable information can be obtained by evaluating this process. These interactions can be discussed during the reflection following the activity.
5. To create their puzzle pieces, group members draw their own images or cut out magazine images that represent their unique characteristics on their piece of the puzzle.
6. The facilitator should be aware of how the art-making process can produce anxiety or self-consciousness. Conversations can be encouraged and facilitated through positive feedback. Students often become engaged in the process and can open up during their conversations. This needs to be facilitated in a nonthreatening and safe environment created by the facilitator.
7. After each piece has been decorated, the group comes together and each member glues his or her own piece onto the remaining poser board with the predrawn outline of the puzzle.
8. The puzzle is created when all the pieces have been glued down onto the poster board.
9. Then, each person describes his or her own piece of the puzzle.
10. After each piece of the puzzle has been explained, the facilitator leads the group in a reflection discussion. The following questions can be used as a guide:
    a. *"What were your initial thoughts when you found out we would be creating a puzzle today?"*
    b. *"How did you feel when you were creating your own puzzle piece?"*
    c. *"How does your puzzle piece fit in with the rest of the puzzle?"*
    d. *"Do you notice any themes among the puzzle pieces?"*
    e. *"What did you learn from other group members as the puzzle was being created and assembled?"*
    f. *"What were your thoughts when you looked at the finished puzzle?"*

Suggested Modifications (for Special Needs Populations): This activity can be modified to meet the needs of various populations. Individuals with fine motor skill deficits can be paired with student helpers or aides to create their puzzle piece. The theme chosen for the group can be broadly defined to allow more options for students with developmental or intellectual disabilities. A peer or facilitator could work with students as necessary to plan what images to place on the puzzle piece. Additionally, magazine pictures could be cut out and available for students to easily add to their puzzle piece. The facilitator might also create an example puzzle piece for students to use as a guide.

Evaluation Plan: The following questions can be used to evaluate student learning from this activity.

Please answer the questions below about your experience with this activity.

1. What are the benefits of this activity?
2. What are the drawbacks of this activity?
3. How did this activity impact group cohesiveness?
4. What did you learn about yourself by participating in this activity?
5. What did you learn about the other group members by participating in this activity?

RECYCLED REFLECTIONS: A VISUAL JOURNAL PROJECT

Laura L. Gallo

This activity is designed to be utilized in small-group counseling. At the start of the group, students are invited to select old books (left over from the school library, picked up from garage sales, etc.) that hold some type of meaning for them; perhaps the title, the illustrations, or words they find within the book capture their attention. The students then spend time using the book as a type of journal—writing on pages, circling words, creating drawings, writing poetry, and adding to illustrations. Group leaders then facilitate discussions about adolescent issues and the visual images being created by the group members within their books. Leaders can utilize structured topics or allow a more open-ended session with students bringing up topics they would like to discuss.

Modality: Visual Arts

ASCA National Model Domain: Personal/Social

Deliver via: Group

Appropriate Level: Middle or high school

Indications: The group can be run as "open," but invite students who are presenting with typical adolescent developmental struggles. Examples include parent conflict, relationship issues, perfectionism, stress, identity issues, or motivational issues.

Materials: Old books, markers, pens, glue, glitter, any other materials available.

Instructions:

1. At the first session, it is important to address the basic expectations related to the formation of counseling groups (informed consent, purpose of group, limits to confidentiality, group rules, etc.). Although typically run as an open group, membership may not vary; if new members join, current members can be invited to inform them of the group "rules."

2. The counselor describes the activity of creating a visual journal. The purpose of the journal is twofold. First, it gives students an opportunity to express themselves in creative ways. Second, it provides a "purpose" for being in the group while they discuss relevant topics. It is also helpful if the counselor has an example for students to see.

3. The counselor provides students with materials to use in the creation of their journals and examples to help them get started. For example, the author has shown students how she had drawn pictures in her own visual journal and how she had focused on the word "grief" from a page in her book and how this word led her to write out some memories of her father, whom she had lost a few years ago.

4. Remind students that there is no wrong way to create a journal. Acknowledge that some of their drawings or creations may not be sparked by anything specific to the contents of the book, but may arise from discussions occurring in the group.

5. At the end of each session, invite group members to share any of their journal creations if they feel comfortable doing so.

6. At the end of the year, incorporate an event that brings closure to the group. This might be sharing of their artwork or inviting each member to summarize their "story" as illustrated by their journals.

Suggested Modifications (for Special Needs Populations): This activity can be modified for most any student. Remind members that the project is not about the product (i.e., that their artwork does not have to be "perfect"), but the process. If students have physical limitations, they can be encouraged to verbally participate or a scribe can be assigned.

Evaluation Plan: Use a pre- and postassessment similar to the example provided; the assessment may be modified to reflect a theme, if necessary. Individual interviews could also be used to gather more data from students as to their lived experience participating in the group. During the "exit" session with each student, gather qualitative data regarding the strengths and weaknesses of the group for each participant. What worked well for them? What did they not like? What was their favorite part? What should be kept for future groups? Counselors may also meet with those students who stopped attending the group during the course of the semester to gather information regarding their choice to leave. Counselors can also track attendance to help evaluate the effectiveness of the group.

1.	I feel good about coming to school	1	2	3	4	5
2.	I have others I can talk to when I need a friend.	1	2	3	4	5
3.	I am able to express my feelings well.	1	2	3	4	5
4.	I do not have many ways to express my feelings.	1	2	3	4	5
5.	I would not tell an adult if I were feeling very sad or had feelings of hopelessness.	1	2	3	4	5
6.	I would not tell an adult if I had a friend that was feeling very sad or had feelings of hopelessness.	1	2	3	4	5
7.	I get along well with others.	1	2	3	4	5
8.	I often have conflicts with my parents.	1	2	3	4	5
9.	I have positive coping methods.	1	2	3	4	5
10.	Being part of something beyond myself helps me feel better.	1	2	3	4	5

Directions: Circle your responses to the following questions/statements using the following scale:

1 = Strongly disagree,   2 = Somewhat disagree,   3 = Not sure,   4 = Somewhat agree,   5 = Strongly agree

---

REFLECTING IN COLOR

Kanessa Miller Doss

*E**motions are often difficult to express in words and sometimes even more difficult to identify. Many students need help in identifying, expressing, and regulating their emotions and this activity uses drawing/doodling to achieve those three goals.*

Modality: Visual Arts

ASCA National Model Domain: Personal/Social

Deliver via: Individual or group

Age Level: Middle or high school

Indications: This activity may be used for individuals who have emotional regulation issues or require anger management. It may also be used to teach students about identifying and expressing emotions.

Materials: White paper, feelings picture or word chart, crayons, colored pencils, and/or markers

Preparation: This is a simple activity that would be enhanced if the facilitator prepared and presented a sample of the activity. The facilitator should also post the feelings chart and provide a list of strategies to reduce stress or produce happy feelings.

Instructions:

1. Distribute the paper and several coloring utensils to each student.
2. Instruct the students to write their names in the center of the paper and pick one to two colors that represent their current feelings.
3. Have the students use those coloring utensils to draw a figure in the upper-left corner of the paper that represents how he or she feels. Next, instruct the students to list three words under the picture to describe his or her feelings. Students may refer to the feelings chart for accurate descriptions of their current feelings.
4. Direct the students to pick three colors that he or she would use when feeling happy. Instruct the students to draw a happy picture in the upper-right corner and list three things he or she does when happy.
5. At the bottom of the paper, have the students write three mood-enhancement strategies that they can use to feel happy when they feel sad, angry, scared, and/or frustrated.
6. Instruct the students to draw an arrow from the left picture to the mood-enhancement strategies at the bottom of the page. Then, direct the students to draw and arrow from the mood-enhancement strategies at the bottom to the right picture.
7. Discuss how the strategies at the bottom can produce happy feelings in times of sadness, anger, fear, and frustration. Explain the connections of the arrows and one's responsibility for managing feelings.

Suggested Modifications (for Special Needs Populations): This activity can be used with all middle and high school students. If needed, modifications can be made for diverse populations, such as only using pictures for students with speech/language disabilities.

Evaluation Plan: Evaluation of this activity involves discussing the individual reflections. The students should be able to identify their emotions, express their emotions in drawings/doodles and/or verbal/written words, and describe techniques to change stressful emotions into less stressful emotions.

THE REMEMBRANCE TREE

Edward F. Hudspeth and Rochelle Moss

*R*emembrance trees are not a new concept. Usually a remembrance tree is planted in memory of a person or event. This intervention is designed to be utilized in small-group counseling or possibly as part of classroom guidance. It may be done as a one-time intervention or as an intervention, with various activities, completed throughout a school year. The intervention and subsequent activities are intended to facilitate the grief process. The counselor *opens the activity by asking the students to remember events that occurred prior to the situation that has generated the grief. When completing the chosen activity, students may work individually or in small groups.*

Modality: Art, Writing

ASCA National Model Domain: Personal/Social

Deliver via: Group counseling or classroom guidance

Age Level: Elementary (This may be utilized with any age group. Modify the activity, the processing questions, and assessments to align with the students' developmental level.)

Indications: This intervention may be used to help support students after a traumatic event or to help them process grief. The intervention is particularly useful when there has been a loss within the classroom (e.g., classmate or teacher).

Materials: A living tree. When choosing a live tree, select one that will grow in a pot indoors. Dwarf trees such as the Norfolk Island Pine, Alberta Spruce, and Arborvitae are good choices and are readily available at garden centers for a reasonable price. Dwarf varieties grow to approximately 4 feet tall; coloring pencils, crayons, or markers; paper (white or colored); paper clips or ornament hangers; tree-shaped cutouts (see Appendix, Figure 4.11); a picture of a family tree; a wrapped box with a slit in the top of the box; 3 × 5 notecards; heart-shaped cutout (see Appendix, Figure 4.12); and other cutout shapes as mentioned below in Other Activities.

Preparation: If a living tree is utilized, make sure it is in a large enough pot to allow for growth. Place the tree in a prominent place in the classroom where it is continually visible. Depending on the activity, have the art media out and available to all. After each activity, the counselor should take a picture of the tree to provide a photographic record of the students' work.

Instructions: Introduce the intervention by speaking about the topic of trees. The counselor may mention that trees make the air we breathe and filter the water that we drink. At this point, as a way to center the students, the counselor may ask the students to close their eyes, take slow deep breaths, and envision and reflect on trees. After a short pause, the counselor asks the students to open their eyes. The counselor continues by saying, *"We also know that some trees have flowers that smell good, some give us food (e.g., apples, oranges), and some give us shade on hot summer days. Trees also have roots that make them strong and connect them to the Earth."*

Initial Activity: My Tree, Our Tree, Their Tree: This activity is often done as the first of a series of activities. The goal is to allow students to acknowledge that someone is no longer in their class and to verbalize this change. Prior to this activity, the counselor has decorated a tree-shaped cutout and labeled it with the missing individual's name.

1. Ask each student to decorate a tree-shaped cutout using his or her choice of colored pencils, crayons, or markers. Limit time to about 5 minutes. Ask each student to put his or her name on the tree cutout.
2. Next, say, *"Sometimes we use trees to represent our family. We may even use a tree to represent our class."* Show an example of a family tree. Then, invite students to attach their tree cutout to the living tree using paperclips or ornament hangers. Once each student has placed a tree cutout on the living tree, ask, *"Is everyone on the tree? Are we missing anyone?"* It is likely that someone will mention the individual who is no longer in the class. If no one mentions the individual, encourage them to remember. Name a specific day, event, holiday, or party when everyone was present and say, "Who are we missing from then?" Once the individual has been mentioned, say, *"Yes, that is who we are missing. I've got a tree for him (her), too. Should I put it on the tree?"* If yes, place the missing individual's tree cutout on the living tree and say, *"Now everyone is there."* If no, simply reflect that ____ is no longer here. Both outcomes have facilitated awareness, remembrance, and acknowledgment of a change.

Suggested Modifications (for Special Needs Populations): The words utilized may need to be modified for different ages or developmental levels. This activity is useful with most student groups and will be particularly helpful for students who have yet to verbalize that their classroom makeup has changed. Students who have difficulty with fine or gross motor skills may need assistance from the counselor or a classmate when decorating their tree cutouts and attaching them to the living tree.

Evaluation Plan: To evaluate the effectiveness of this intervention, you may use the following survey as a postassessment. Unless there has been a previous discussion about the loss of an individual, using the assessment as a preassessment has little value. The primary goal of the activity is awareness and verbal acknowledgment of change.

Activity 2: I Miss You Box: This activity may be timed to occur during a holiday when presents are given or around the birthday of the individual lost. The goal of this activity is to give students the opportunity to express sorrow associated with a loss. The counselor reflects aloud about the change the class has experienced. Specifically mention the individual who is no longer present. Next, invite students to respond on a notecard to the statement, "I miss [individual's name], because_____" or "I miss _____ about [individual's name]." Once all have had an opportunity to write a response, the counselor invites the students to place the card in the prepared box, which has been placed near the living tree. Allow time at the end of the activity for students to share their reminiscences and stories together.

Suggested Modifications: For younger children, depending on their age and writing ability, the counselor may need to ask each student if he or she has a response and then write it for them. A substitution may be to allow students to find images from magazines that represent what they miss about the individual. The images are cut out and placed in the box.

Evaluation Plan: To evaluate the effectiveness of this intervention, use the assessment that corresponds to this activity as a pre- and postassessment of their recognition of whom and what they miss.

Activity 3: A Part of My Heart: This activity allows students to identify emotions associated with grief. Prior to the activity, the counselor removes the objects that were previously attached to the tree. To begin the activity, the counselor gives each student a heart-shaped cutout. The counselor says, *"When we lost* [individual's name], *I felt _____."* Next, the counselor invites students to write the emotion(s) named on the heart and color the part of the heart that the emotion occupies. Once completed, the counselor invites students to attach their heart to the living tree. Allow ample time for this activity to acknowledge and validate each student's responses. When multiple students name the same emotion, link the individuals by saying, *"That is what _____ said/felt."* This provides normalization for these students.

Suggested Modifications: For younger children, depending on their age and writing ability, the counselor may need to ask each student if he or she has a response and then write it for the child. The student can then color the parts of the heart once the emotion is written.

Evaluation Plan: To evaluate the effectiveness of this intervention, you may use the assessment that follows as a pre- and postassessment of their recognition of emotions.

Other Activities: Further activities may be utilized throughout the school year. Activities may coincide with holidays, school events, or the seasons. Substitutions, in the previously mentioned activities, may include (a) for holidays, cutouts of eggs, hearts, or flags; (b) for school events, cutouts of red ribbons, footballs, or graduation caps; and (c) for seasons, cutouts of green leaves, colored leaves, or snowflakes. The counselor would use similar wording when initiating the activity with modifications for the image being utilized.

Suggested Modifications: As with other activities, younger students may need help with writing or manipulating smaller objects.

Termination Activity: This activity may be done at the end of the school year or at the end of a predetermined period of time. The counselor and students take the tree outside and find a place to plant it. The counselor recounts the activities that the class has done with the living tree. Next, the counselor shows the pictures of the living tree that were taken after each activity. The counselor states,

"Remember when we talked about the tree and its roots? We said the roots help it grow strong and connect it to the Earth. I think this tree helped us remember a lot of things, especially things about [individual's name]. I think we are connected to the tree like it is connected to the Earth. I hope after today, when you see this tree, it will help you remember that we are all connected and that we are all growing stronger each day."

My Tree, Our Tree, Their Tree Assessment of Understanding and Awareness
Students will complete this assessment as a postassessment of their understanding of the concepts addressed during the activity and awareness brought about by the activity My Tree, Our Tree, Their Tree and then again as an overall assessment at the end of the intervention. For younger students, this may be done verbally.

1. What are three things trees do for us?
   a. _____
   b. _____
   c. _____
2. True or False: Sometimes we use trees to represent our family or class.
3. True or False: Trees have roots that make them strong and connect them to the Earth.
4. How has our class tree changed since _____ (insert the date, event, holiday, party mentioned during the activity)?

I Miss You Box Assessment
Students will complete this assessment as a pre- and postassessment of their recognition of whom and what they miss as mentioned in the I Miss You Box activity. For younger students, this may be done verbally.
1. What things do you miss about [individual's name]?
   a. _____
   b. _____
   c. _____
2. Sometimes we miss friends because:
   _____

A Part of My Heart Assessment of Emotions Recognition
Students will complete this assessment as a pre- and postassessment of their recognition of emotions as mentioned in the A Part of My Heart activity. For younger students, this may be done verbally.

1. How many feelings can you name? Name them:

   _____, _____, _____,

   _____, _____, _____.

2. Which feeling(s) have you felt today?

   _____, _____, _____,

   _____, _____, _____.

APPENDIX

Figure 4.11 Tree pattern.

Figure 4.12 Heart pattern.

SELF-DISCOVERY THROUGH NATURE

Sherrionda Heard-Crawford

Students will learn how to build self-esteem and embrace the importance of individuality by utilizing leaf rubbings to identify personal strengths, as well as to discover what's important and unique about themselves.

Modality: Visual Arts

ASCA National Model Domain: Personal/Social

Deliver via: Small group

Age Level: Elementary

Intervention: This intervention can be used as a self-awareness activity for small groups of students who are experiencing difficulty with low self-esteem, interpersonal conflict, and/or identity issues. Ideally, this group would be a closed group and this particular session would supplement additional sessions related to the group topic.

Materials: Various types of leaves or leaf templates, plain white paper, crayons and pencils. (To complete leaf templates, gather the following materials: craft glue, 4 × 6 cardboard pieces and leaves.)

Preparation: If this activity is being delivered during the fall, the group can go outdoors to select their own leaves. If planning to facilitate this group throughout the year, leaf templates are recommended. To prepare leaf templates, you will need clear craft glue, a large variety of leaves, scissors, and cardboard. Cut the cardboard into 4 × 6 pieces. Use the clear craft glue to paste leaves onto the cardboard.

Create goals and objectives for your group session. These may include the following: (a) Define self-esteem, (b) discuss potential factors that may affect self-esteem, (c) identify personal strengths and unique characteristics about oneself, and (d) completion of a leaf rubbing.

Instructions:

1. Discuss the purpose of the group, discuss group rules, and complete informed consent (if required by your school).
2. Discuss objectives for the group session:
   a. Define "self-esteem."
   b. Discuss potential factors that may affect self-esteem.
   c. Identify personal strengths and unique characteristics about oneself.
   d. Complete a leaf rubbing.
3. Show students a completed leaf rubbing. Share how each vein represents a personal strength and how personal strengths can be used in a variety of situations (read the identified personal strengths and unique characteristics descriptions to the group). Also, emphasize that everyone's leaf will be unique. Discuss the advantages of being unique (we all have our own special characteristics and strengths).
4. Provide instructions for leaf rubbings:
   a. Choose a leaf.
   a. Position leaf (vein side up) on a sheet of plain white paper.
   b. Place another sheet of plain white paper over the leaf.
   c. Take a crayon or pencil and turn it sideways.
   d. Gently rub the top of the paper.
   e. The leaf will appear on the top sheet.
5. Challenge the students to complete their own leaf rubbings and attach a personal strength to each vein of the leaf. Then, have the students share their completed leaf rubbings with the other group members.

Suggested Modifications (for Special Needs Populations): Students of all levels and abilities can actively engage in the group. If your group includes students who are English Language Learners (ELL), visuals and translated materials should be included. Also, for primary students (or others) who are not able to write, drawings can be utilized.

Evaluation Plan: Both formative and summative evaluations should be utilized. Group discussions, individual feedback, and nonverbal cues are effective as a formative evaluation. A summative evaluation for the group session may include an assessment of the student's ability to provide written documentation of the following: definition of self-esteem, factors that affect the student's individual self-esteem, and identification of personal strengths that may provide a barrier to factors that affect self-esteem.

SELF-EXPRESSION: LETTING YOUR WORRIES GO

Anne Stuart Henry, Alicia H. Schwenk, Genevieve Shaw, and Sherry A. Bosarge

This activity is designed for use with small groups and is ideally conducted by a counselor in collaboration with an art teacher. The activity emphasizes positive self-expression through art.

Modality: Visual Arts

ASCA National Model Domain: Personal/Social

Deliver via: Group counseling

Age Level: 4th/5th grade

Indications: Group candidates may demonstrate academic or behavioral concerns. However, these activities can also be used with any small group focusing on coping (divorce/separation, chronic illness, grief).

Materials: Model Magic clay (two to three packets for each group member), Guatemalan worry dolls or an image of worry dolls, Smart Board, *Frida Kahlo* book.

Preparation: Before the group session, you may want to purchase Guatemalan worry dolls. Alternatively, you can complete an Internet search for images of Guatemalan worry dolls.

Take the Model Magic clay and create an example of a worry doll.

On the day of this activity, get into a circle for discussion. Tell students, *"We each have events/problems in our lives we cannot change. When this happens, we have to learn how to cope, or deal with our feelings. Feelings are very important. When we pay attention to them, we can understand what we want or need. Self-expression is how we express or show our feelings. Today we are going to discuss healthy ways of dealing with and expressing our feelings, which is a coping skill."*

Instructions:
1. Tell students that there are four steps to dealing with feelings (*The Coping Skills Workbook,* Schab, 1996):
   a. Label what you are feeling.
   b. Accept your feelings.
   c. Express your feelings.
   d. Decide what you need to feel better.
2. Ask students to list some feeling words (comfortable, lonely, frustrated, guilty, anxious, excited, etc.). Tell students they have the right to express their feelings.
3. Show students a balloon, and tell them the balloon represents their body. Say a feeling word, and then blow into the balloon. Ask students what would happen if they kept all of those feelings inside.
4. Tell students that they might feel like they would pop! Keeping feelings stuffed inside can make you feel uncomfortable, but letting the feelings out a little at a time helps you feel better.
5. Tell students that when they let their feelings out, they should think of a safe way to express themselves. It is very important not to harm themselves or anyone else.
6. Read the story *Frida Kahlo.* Ask students to label her feelings and think of ways she safely expressed her feelings. Students may discuss challenges in their own lives and healthy ways of expressing the feelings accompanying those challenges.
7. Explain to the students that they are going to participate in an art activity in which they express their feelings in a safe way. Tell students about Guatemalan worry dolls, and show them an example. Children can tell one worry to each doll at night, and place them under the pillow. In the morning, the dolls have taken their worries away.
8. Have students mold the clay into posed figures symbolizing emotions with which they struggle. These will become their own worry dolls.
9. Students will use approximately half a Model Magic packet for each doll.
10. Demonstrate how to attach two pieces of clay together by firmly pressing the clay together.
11. Allow the dolls to air dry.
12. Ask closing questions:
    a. *"What was it like to express your feelings in clay?"*
    b. *"What were some similarities/differences among the clay figures?"*
    c. *"How did it feel to hear your feelings are always acceptable?"*

Suggested Modifications (for Special Needs Populations): School counselors may need to modify vocabulary to meet all student needs during discussions. Counselors and art teachers can provide individual assistance to

students who need extra help with specific projects. Students who have difficulty writing may either complete artists' statements on the computer, or may
dictate answers to group leaders. Additionally, assessments may be conducted
orally if necessary.

Evaluation Plan: Ask students, *"What does 'to cope' mean? What are some
healthy ways to express your feelings?"*

REFERENCE

Schab, L. M. (1996). *The coping skills workbook.* Plainview, NY: Childswork/Childsplay.
Verezia, M. (1999). *Frida Kahlo.* New York, NY: Grolier Children's Press.

SOUNDTRACK TO YOUR LIFE

Shannon Halligan

*P*articipants will create a soundtrack that reflects who they are and/or
major events in their lives. It combines images, words, and lyrics and
*music to express personal meaning. This project is a self-reflective exercise,
similar to creating an autobiography.*

Modality: Visual Arts

ASCA National Model Domain: Personal/Social

Deliver via: Individual, group, or classroom guidance

Age Level: 6th to 12th grade

Indications: This activity works well with adolescents due to their tendency to
identify with music and lyrics. It also incorporates some of the healing benefits
of music therapy (lyrical analysis, active listening, etc.) as well. It can be used for
various diagnoses/symptoms, including depression/anxiety, mood disorders, attention deficit hyperactivity disorder/attention deficit disorder, trauma, and so on.

Materials: Magazine images, markers, pencils, paper, glue sticks, scissors;
optional: CD inserts if available as examples.

Preparation: Have materials ready to be used on a table; have each student
work quietly and individually.

Instructions:
Ask the students to do the following:

1. Make a list of significant events in your life.
2. Write down the names of five to ten songs that accompany those events.
3. Create cover art to accompany the song selections. This can be in the form
   of drawing, painting, or collage.

Suggested Modifications (for Special Needs Populations): Simplify the task
by asking students to select only three to five songs. Or provide participants a

list of songs from which to choose. Some participants may need to hear songs in order to choose. Have a selection of appropriate songs that you may play in session for the group.

Evaluation Plan: Have each participant share his or her song list. Discuss the meaning for each song and its relevance to the life event. This directive allows participants to express their unique and common experiences in a creative way. It can increase their ability to express their emotions, self-esteem, and self-worth, as well as increase socialization and their support network by finding commonality with experiences and their coping skills.

Group Processing: Encourage participants to see who has music similar to theirs on their CD. Discuss the music's relevance and what areas the students may have in common, what similar challenges they may have faced. Students can also be encouraged to burn the CD so it is in audio format.

THE STARS IN YOUR WORLD

Hennessey Lustica and Atiya R. Smith

This activity is designed for individual or small-group counseling settings. It facilitates understanding of the students' collective culture and the nature of the relationships of the people in their world. Students will work to create a poster illustrating these relationships.

Modality: Expressive Arts

ASCA National Model Domain: Personal/Social

Deliver via: Individual or group counseling

Age Level: Elementary and middle school (modify the processing questions to align with the students' developmental level)

Indications: This activity can be used individually and in small groups focused on family dynamics or peer relationships as a modality other than traditional talk therapy.

Materials: Small and large star cutouts, construction paper, glue, markers/crayons/colored pencils, and glitter.

Preparation: Provide each student with one large star and multiple smaller stars, construction paper, and art supplies.

Instructions:

I. Introduction

Introduce the activity by asking, *"Who are the important people in your life?"* Explain to students that this could include the people who live in their home; grandparents, aunts, uncles, and other relatives; pets; friends; and teachers. Discuss with the students how different people have different relationships with the important people in their lives. Encourage exploration of how these relationships can be positive or negative depending on the situation. Also, it will be important to work with the students to create, or simply provide for them, a definition of the following types of relationships: *positive*, *okay*, and *negative*. From this discussion, explain that this activity will focus on how each student is the "star of his/her world" and that today they will create a poster that not only depicts the important people in their lives, but also their relationships with these important people. Discuss the importance of talking about these different relationships, their strengths, and how they can be made more positive.

II. Activity

1. Ask students to write their names on the large star and place it in the middle of their poster.
2. Explain to students that this star represents them and that all the stars around them represent the important people in their lives.
3. Have the students write the names, or draw pictures, of these important people on the smaller stars and then paste them around the larger star. Explain to students that they will use color coding to describe their relationships with the people on the smaller stars:
   - ■ Blue = positive relationship
   - ■ Green = okay relationship
   - ■ Red = negative relationship
4. Have the students color in their stars based on the color chart and finish decorating the poster with glitter.
5. Invite students to present their posters and to ask questions that facilitate open conversation about their relationships.

III. Discussion

1. List the qualities that make up positive relationships on the chart paper and discuss (e.g., *My mom and I get along very well because she is nice, kind, funny, patient, etc.*).
2. List the qualities that make up the okay/negative relationships on the chart paper and discuss (e.g., *My mom and I argue sometimes because she gets angry, makes me do my chores, won't let me watch television, etc.*).
3. Discuss with the students what responsibility they might have in changing the okay/negative relationships to positive relationships (e.g., *My mom and I argue sometimes when I don't want to do my chores. I should try harder to do my chores so my mom doesn't get angry.*).
4. Last, as a group brainstorm additional ways to help the okay/negative relationships become much more positive.

Suggested Modifications (for Special Needs Populations): You may need to modify the language used in descriptions of the relationships with others to align congruently with students' developmental levels. This activity is appropriate for use with most student groups and will be particularly helpful with students who are hesitant to participate in talk therapy but enjoy creative activities. Students who have difficulty with writing may be encouraged to draw pictures or work with the counselor on filling in their stars.

Evaluation Plan: To evaluate the effectiveness of this intervention, school counselors can use observation and discussion questions postactivity.

School counselors can assess student understanding by direct observation of student participation in the activity. Student learning can also be assessed by asking the following questions:

1. Who are the important people in your life?
2. What makes these people important to you?
3. What are your relationships like with the important people in your life?
4. What does a positive relationship look like?
5. What does a negative relationship look like?
6. What strategies can you use to help the negative relationships become more positive?

SUCCESS, STONES, AND SOLUTIONS

Elsa Soto Leggett

*T*his activity is devised to be used with small groups. It can also be adapted for classroom guidance or individual counseling as well. As students move between grades and schools it can be challenging for them. Likewise as students move from one home to another there are trials. Helping them to recognize what has worked for them in the past will help them find solutions in their future. The counselor should begin by discussing upcoming changes in the lives of the students. Together, the students will recognize upcoming challenges and discover past successes they have had facing similar challenges. This will lead them to solutions for their future situations.

Modality: Visual Art and Narrative Discussion

ASCA National Model Domain: Personal/Social, Academic Development

Deliver via: Group counseling

Age Level: Elementary, middle, or high school (Appropriate for use with any age group—modify the processing questions to align with the students' developmental level)

Indications: This activity can be used with small groups. The focus is on acquiring skills to help students to understand and respect self, others, make decisions, set goals, and take necessary actions to achieve goals. In addition, it will facilitate academic preparation that is essential when choosing from a wide range of substantial postsecondary options, including college, as well as the ability to balance school, studies, extracurricular activities, leisure time, and family life.

Materials: One river stone, either multicolored or natural, per student. Smooth flat stones work best for this activity but need not be limited to these. Stones are easily located in craft, hobby, or gardening stores. A variety of writing tools may be used, but Sharpie oil-based paint pens (fine point) are suggested to reduce the amount of mess. These markers are resistant to water, fading, and abrasion. They are also quick drying and nontoxic. A variety of colors should be made available. Other materials to consider are paper of any type and a table or surface suitable for accommodating use of paint markers.

Preparation: Place the river stones in a bowl or basket and have these and the Sharpie paint pens available for selection by students upon instruction.

Instructions: Open this session by introducing the upcoming change or transition the students are about to face. When exploring the upcoming event, assist the students in understanding that changes are a normal part of life. Also, discuss any questions they may have about this event. Keep in mind the need to normalize their feelings and questions. Help them to identify their feelings about this change.

Using a solution-focused paradigm, the school counselor will shift the focus from the upcoming event to times in the past that were similarly challenging for students. With this opportunity the discussion will turn to investigating the challenge each student faced.

Questions and statements used to facilitate the discussion of past successes:

"Think about a time recently when you were in a new place. Maybe you moved from your home or you moved to a different school. Share that experience. What were some of the challenges you faced with that situation? How did you feel in that moment?

"Now let's think about how you were able to handle that situation. What were some things you did to make things better or to help you adjust to the new situation? Share those details."

After the initial sharing by the students, respond:

"It sounds like some very successful steps were used to make the adjustment to the new place. How did these actions change your feelings about what was happening, about being in a new place? Describe one action or choice you made and how it changed or affected your feelings about the situation."

Using Past Successes for Future Solutions

Assisting the students in recognizing how their action or choice helped them through the previously difficult period of time is the turning point of this activity. Understanding the details of what they did differently to alter the situation will help them replicate the action or choice with the upcoming change.

Questions and statements to facilitate the discussion of future successes:

"Thinking about that time, can you pick one action, thought, or choice that was the most helpful to contributing to the change? And what feeling do you have tied to it? Let's talk about that one action, thought, or choice.

"Now let's think about how you can use that action or choice to help you in the future with your upcoming change. What are your thoughts about how you can use this action or choice again?

"Okay, let's describe this in detail. Tell me how this one action or choice would work."

Stones for Success

Using the details the students have shared, prepare them for a creative expression activity that will help them to carry their success into the future. Summarize what has been discussed and the importance of knowing how the chosen action or choice will become a solution in the future situation. Also, point out that this action or choice can also be helpful with other situations and settings further in their future.

1. Invite the students to look over the collection of river stones and select one stone that reminds them of the success they have discussed. Let them know that they will use this stone to remind them of the success they experienced with their past transition.
2. Ask the students to consider how they might decorate the stone to help them recall their success. They may want to decorate the stone with a word, a small drawing, geometrical shapes, doodles, or simply painting the stone one or more colors. Encourage a discussion with the students as they consider how they will decorate their stones.
3. Instruct the students to select from the Sharpie paint pens and begin decorating their stones. (Note: It may be helpful to try the pens out on paper to allow the students to become familiar with the texture and colors.)
4. Decorating the stones can take time. It is important during this time to allow each student the time needed to creatively synthesize his or her thoughts and feelings into the decoration of the stone. You may or may not choose to softly track their activities as you monitor their work. Allow the students to initiate any communication about the content or process of the activity. Using Sharpie pens should allow the stone to dry quickly and not smear.

Once students have completed their creative work, you will want to close the activity.

Success, Stones, and Solutions

Finally conclude the session by processing the activity. Integration of the thoughts, feelings, and successes discussed during this session and activity will create a stronger understanding. Use the following questions and statements to facilitate the discussion:

"During this time today we have talked about changes in our lives. It was pointed out that our lives will always have changes. We talked specifically about the change you are about to face in the near future. You shared your feelings, thoughts, and anxiety about that situation. And it was evident that we all shared similarities in these, so we recognized it was normal to have these feelings and thoughts and even to be anxious or nervous.

"You also examined a time in your recent past when you faced a similar situation. You were able to find an action, thought, or choice that helped you to adjust to the situation, to help you feel better. More important, through our discussion, you recognized that you could use this success to support you in this upcoming change or move.

"The stone you selected and decorated helped you to illustrate your success in a creative expressive way. So now you have a stone that you can carry with you into this new change or move. Your stone will remind you of your past success and future solutions.

"Share with the group your thoughts about your stone. When you look at your stone, what feelings do you have? Do you think that when you find yourself in your new place or situation that your stone will help you to recall that feeling? Will it help you to think of an action or thought or choice to make in your new place or situation to help you adjust?

"Do you think you will share the story about your stone with anyone else outside this group? What will you say? Does anyone have any additional thoughts to share before we end this session today?"

Suggested Modifications (for Special Needs Populations): The language used should be modified as needed to match students' developmental levels. This activity is appropriate for use with most student groups. Students of younger ages or lesser developmental skills or cognitive abilities may need to be directed with suggestions for creative decorations. The selection of a word or a color may be appropriate as well as drawing an expression.

Evaluation Plan: To evaluate the effectiveness of this intervention, the following can be used as a pre- and postassessment. Students will complete this assessment as a pretest and as a posttest of their understanding of the concepts and materials addressed during the activity.

Think about the upcoming change you are about to make. Use the scale of 1 to 6 to answer the following questions about this change. Circle the number that describes how you feel about this change.

1. I feel I am pretty well ready for this change.

1	2	3	4	5	6
None of the time	A little of the time	Some of the time	A lot of the time	Most of the time	All of the time

2. I am doing as well as other kids my age making this change.

1	2	3	4	5	6
None of the time	A little of the time	Some of the time	A lot of the time	Most of the time	All of the time

3. When I think about this change I can come up with ways to make me feel prepared.

1	2	3	4	5	6
None of the time	A little of the time	Some of the time	A lot of the time	Most of the time	All of the time

4. When other kids want to quit, I know I will find ways to face this change.

1	2	3	4	5	6
None of the time	A little of the time	Some of the time	A lot of the time	Most of the time	All of the time

Adapted from Children's Hope Scale (Snyder, Sympson, Ybasco, Borders, Babyak, & Higgins, 1996).

REFERENCE

Snyder, C. R., Sympson, S. C., Ybasco, F. C., Borders, T. F., Babyak, M. A., & Higgins, R. L. (1996). Development and validation of the State Hope Scale. *Journal of Personality and Social Psychology, 70*(2), 321–335.

TEE-SHIRT ART AS AN EXPRESSIVE THERAPEUTIC INTERVENTION IN SCHOOLS

Gaelynn P. Wolf Bordonaro

Wearable art, including tee-shirt art, presents a unique media for exploration in therapeutic settings. It moves beyond traditional art media and embraces contemporary applications of therapeutic art in personal expression and communication, social activism, historical contextualization, and "making special" (Dissanayake, 1995).

Tee-shirt art as an expressive art intervention has been implemented with individuals and groups in public schools, community bereavement programming (Wolf Bordonaro, 2011a), with children impacted by natural disasters and their direct care providers in international settings (Anderson, Arrington, & Wolf Bordonaro, 2012; Hurlbut & Wolf Bordonaro, 2010), art camps for kids with autism and their typically developing peers (Easter Seals Capper Foundation Art Star Camp, 2011), and as an experiential response to academic lectures (Wolf Bordonaro, 2011b). Importantly, wearable art necessarily engages the clinician and student in ethical decision making, as students may choose to wear their art expressions outside the therapeutic settings.

Modality: Visual Arts

ASCA National Model Domain: Personal/Social

Deliver via: Individual or group

Age Level: Elementary, middle, or high school

Indications: Tee-shirt art may be initiated individually or in therapeutic groups to address specific interpersonal or intrapersonal issues, increase self-awareness and self-advocacy, demonstrate personal or group values, address locus of control, identify or build support networks, or explore membership in a group.

Materials: White or light-colored shirts, fabric markers and/or fabric paint, embroidery hoops, pencils, white paper. Acrylic paint and permanent markers also work well on fabric.

Preparation: The school counselor will need to have appropriately sized tee-shirts for each student. Additionally, the counselor can decide how many sessions he or she plans to devote to the experience. Alternately, students could provide their own tee-shirts.

Instructions:

1. The clinician can begin the activity by introducing the historical function of tee-shirts as political and social advocacy. For example, in the United States in the 1960s, individuals demonstrated their support for specific causes by wearing the cause on their shirts! Simply wearing tie dye announced an individual's affiliation with specific social values. Ask students to think about what the tee-shirts they are wearing or have at home communicate to others.

2. At this point, clinicians can explain that the group will be making tee-shirts that demonstrate personal advocacy, support for a specific cause, and so on. Examples are provided in Figures 4.13 to 4.16.

   Importantly, art therapists consider art making done within the context of the therapeutic group or relationship to be confidential. Therefore, the school counselor will want to take this opportunity to explain the limits of confidentiality if tee-shirts are worn outside the therapeutic setting. If they will be displayed or photographed as a project or worn as a group, informed consent can be obtained as well.

3. As preart-making exercises, students can be asked to make lists of the concepts/things they value or hold as very important. Some students may respond best if asked to make a list of "six" things. Language can be adjusted to meet the developmental level of the participating students, and the school counselor can record the list for the students if needed. Rather than examples, open-ended sentences may help students get started; for example, the counselor might prompt "My _____ is very important to me."

4. The school counselor can facilitate a discussion about values and invite students to share items on their list.

Figure 4.13 Dogs are man's best friend. Treat them like family.

Figure 4.14 Don't drink and drive.

Figure 4.15 Boat sober.

Figure 4.16 Be kind to spiders and they will be kind to you.

Figure 4.17 Share thy humor.

5. Next, for each item on the list, ask students to identify two or three things that support, make possible, or are needed to maintain that value or thing. An example of this was a high school student with whom I worked. He identified friendship as something he valued deeply; to be a good friend, he said he needed to treat friends the way he wanted to be treated, talk with his friends and understand their "side," and above all, have a sense of humor (see Figure 4.17).

6. Ask students to select two or three items from their lists that particularly resonate with them, or feel "most important." On a piece of paper divided (with a line or a crease) for the number of items, ask students to write each word in one of the sections. For some students, narrowing to a specific number may be difficult; there is certainly room for negotiation or combining of concepts (friends and family may become one concept, for example). The two or three items can be narrowed, again, to one. This editing process can be an important part of creative planning and thinking, and can even provide a discussion as a metaphor for self-censorship.

   Note: Depending on how much time is available, or how many sessions have been dedicated to this intervention, the counselor may decide to have the students each identify just one "favorite" or "most important" concept.

7. For each identified concept, ask the students to create symbols or imagery. These concepts may need explaining. Students may also write short phrases to teach others about their concept. The symbols and phrases can then be developed into tee-shirt designs (see Figures 4.18–4.20).

   It may help students think about the design if, rather than blank paper, sheets with predrawn tee-shirt shapes are provided. In high school groups with whom I have worked, the students decided on the front of the shirt they would write a catch phrase (e.g., "Adopt a Pet" or "Don't Drink and Boat") and on the back of the shirt, write and illustrate a teaching point.

Figure 4.18 Art is life. Make more art and color.

Figure 4.19 Fire up the grill, but don't burn the woods.

Figure 4.20 Beauty is in everything.

8. When students are ready to transfer completed designs to the tee-shirts, help them stretch the shirts onto embroidery hoops. The hoops can actually contribute to the design by providing a mandala form in which to work.

9. Placing cardboard or newspaper between the front and back of the shirt will keep fabric markers or paint from bleeding through.

10. Pencils can be used to begin the design before permanent pigments are used. Some students may even want to trace their designs. This can easily be achieved by using a dark marker to outline the design on paper; when slipped under the fabric, the design will show through.

11. Provide opportunities for students to share their ideas, images, and finished tee-shirts within the context of the group. If students keep a journal, the on-paper planning stages can be taped into the journal as well as a photo of the finished tee-shirt, with a brief narrative.

12. To process the experience, school counselors can facilitate appropriate dialog related to the wearable art created by group members. Topics may include:
    a. Self-advocacy
    b. Community action
    c. Tolerance of ideas

    Where the students will or will not wear their shirts may also provide fruitful discussion.

13. Follow instructions for setting the pigments. This may mean ironing or heat drying the tee-shirts, or sending directions for this to be done at home.

Suggested Modifications to the Materials:

- Fabric markers offer younger students (elementary and middle school) control of the media. For high school students, fabric markers should also be available, but the clinician may also make available fabric or acrylic paint and markers.

- "Starter shirts" or preprinted shirts with an expressive arts directive implied by the printed design have been designed for directed use with specific populations or to address specific issues such as bereavement; this parallels the "starter sheets" suggested as developmental adaptations by Anderson (1999).

- "Puff Paint" or "Slick Paint" will maintain dimension when dry; this may be particularly appreciated by students with low vision or blindness.

- Embroidery hoops stretch the surface of the tee-shirts and make application of the fabric marker or paint smooth. If none are available, tee-shirts may be stretched over sturdy cardboard and taped with masking tape to keep the fabric taut.

- High school students may be interested in designing imagery using technology. They could use graphic design or drawing programs to create a design, print the image, place it under the tee-shirt fabric, trace it with fabric or permanent markers, and finish with color. Inexpensive iron-on transfer paper is also available, but may not last through too many launderings.

- Often, young children like to write their names on the shirts they make. School counselors should purposefully redirect this to the inside of the collar, so the name does not show when the shirt is worn. This is an important safety consideration, as it inadvertently advertises the child's name to strangers.

- Tie dying has built-in success, even for students with developmental disabilities. Students could simply use school-colored dyes to demonstrate being a part of something larger than themselves.

- If the cost of providing tee-shirts is prohibitive, participants could be asked to bring their own.

- Depending on the policies of the school, clinicians may want to become familiar with problematic imagery (i.e., gang symbols) and be prepared to redirect students.

Suggested Modifications to the Directive:

- To build group cohesion or demonstrate shared vision, the directive for tee-shirt art may be simplified. For example, a group or class as a whole could design shirts cooperatively, and the same design could be created on each shirt.

- If a group of students is addressing a singular social/interpersonal concern, each student could create his or her own image to demonstrate support. One example of this is antibullying tee-shirts. The front could have the text "I've got your BACK." The back of the shirt could have a place for students to create an image.
- Tee-shirts could be used with individual students, as appropriate, to address issues of transition. For example, a first grader acting out following the arrival of a new sibling could create an "I'm the big brother" tee-shirt and process the experience through the art making and art object.
- At a Teacher Inservice Workshop, the school counselor could lead teachers and staff in creating undershirts adorned with symbols of the strengths and gifts they bring to education. The shirts could be worn under regular clothes as "armor" to remind education professionals of their motivation and the differences they make every day.
- Particularly for students with developmental or cognitive disabilities, self-advocacy objectives may be addressed in students' individualized education plans (IEP). The tee-shirt intervention could be used as an activity to initiate teaching and learning opportunities to identify likes and dislikes, seek assistance as appropriate, and communicate needs or desires (see Figure 4.21).

Figure 4.21 Get more ice-cream scoops.

Evaluation Plan: Tee-shirt art interventions could be designed to specifically address goals written into students' IEPs. Additionally, a simple pre- and post-test with items such as those listed next could be paired with psychometric instruments addressing self-advocacy, personal insight, or locus of control.

Student Self-Awareness and Advocacy Survey

1. Identify three of your personal values:
   (a)
   (b)
   (c)

2. Identify three ways you can appropriately advocate for something important to you:
   (a)
   (b)
   (c)

3. I can communicate that something is important to me.
   ☐ True   ☐ False

4. I can make a difference for something that is important to me.
   ☐ True   ☐ False

5. You have to be an artist to make art.
   ☐ True   ☐ False

6. I can teach others how to make a difference.
   ☐ True   ☐ False

REFERENCES

Anderson, F. E. (1992). *Art for all the children: Approaches to art for children with disabilities.* Springfield, IL: Charles C Thomas.

Anderson, F. E., Arrington, D., & Wolf Bordonaro, G. P. (2012, July). *Weaving the global tapestry of art.* Panel presented at the 43rd Annual American Art Therapy Association Conference, Savannah, GA.

Dissanayake, E. (1995). *Homo aetheticus: Where art comes from and why.* Seattle, WA: University of Washington Press.

Easter Seals Capper Foundation Art Star Camp. (2011). Retrieved from http://capper.easterseals.com/site/DocServer/Art_Star.pdf?docID=145245

Hurlbut, G., & Wolf Bordonaro, G. P. (2010). *Introducing expressive therapy constructs and applications to medical professionals following a national disaster.* Kings Hospital Symposium, Port au Prince, Haiti.

Wolf Bordonaro, G. P. (2011a, November). *Art therapy techniques in response to grief and loss.* Kansas School Counselor Conference, Emporia, KS.

Wolf Bordonaro, G. P. (2011b, April). *International art therapy responses to natural and human-created disasters.* SATA Annual Fall Conference, Southern Illinois University, Edwardsville, IL.

USING ARTIST TRADING CARDS TO ENHANCE SELF-ESTEEM

Marta Garrett

*A*rtist trading cards (ATCs) are basically miniature artworks that are created within the dimensions of standardized trading cards or playing cards (2½ in. × 3½ in.). ATCs can be made with any media that might be used in a larger art format—pencils, pen and ink, chalks, crayons, markers, paints, collage materials, foam, smaller arts and crafts materials, photos, digital creations, and so on. Each work of art is typically signed, dated, and labeled as a unique or limited edition work. They can be shared easily, traded, stored in protective sleeves, carried around, laminated, mailed, made into key chains or necklaces, or framed.

This compact art format allows counselor flexibility and significant time and money savings over using larger traditional art formats. This compact art format provides the school counselor with most if not all of the same benefits of larger art media such as expressive release, creativity, artistic communication, symbolic self-expression, self-exploration, and so on, but the miniature works of art can be more easily completed in a shorter time frame, take less space and use fewer materials to complete, and can be taken with the student (as a way of extending the counseling or guidance work beyond the limited time spent in counseling). ATCs can be introduced as a guided or directed project or they can be spontaneous or nondirected, allowing great flexibility for the school counselor.

A quick Internet search may provide the school counselor with additional information of interest on the history and use of ATCs. The ATC format evolved as an acceptable art format for artists in a variety of media who wanted to be able to finish smaller works and share them with others. There are no real "rules" for ATCs other than they must be created within this standard size (2½ in. × 3½ in.) and they must not be sold. There are a variety of websites that offer ideas for ATCs and a location for posting and trading ATCs among artists.

This example uses the ATC as an art intervention format for students by asking them to create a wallet-sized card of "qualities" that they can carry with them to enhance their self-esteem by reminding them of their positive qualities when they are outside of the counseling environment.

Modality: Visual Arts and Expressive Writing/Poetry

ASCA National Model Domain: Personal/Social; may also be used in Career

Deliver via: Individual, group, or classroom guidance

Age Level: This activity is appropriate for use with any age group by modifying the directions and art media used to align with the students' developmental level. This particular exercise is designed for middle school students.

Indications: ATCs can be used to support counseling work on many topics, such as self-esteem, decision making, self-expression, career exploration, goal setting, or others. ATCs can also be used in small or large groups to support similar topics or team-building exercises and can be used in classroom-guidance lessons to create a short art break or to provide a fun way to emphasize a specific topic or lesson (e.g., creating ATCs as an alternative to journaling exercises or as a therapeutic transitional object). This specific exercise is designed to be used as a means of boosting students' self-esteem by providing them with a reminder of their positive personal characteristics that they can see, read, touch, and hold (or wear).

Materials: Paper, canvas, or cardboard (as desired, a deck of cards can also be used); drawing instruments or paints; pictures, magazines, or other collaging materials, rubber stamps; a variety of yarns, beads, or other small craft scraps can also be used. Scissors and glue as needed. "Author" stamps (ready-made rubber stamps to give the artist a location and format for naming, signing, and dating the creation) are available in arts or crafts stores or online.

Depending on the intended use of the ATCs, counselors may want to have sleeves available (plastic, wax paper, or paper envelopes) to store or share the creations (many options are available premade or traditional office stationery products can be used). If the intended use involves making the ATCs into a keychain, necklace, attaching them to a book bag or cell phone, or laminating the ATCS, additional supplies may be needed.

For middle school students working on self-esteem issues, general art materials are suggested as well as collaging materials (magazines, scissors, glue sticks, etc.). Middle school students may also want to wear or carry their creations, so additional materials might be required (such as laminating materials and/or cords or key chains). These quality cards can be made into necklaces, backpack tags, key chains, or bookmarks.

Preparation: Have art materials ready for selection and use by students. For time saving, precut ATC forms may be used or intact playing cards can be used as the base or background for this assignment. For this particular exercise, white or off-white backgrounds sheets may be most helpful.

Middle (or high) school students may be able to cut their own 2½ in. × 3½ in. sheets if time permits. Precut sheets may also be purchased in a variety of paper types, thicknesses, and colors (at Walmart or crafts stores). For elementary students, school counselors may want to precut the paper, canvas, or cardboard into ready-made 2½ in. × 3½ in. sheets.

Instructions:

1. Using age-appropriate language and directions, the counselor should introduce the format of the ATC and describe its background. Additional information on ATCs can be found on the web if needed.
2. Model a variety of completed ATCs in differing art media made by similar-aged students to help students see the possibilities of creating within this smaller format (e.g., show examples of photo ATCs, collage-based ATCs, drawings, or paintings completed in this format).

3. Continue introduction or instruction as needed depending on the intentional use of the ATC. For this example, making a quality card to boost self-esteem, students can work individually or in pairs or small groups. Set a time limit as appropriate so students will know how much time they will have to complete the project.

4. To prompt students for this assignment, students can be asked to come up with one idea or image or word that reminds them of a positive accomplishment, characteristic, or trait they see in themselves or have been told by others they have (e.g., "My mother says I should be proud of how well I did on my last science test . . . "). When working individually with students, counselors may be able to help or guide students to come up with three positive traits or characteristics. For example:

   a. Close your eyes for a moment and think about a time in your life when you felt really happy or proud of an accomplishment or when someone paid you a compliment (even if it was hard for you to accept the compliment).

   b. Using the art materials in front of you, create a small work of art that reminds you of this positive trait or accomplishment. It can be a specific, concrete image such as a number that represents how fast you can run in track or your GPA, or a word such as "smart" or "clever." You can use letters, words, or images from the magazines, or you can draw something. You can even write a poem or verse. If you feel more comfortable with a more abstract picture or an implied artwork, you can draw something or create something that only you will understand—perhaps a picture of a rose because it reminds you of your grandmother's garden and she always told you that you were funny.

   c. Decorate the rest of your ATC around your word or artwork.

   d. Title, date, and sign the work on the back of the card.

   e. After the project is completed, spend time discussing the creation and explain how the student can keep the card around to pull out and look at any time he or she needs a boost to his or her self-esteem.

Suggested Modifications (for Special Needs Populations): Because ATCs are a form of artwork versus a particular medium or instruction set, they are appropriate for use with almost any special needs population with appropriate adaptation. Providing precut cards or papers for special needs students may be required.

Additional Suggestions for ATCs

   ▪ ATCs can be used as an alternative to journaling exercises—students can be asked to create a themed card based on the assignment or to emphasize a theme or emotion (e.g., instead of completing poetry stems, students can be asked to create a poem or story on the ATC or on multiple ATCs).

   ▪ ATCs can be used to express feelings in the same way that other larger art projects are used but can be completed faster and using fewer art materials (e.g., an ATC can be constructed to demonstrate what anger means to a student).

- ATCs can be used to emphasize or memorialize a specific event or moment (e.g., to support guidance lessons or as a token to remember a deployed or departed parent or loved one).
- ATCs can be created on both sides of the card to demonstrate two sides of a problem or issue or two choices (e.g., "Create a card that demonstrates what you think your life will be like if you go to college next year or decide to join the Navy . . . ").
- ATCs can be used in narrative or projective storytelling work because their size allows multiple cards to be created in a shorter amount of time (e.g., each student in a group can create a card and then use the cards as a means of telling a joint story).
- ATCs can be laminated and used similarly to other commercially available cards for a variety of games, interventions, and assessments (e.g., memory games; "create a card that shows what might happen next . . . ").

Evaluation Plan: Evaluation of how well the ATC format helped to reach counseling or guidance goals would be measured similar to evaluation of other art-based interventions (and is highly dependent on *how* the ATCs were used).

THE WEIGHT THAT I CARRY

Ajita M. Robinson

This activity is an exercise that is designed to help clients increase their awareness of the weight of the emotions that they carry on a daily basis.

Modality: Visual and Writing Activity

ASCA National Model Domain: Personal/Social

Delivery via: Individual or Group

This activity is effective and appropriate for both individual and group counseling. The facilitator should have knowledge of the history of loss for each group member. Group leaders should be mindful of the need to facilitate and mediate the discussion to promote emotional and psychological safety of all group members.

Age Groups: Age 8+

Indications: This activity is useful to students who are experiencing a variety of emotions that are negatively influencing them socially/personally as well as academically. This activity has been used in children who report high levels of stress, feelings of grief and loss, issues with self-esteem and interpersonal relationship conflicts. This activity is designed to assist students with identifying and exploring their emotions.

Materials Required: Rocks (Mexican Pebbles work well), bag or backpack, paper (journal is preferred), pens, colored pencils, acrylic paint and paintbrushes for preparation stage.

Preparation: It is necessary to paint the rocks prior to the activity. Make sure to have adequate pebbles ready for the session. Acrylic paint has been used successfully to paint and write on the pebbles. The facilitator will also need to determine what "emotions" to write on the pebbles.

Instructions:

1. Invite the group (or individual) to sit down either on the floor or on chairs so that the pebbles are visible to all members. Sitting in a circle may be ideal depending on the nature of the group.
2. Open the session by explaining that during the check-in process, each member will wear or hold the backpack filled with the pebbles while he or she tells the group how he or she is feeling today.
3. After each member has had an opportunity to check-in, begin to unpack the rocks from the bag and place them in a way that all members can see the pebbles.
4. Members are invited to discuss their thoughts and feelings regarding the words written on the pebbles.
5. Members are invited to discuss what they carry with them on a daily basis.
6. Members are tasked with identifying which emotions can be "unpacked."
7. Members are invited to share what helps them cope with the "weight that they carry" on a daily basis.
8. Have members write in their journals addressing which emotions they carry with them on a daily basis, which emotions they believe they can "unpack," and what helps them carry the weight of their emotions.
9. Invite members to share their reflections with the group.
10. Help members establish goals related to managing/unpacking the weight.
11. Help members identify coping strategies.
12. Give members homework: To come prepared to the next session ready to explore where in the body they hold their emotions so as to help increase mind–body integration awareness.
13. Close the session by having the members finish the sentence "I am enough because . . ." (or another closer that is appropriate to the group).

Suggested Modifications: The words used on the pebbles should be appropriate for the target population. Additionally, if having the clients wear the backpack is unsafe or inappropriate for the clients, then this portion of the check-in process can be skipped.

Evaluation Plan: You should be able to evaluate student progress by the student's readiness to identify emotions and engage in healthy discussion (verbally or written) about the factors that contribute to the weight and the student's level of success in identifying coping strategies and level of interest in developing coping strategies. Students' willingness to increase awareness is important in determining readiness for change.

WHAT MONSTERS ARE HIDING IN YOUR CLOSET?

Marie Bonner Huron and Karen L. Lee

*T*his activity is designed for use in small-group counseling, although it may be modified for use in individual counseling, and focuses on social emotional learning for high school students. The foundation of the activity is based on narrative, art, and group therapies. Students experience three different types of learning during this session: visual (PowerPoint presentation), kinesthetic (hands-on construction), and verbal (presenter and participant discussion). The counselor should encourage students to participate in a candid conversation about how some of their thoughts and behaviors may be unproductive and to identify at least one action that can be taken to be more positive. Students will create a concrete visual of their "monster" as a reminder of their progress toward more positive thoughts and behaviors.

Modality: Visual Arts and Drama

ASCA National Model Domain: Personal/Social

Deliver via: Group or individual counseling

Age Level: High school

Indications: The activity emphasizes goal-setting and attainment skills by having students define a problematic behavior and then identify appropriate ways to modify that behavior.

Materials: Easy-to-use art materials, such as clay, Play-Doh, scissors, markers, colored pencils, pastels, crayons, Cray-Pas, tempera paint, paper, glue, glitter, craft items, stickers, and extra materials that are not going to be used any more. The students should be encouraged to be creative and use everything and anything. This is "their monster" and it need only make sense to them.

Preparation: Prepare a visual for the students addressing the "monsters" that are found within the school or community. The visual can be either a handout or slide-show presentation. This will be specific for your population by using examples of "monsters" that you have seen within your school or community. Have more than enough materials for the students so they can be creative and not feel confined to specific materials. Students may use found items, or items that might be considered trash (e.g., plastic containers for clay) for their "monsters."

Instructions:

1. Once the students have arrived, introduce yourself and any other facilitators and provide the following explanation of the activity: *"We all have things that we would like to change or improve on, right? In this session you not only name that thing, you will get to meet it face to face and find out how you can improve it. The only thing required of you is to come in with an open mind and be willing to try to have some fun. Caution! This session will be an active one; we will be playing with different building materials and a lot of other exciting stuff!"*

2. If it is a small group, allow the students to introduce themselves. If it is a bigger group, after reviewing the handout or slide show, break into small groups to allow for introductions and discussion.

3. Present a handout or slide show that gives the students a background of what behavior is and how they can change it. Provide enough examples for the students to feel comfortable with the abstract project of picking a behavior of their own to change.

4. Once the presentation is over, allow the students to go to where the crafts are located and allow them to pick out materials for the "monsters." Remind them that this is their vision and does not have to make sense to anyone else. Allow the students ample time to think about their "monster" and what they want to create. Have students work individually to create their "monster" out of various art materials and supplies. They could be either two dimensional or three dimensional in nature. They may even want to give it a name. Tell students there is no right or wrong way to develop and express the "monster." This is their opportunity to be creative and have fun with it.

5. Depending on your time limit, bring the students back together (either in one big group or keep your small groups) to discuss their "monsters." Some students may not know how they will change their behavior and this is where the discussion will be most valuable. Other students may have ideas about what they would do in that situation.

6. After the discussion about the "monsters," bring the group back to allow for an overall discussion about the process and what members felt about the session as a whole.

Suggested Modifications (for Special Needs Populations): When working with students with special needs, you may need to be more specific about the types of behaviors on which to focus. You may need to provide them with additional help when working with the materials. At the same time, it is important to give these students enough opportunity to be creative and make something that they feel accurately expresses who they are.

Drama can be the modality if it is more appropriate for your setting. Instead of creating "monsters" out of art materials, students could "become" the monster and act it out, or they could write and discuss a journal entry, and so forth.

Evaluation Plan: Allow 2 or 3 minutes for students to record in writing their level of satisfaction of the activity. (A half sheet of paper should be sufficient.) This will allow you as the facilitator to modify the activity to fit your school's needs in the future. You may ask students to answer the following questions:

1. On a scale of 1 to 5 (1 being "did not enjoy myself" and 5 being "really enjoyed myself"), please rate how you felt about this activity.

   1   2   3   4   5

2. Do you feel that you learned something about yourself?   YES   NO
   Please explain:

3. What did you like most about this activity?

4. What would you have changed about this activity?

   Suggestions or comments?

WHAT'S IN YOUR LOCKER?

Barb Wilson

This activity utilizes the visual arts as a method of conceptualizing our inner and outer selves. Students will gain insight about their role(s) among their peers and in society. The image of the locker is used as a metaphor of the "self" to represent how we present ourselves to others on the outside and what we keep hidden on the inside.

Modality: Visual Arts

ASCA National Model Domain: Personal/Social

Deliver via: Individual or group counseling

Age Level: Middle or high school

Indications: This intervention is particularly useful for students working on self-esteem building, reducing self-harm, enhancing social skills, coping with being a new student, and dealing with changing families.

Materials: 8.5 × 11 cardstock paper, writing instruments, assorted decorating items (e.g., glue, stickers).

Preparation: Prior to the individual or group attending the session(s), gather the necessary materials. The school counselor may want to create separate work environments or to offer the activity in a location where participants may go for privacy.

Instructions:
1. The counselor welcomes the group and introduces the activity.
2. The counselor invites group members to provide a definition of "self-identity."
3. Discuss with the group how others' impressions of us can affect our own self-identity.
4. Distribute the cardstock paper to the participants and provide access to the writing instruments and decorating items.
5. Ask group members to fold the cardstock paper lengthwise to resemble a locker.
6. Instruct the group members to begin the activity reflecting on the outside of their lockers. Ask them to think about what others know about them, what others see, and what they are willing to allow others to know about themselves. Each group member is encouraged to decorate the locker with pictures, words, and/or symbols representing what he or she shows on the "outside."
7. After group members have had time to decorate the outside of their lockers, ask them to open their lockers. Discuss what might be on an individual's "inside," such as thoughts, talents, specific life events, and personal struggles. Now, invite members to add elements to the "inside" of their locker.
8. After the inside of the lockers have been completed, allow group members time to share their work. *This is completely voluntary.*
9. At the close of the meeting, allow group members to take their lockers with them.

Suggested Modifications (for Special Needs Populations): Due to the potentially sensitive nature of some items, the group leader may consider allowing group members to move to separate areas of the room for privacy. Additionally, it is imperative to allow group members to use words or pictures to represent their thoughts and not require a specific form of expression. The time required for this activity can be adjusted according to the specific work setting and/or the developmental level of the group members.

Evaluation Plan: The school counselor should observe the participant(s) to assess for understanding. The school counselor may also have a discussion with the participant(s) to assess for understanding. The following sample pre-/posttest may be used for data-collection purposes.

Using the following scale, rate your agreement with the following statements:

1 = Strongly disagree
2 = Disagree
3 = Neither agree nor disagree
4 = Agree
5 = Strongly agree

Please rate your answers on each of the following questions.

1. _____ I like myself.
2. _____ I like others.
3. _____ I understand what it means to have an "inner" self.
4. _____ I understand what it means to have an "outer" self.
5. _____ I know what my "outer" self looks like.
6. _____ I know how my "inner" self can affect my "outer" self.

III �֍ Music

5 ❈ Music-Based Interventions in the Academic Domain

LYRICS AND MY LIFE

Erin N. Friedman and Benjamin P. Friedman

*T*his activity will help students explore what difficulties they may be experiencing in school (academic, emotional, relational, etc.) through music. Student(s) will find song lyrics that reflect how they feel about school, giving them an opportunity to express their feelings as well as normalizing their difficulties. They are likely to discover that other individuals have had similar feelings and/or experiences that may help reduce the stigma(s) that they may have experienced in the school setting.

Modality: Music and Creative Writing

ASCA National Model Domain: Academic and Personal/Social

Deliver via: Psychoeducational group (approximately six to eight students) or modified for individual counseling

Age Level: Middle school or early high school

Indications: Building self-esteem and academic self-concept through music-oriented creative writing and group reflection. Lyrics and My Life would work well in concert with Imagining a Future Me and My (Gritty) Collage activities (see Chapter 11).

Materials: Access to computers so students can find song lyrics, and headphones.

Instructions: Students will look up various song lyrics that reflect what they are concerned about regarding school. Counselors can ask students to reflect on some salient obstacles or difficult experiences students have recently encountered. Students can pull from different songs and splice lyrics together or students can pull from a single song. Students will need to modify songs if the language or thematic issue is inappropriate for school; however, students should have the freedom to choose from songs that are meaningful to them. It is better to err on the side of students modifying songs than to make students choose songs that they do not connect with. The counselor may allow students who wish to present their song to the group with an opportunity to do this at the end of the lesson. If counselors would like to continue this activity and add another layer of depth to this experience, counselors can have students write their own lyrics to reference these feelings and changes.

Individually Focused Process Questions: Ask, *"What are some of the difficult experiences you have in school? How do you try to cope with those difficulties? Explore what your natural instinct is when you are having a difficult experience at school. How do you react? How do you feel that you should act?"*

Relational Process Questions: Ask, *"How did you feel when you read someone's lyrics that reflected a feeling you've been having? Was it helpful to know that someone shared similar feelings that you've recently had? Did it change how you viewed the experience? Did it change how you viewed yourself? What advice would you give the person that wrote the lyrics you referenced in your lyrical story?"*

Notes: This activity works well in concert with Imagining a Future Me and My (Gritty) Collage (see Chapter 11).

Suggested Modifications: Given that students' feelings about school may change, often this is an activity that can be revisited as needed, especially for students who find it helpful. Counselors concerned about the appropriateness of song lyrics chosen by students may assign this activity as homework. Students would then summarize song content rather than play it during the group session. Alternatively, the counselor may ask students to pick songs that have no lyrics that may widen the array of genres students choose from (to include jazz, classical, etc.). This may require more of an active role by the counselor since students may need to explore genres of music they are less familiar with; this is something that may also take more time.

Evaluation Plan: Identifying feelings and emotions and what situations they grow out of is often the first step in addressing problem areas. During future sessions, students may reflect on how their song choices reflect their changing attitudes about school. Students should also feel free to communicate how songs have helped them cope during difficult times in their school lives.

REFERENCES:

See *Imagining a Future Me* in Chapter 11 for relevant references.

6 ✤ Music-Based Interventions in the Career Domain

RETIREMENT CELEBRATION "DJ PLAYLIST"

Katherine M. Hermann and Lindsey B. Guidry

*H*igh school students often experience confusion and trepidation as they explore career choices and have difficulty deciphering current and future interests and formulating long-term goals. One effective method for exploring these trajectories is imagining future career paths. This activity provides students with the opportunity to envision their future, establish goals related to career plans, and celebrate upcoming career accomplishments.

Modality: Music

ASCA National Model Domain: Career

Deliver via: Group counseling

Age Level: High school (Grades 9 to 12)

Indications: This activity is effective for high school students contemplating future career paths. Students who are uncertain about education or career decisions, first-generation college students, and other individuals who have not reflected on lifelong goals may be a particularly appropriate match for this intervention.

Materials: Paper and pens, depending on time and technology available; students may find it helpful to have access to a music library (CDs, iTunes, or other digital, downloaded, or hard-copy music).

Preparation: Although no preparations are required, if counselors plan to use digital media, they will need to gather and be familiar with technology that has music capabilities. Counselors may also find it helpful to instruct students to bring a digital device with access to their personal music libraries (e.g. MP3 player, cell phone, tablet, or laptop).

Instructions:

1. Before beginning the intervention, revisit established group rules addressing confidentiality, respect, and support, as members are likely to share personal information, desires, fears, and goals.
2. Introduce a discussion on the usefulness of planning and goal setting. Explain to students that envisioning what a goal entails can provide clarity and focus to the decision-making process and aid in the implementation of the steps necessary to achieve the goal.
3. Have group members close their eyes and reflect on their future lives (5 years in the future, 10 years, and upon retirement). Ask members to think about what they would like to be doing, where they would like to be working, and what their lives will be like. As they ponder these options, ask them to notice when they feel excited or fulfilled. In this particular task, members do not need to develop specific career choices, but counselors may find it helpful to observe how the group members describe their lifestyles. For instance, do they have big houses? Do they have a big family? This information will be important in creating goals since career choices will likely have a significant impact on future lifestyle.
4. After reflecting on career choices, ask group members to choose one career. Have members write down (in any format) as many details as possible about their chosen careers. Below are a list of questions that may be used to aid members in this process:

   - *"What do you do each day?"*
   - *"What do you like about your job?"*
   - *"What hours do you work?"*
   - *"What do you wear to work?"*
   - *"What is your salary?"*
   - *"Where do you live?"*

   Members should be encouraged to be as realistic as possible when choosing and writing details about their chosen careers. After reflecting on these details, ask individuals to select one career path.
5. Invite members to share their career choice and the information they wrote down. This may be especially helpful to students who are having a difficult time choosing and writing details about a career.
6. After members reflect on and discuss their career, introduce the Retirement Celebration DJ Playlist activity by asking the group to imagine they are retiring from their chosen career and have decided to have a retirement party in which they need to create a playlist. This playlist should include five to seven songs related to their chosen career. Students may find it helpful to use their personal playlists or digital media to help develop this list.

Songs may reflect special aspects of their jobs (e.g., a teacher may choose "Summertime" by Sublime) or even particular challenges (e.g., a writer may select "Rewrite" by Paul Simon). Focusing on the entire career rather than specific periods, such as being a new employee or retiree, may help stimulate creativity, but allow for maximum flexibility in the activity for students.

7. Once the songs have been selected, have students title their Retirement Celebration DJ Playlist, encouraging them to find a title that summarizes their lifelong career experience.

8. Invite members to share their album and playlist with the group and discuss what drew them to these playlist selections. Counselors can process the activity with questions such as:

   ■ *"What are your feelings after developing this playlist?"*
   ■ *"Do you feel differently about your chosen career path having completed the activity? If so, what changed?"*
   ■ *"Did you experience any fears or feelings of uncertainty during the activity?"*
   ■ *"How can envisioning a goal in detail help decision making?"*
   ■ *"Now that you have this playlist, what decisions can you begin to make to reach the goals to have this chosen career? What are the steps to take? What can you do now?"*

Suggested Modifications: While this activity is designed for a single session with a high school group, it can be modified to span several sessions. It could be used with middle school students or be incorporated into individual counseling using the same format and guidelines but taking additional time to process. In addition, if time and resources permit, counselors may find burning a Retirement Celebration DJ Playlist CD for each group member creates a positive memento of the student's goal and path to reaching that goal. CD cases can be decorated by students; the process of creating an album cover with markers, paints, glitter, etc., can provide an additional creative modality to process, explore, and discuss the lifelong career experience.

Evaluation Plan: To evaluate this plan, counselors may find it helpful to discuss aspects of the activity students found helpful. Depending on the grade or time of year the activity is implemented, counselors can revisit the playlists in subsequent years, later in the semester, or before graduation to facilitate discussion, assess effectiveness, and make career plan adaptations. In addition, school counselors may find using both pre- and posttest assessments about career goals with students is particularly useful in gathering feedback on implementing and maintaining a comprehensive school counseling program.

7 ✵ Music-Based Interventions in the Personal/Social Domain

CONNECTING STUDENTS TO THE CIVIL RIGHTS MOVEMENT THROUGH MUSIC

Barb Wilson

*T*his activity uses music from various eras to connect students with the history of the Civil Rights Movement. Music played a key role in the movement and marked pivotal milestones as the movement progressed. Through this activity, students will gain a better understanding of the Civil Rights Movement, be able to identify at least one song related to this time in history, identify the social injustices that spurred the Civil Rights Movement, and be able to identify at least one current social injustice.

Modality: Music/Movement/Dance

ASCA National Model Domain: Personal/Social

Deliver via: Classroom guidance

Age Level: 5th to 12th grade

Indications: Can be used in conjunction with social studies curriculum related to U.S. History, Black History Month, and/or Civil Rights curriculum.

Materials: Audio/visual equipment to play the music, song lyrics (www .azlyrics.com, www.metrolyrics.com), and copies of Music of the Civil Rights Movement (Wilson, 2011) worksheet.

Preparation: The school counselor may want to collaborate with the social studies teacher(s) in order to maximize learning potential. This lesson can be split into two shorter lessons as well.

Instructions:
1. The school counselor should say, *"The Civil Rights Movement was a time of transformation in American history. The movement was deeply rooted in expression and music as methods of coping and sharing information.*

This activity explores songs related to the Civil Rights Movement and as an expression for discussing social justice. Current-day social injustices will also be explored. By the end of this activity you will be able to identify at least one song from the Civil Rights Movement and will understand how music played a role during this time in history."

2. The school counselor will then describe the connection between expression and music. Tell the students that words can become a song when put to music. Through words and music people are able to express feelings, emotions, and share information about events. Think about songs that make you feel happy (i.e., upbeat dance music). Think about songs that celebrate life (i.e., the "Happy Birthday" song). Songs can also mark moments of sadness and struggle. Sometimes the act of writing a song can be healing in addition to listening to the song itself.

3. Ask students to identify a few current popular songs. Write the names of the songs on a board or large paper if possible. Prompt students by asking them what artists they like or what songs they downloaded recently. Ask students to share why they like the songs and/or what feeling the songs give them. You may want to write keywords as the students discuss the songs.

4. Discuss any overlapping themes or words among the songs that the students have named.

5. The counselor can then move into a brief discussion of the Civil Rights Movement, saying, *"The Civil Rights movement was a time in American history focused mainly on achieving and protecting equal rights for all people. Minorities, such as African-Americans and women, had historically been treated with less equality than their White and/or male peers. The movement was marked by protests and changes in laws. Music played a major role in the Movement."*

6. Give each student a copy of the worksheet found at the end of this section, Music of the Civil Rights Movement (Wilson, 2011). Explain to the students that one song, "This Little Light of Mine," is a gospel song and can commonly be heard in Christian churches. However, remind the participants that the purpose of listening to this song is not to focus on its religious connection, but to think about acceptance of oneself and others.

7. Three songs are listed on the worksheet: "This Little Light of Mine," "A Change is Gonna Come," and "Pride." Play each song and allow students to read the lyrics as each song is playing. After every song has played, briefly discuss the lyrics and emotional responses they evoke (i.e., sadness, hope). Ask the students to think about the feelings and emotions they experienced as they listened to the songs. Ask them to think about the message the songwriter was trying to relay through the song. Encourage empathy within the students for those who are oppressed, especially those during the Civil Rights Era.

8. Have students complete the worksheet as they listen to the songs.

9. As students complete the worksheet, wrap up the session by summarizing the lesson and asking each student to identify one "take-away." The

take-away should be related to equality, accepting others, or the use of music to evoke emotion. How was music used during the Civil Rights Movement? How did you identify with any songs discussed?

Allow time for additional sharing of thoughts, song titles, and questions from the students. Allow students time to share the answers they have written (voluntarily). Walk through each question and prompt when needed. Prompts may include emotion words or sharing examples of groups in current society that might identify with the songs (i.e., the lesbian/gay/bisexual/transgender/questioning [LGBTQ] community, teenagers). What are the social injustices of today? At our school? In our communities? In our country? The emphasis is on helping the students process the songs they heard and bring them to current trends in society and in their own lives.

Suggested Modifications (for Special Needs Populations): Copies of the lyrics may be printed for hearing-impaired students.

Evaluation Plan: The included pre-/postassessment may be used as a paper assessment or as a guide for class discussions.

1. Briefly describe the Civil Rights Movement.
2. How can music be tied to historical events?
3. Identify at least one song related to the Civil Rights Movement.
4. Describe the social injustices of the Civil Rights Movement.
5. Describe a social injustice in our current society.
6. What can you do to create positive change?

Activity Worksheet Instructions

Possible songs:
- "This Little Light of Mine" by Harry Dixon Loes
- "A Change Is Gonna Come" by Sam Cooke
- "Pride" by U2

After we listen to the songs, take a few minutes to answer the following questions:
1. Which song(s) really stood out to you? Why?
2. Have you heard any of these songs before? Which one(s)?
3. Did any of these songs make you uncomfortable? Why?
4. Thinking of society today, what are some examples of social injustices?

EXTRA (if time is allotted): If you could write a song about your own life, your family's history, where you live, and so on:
1. What would be the title of your song?
2. Write down lyrics, lines, or words you want to include in the song.

REFERENCE

Wilson, B. (2011). *Music of the Civil Rights Movement activity worksheet*. Unpublished document.

FEELINGS SONG ABOUT MANAGING ANGER: "WHEN YOU'RE ANGRY AND YOU KNOW IT"

Hennessey Lustica and Atiya R. Smith

*T*his activity is designed to be utilized in small-group counseling. It facilitates understanding of angry feelings and offers strategies to use when students feel angry. The counselor should start the discussion by asking the students to reflect on a time when they felt angry. The counselor should then ask students to think about what angry feels like in their bodies and some ways they have expressed this feeling to others. Students will work to brainstorm a list of what anger feels like in their bodies and work together to learn a song depicting specific strategies to use when they feel angry.

Modality: Expressive Music

ASCA National Model Domain: Personal/Social

Deliver via: Group counseling

Age Level: Elementary school (modify the processing questions to align with the students' developmental level)

Indications: Could be used in small groups focused on feeling management as a modality other than traditional talk therapy

Materials: Chart paper with the outline of a body and markers

Preparation: Review and learn the lyrics to the song about acknowledging and dealing with anger, "When You're Angry and You Know It." Lyrics are available online at http://www.songsforteaching.com/jackhartmann/ifyoure angryandyouknowit.htm. It is sung to the tune of "If You're Happy and You Know It."

Instructions:

I. Introduction

Introduce the activity by asking students to think about a time when they felt angry. Discuss with the students the different ways that anger can feel within one's body. Talk with students about the importance of being able to recognize angry feelings in order to remain in control of their emotions and behaviors. From this discussion, explain that this activity will focus on how anger feels in our bodies and that together they will learn a song with specific techniques to help them when they feel angry.

II. Activity

1. Have the students think about a time when they felt angry. Ask the students to identify how the anger felt in their bodies and write down a list on the chart paper. (Examples can include: hot, balled-up fists, tight lips, clenched jaw, furrowed brow, heavy breathing, etc.).

2. Ask students to volunteer to transfer the descriptions of their words on the chart paper to the picture of the human body. Explain to the students that they can recognize when they are feeling angry by the responses of their bodies.

3. Ask students to brainstorm ways in which they can appropriately deal with their anger. (Examples can include punching a pillow, telling an adult, counting to 10, taking a deep breath, etc.). Explain to students that anger is a normal feeling that is very important and that using strategies to channel their anger will help them to feel better.

4. Tell the students that you are going to teach them a song that will help them with some strategies to deal effectively with their anger. Teach the students the song lyrics and practice singing it with them.

III. Discussion

Discuss with the students why it is important to control their anger. Ask students to think back to the situation they identified in the beginning of the activity about a time when they felt angry. Ask students to share one strategy they learned about that could help them with a similar situation in the future.

Suggested Modifications (for Special Needs Populations): You may need to modify the language used in descriptions of anger to align congruently with students' developmental levels. This activity is appropriate for use with most student groups and will be particularly helpful with students who are hesitant to participate in talk therapy but enjoy creative activities and music. Students who have difficulty with writing may be encouraged to participate because of the limited amount of written work.

Evaluation Plan: To evaluate the effectiveness of this intervention, school counselors can use the following observation and discussion questions after completion of the activity.

School counselors can assess student understanding by direct observation of student participation in the activity. Student learning can also be assessed by asking the following questions:

1. Identify a time when you felt angry.
2. What did that anger feel like in your body?
3. What are some ways that you expressed feeling angry?
4. What are some new strategies you can use when you feel angry as a result of this lesson?
5. How will you know when you did a good job expressing your anger in the future?

REFERENCE

Hartman, J. (2012). *If you're angry and you know it.* Retrieved June 12, 2014, from http://www.songsforteaching.com/jackhartmann/ifyoureangryandyouknowit.htm

MULTIMEDIA TIMELINE LIFE MAP

Suzanne D. Mudge and Katrina Cook

> *S*tudents will select three to five songs that represent meaningful times or stages of their lives. They will also select photos or images that reflect those times. They will create a slide-show presentation that includes the photos and images, synced with selected music, to demonstrate a personal timeline life map of their lives thus far.

Modality: Visual Art, Music, Computer Images

ASCA National Model Domain: Personal/Social

Deliver via: Group counseling or individual counseling

Age Level: High school

Indications: This activity can be used with individuals or small groups and is designed to help students acquire self-knowledge, make decisions, deal with life transitions, or identify/discuss changing personal, social, and family roles.

Materials: Access to computers with a slide-show program such as PowerPoint, scanning ability, and music-syncing capability is helpful, as are a projector and speakers to display the completed timelines. Students will provide music, photos, and images that they want to include in their timelines.

Preparation: During the Planning Session, prior to the Creating the Timelines Session, have notebook paper and markers available for students to create the rough drafts of their timelines. Also, reserve the computer lab or otherwise secure computers for students to use during the next session.

Instructions:
Planning Session

1. Explain to students that the timeline depicts major events in their lives and how those events may have impacted them.
2. Ask students to create a rough draft of a timeline of their lives on notebook paper, beginning with their birth up until the present moment. Help them identify important markers in their lives (e.g., first going to school, parents' divorce, athletic award, loss of a loved one). Explain to students that at the next session they will be making a multimedia version of this timeline.
3. For the next session, instruct students to bring three to five songs that represent meaningful times in their lives as well as photos or computer images that reflect important events or people. For this session, the group will need to meet in a room where there is a computer available for each student

(i.e., a computer lab) so students will be able to create their multimedia timelines.

Creating the Timelines Session
1. This group session will meet in a computer lab or some other room where there are enough computers for each student.
2. Ask students to review the timeline rough draft they completed in the previous session.
3. Instruct the students to use the photos, computer images, and music they brought with them to create a PowerPoint presentation depicting the important events of their lives. Allow the entire group session to work on this if needed. Make technical support available for the students as they complete their timelines.

Sharing the Timelines Session
1. For this session, meet in a room where a projector and speakers can be set up.
2. Allow each student time to play the PowerPoint timeline he or she created for the rest of the group members.
3. Questions to facilitate discussion include:
   - *What was it like for you to complete this timeline?*
   - *What is the significance of each of the songs you chose to add to your timeline?*
   - *What is the significance of each of the images you chose for your timeline?*
   - *What did you learn about each of the other group members when viewing their timelines?*
   - *Based on the timeline, what are some challenges that individual group members have experienced and overcome?*
   - *Based on the timelines you viewed today, what are some experiences that most or all group members have in common?*

Suggested Modifications (for Special Needs Populations): If students have limited technology skills, or if there are no available computers, it is possible to modify this activity into a low-tech version. This version would involve using poster board to create a collage from magazine photos as well as personal items to create the timeline. The activity as it is described here includes a session to create the timelines as well as a subsequent session to share the timelines. Depending on available time, asking the students to create their timelines as homework between sessions is an option if all group members have access to computers at home.

Evaluation Plan: The completed timelines and the students' sharing of the timelines will provide the means for evaluation to determine the effectiveness of the intervention.

THE MUSIC OF MY LIFE

Jennifer M. Foster

> *T*his expressive arts intervention provides students with an opportunity to create a timeline of significant events in their life (positive and negative) using different mediums. Students then select songs to represent several important times in their life. Together the music and timeline are shared and processed with the counselor. This intervention provides an avenue for students who have difficulty putting their thoughts and feelings about their personal life experiences into words. Furthermore, it promotes self-disclosure and exploration of the parts of their story that they might not share during talk therapy. The intervention concludes with looking ahead to the future and encouraging students to explore their unwritten chapters, including their dreams and goals.

Modality: Visual Arts, Music

ASCA National Model Domain: Personal/Social

Deliver via: Individual or group

Age Level: Middle or high school

Indications: This intervention could be used with students with a wide range of presenting concerns (e.g., grief/loss, anger, abuse/neglect, family change, social problems, depression, or anxiety) in an individual-counseling format. Additionally, it could be implemented in a small group focused on any of the above concerns.

Materials: To create the timeline, each student needs one large sheet of heavy-weight paper or a canvas. An assortment of tools for drawing, coloring, collaging, and painting (e.g., paint brushes, paints, colored pencils, markers, a variety of magazines, scissors, and glue) is needed to illustrate events on the timeline. To play the music, the counselor will need a computer, docking station, or speakers for students to share their songs on compact discs, their cellphones, or from their portable music players (e.g., MP3 player).

Preparation: Gather and set out materials for creation of the timeline.

Instructions:
Session One
1. The counselor introduces the activity by talking about how each person's life story is different. Each individual's story is filled with a mixture of positive events and those that are difficult or painful. The important thing is to know your story and how it has influenced you. After exploring the chapters of your story up until now, you can start to think about how you would like to write the next chapters.

2. The counselor then provides an example that the students would be familiar with from popular media or a classic story. For example, the counselor could say, *"Let's think about an example of a life story that we already know; the story of Cinderella. In the beginning of the story, she is a young girl living happily with her father and mother who love her very much. Everything changes for Cinderella when her mother dies. Following her mother's death, her father remarries a woman who treats Cinderella badly. When it seemed like life couldn't get worse, it did when her father passed away. Cinderella continues to be treated poorly by her stepmother as well as her stepsisters, who are jealous of her. The next big event in Cinderella's life is an invitation for every eligible maiden in the kingdom to attend a ball for the prince to choose a bride. Although Cinderella was invited, her stepsisters made it impossible for her to attend by ruining her dress right before she was to leave for the ball. Cinderella felt like losing hope, but then her fairy godmother appeared and used her magic so Cinderella could attend the ball. As you know, she meets the prince and they fall in love. The prince finds Cinderella and they are married. Let's think about the events in Cinderella's life. What are some of the positive events that she experienced? What are some of the difficult and painful ones?"*

3. Following the example, the counselor encourages the students to brainstorm on a piece of paper using a word or short phrase that represents the happy and difficult memories that make up their stories.

4. The counselor then asks the students to write next to each word or phrase the age they were at the time.

5. Next, the counselor instructs the students to draw a line on the paper from left to right; this will be the timeline. Students will write on the left the date they were born and approximately three quarters of the way across they will add the date and their current age.

6. The counselor then directs the students to put the events they brainstormed earlier on their timelines in chronological order.

7. The students then illustrate events using colored pencils, markers, crayons, or paint. Students may also use magazines to find pictures that symbolize the events or feelings remembered from that time.

8. For homework, the students are asked to think about their timeline during the week and find two or three songs that correspond with significant events they have experienced. For the next meeting, the students are asked to bring in their music on a CD, phone, or portable music player (which can be kept in the counselor's office if needed).

Session Two

1. During the follow-up session, the counselor starts by reviewing the idea of a life story from the previous session. The counselor reiterates that each person has a story that is unique and includes a mixture of events

that have impacted that person. There is also a part of that story that is unwritten.

2. The students are asked to share their stories by showing their timelines, describing in as much detail as possible the important events, and then share the music they selected to go with several of their experiences.

3. After the students have shared their timelines and music, the counselor asks several process questions to explore the experience, such as:

   a. *"What did you experience while making your timeline and finding music?"*

   b. *"What was the hardest part of this activity? What was the best part?"*

   c. *"What was it like to share your timeline and music with me (or with the group)?"*

   d. *"In a sentence or two, what stood out to you about this exercise?"*

   e. *"What did you learn about yourself from your timeline and music?"*

   f. *"For groups: What did you learn today from what others have shared?"*

4. Following the processing time, the counselor directs the students to think about the unwritten chapters, which are represented by the part of the timeline that is still blank. Counselors can prompt this exploration by asking questions such as:

   a. *"What are your hopes and dreams for the next chapters of your story?"*

   b. *"What are the goals that you can set to help achieve your dreams?"*

   c. *"What choices can you make today to help you meet these goals?"*

   d. *"When you have another hard chapter in your story, how can you get through the difficult time?"*

   e. *"Who are people in your life who support you and encourage you on your journey?"*

5. The counselor concludes the activity by noting the courage it took for students to explore their stories and affirming the students by noting their strength and resilience.

Suggested Modifications (for Special Needs Populations): School counselors may need to modify various aspects of this intervention to meet the needs of students with varying ability levels. Counselors can make materials more accessible for students who have difficulty with fine motor stills. For example, counselors can help students who have difficulty grasping markers or paint brushes by securing a piece of foam around them to make them easier to hold. Students who are adding collage materials to their timelines may benefit from glue dots, which are an alternative to liquid glue, that are easier for students to manipulate. Students who have difficulty writing can create their timelines on the computer and could use clip art to illustrate different events. The intervention can also be modified for students who need additional time by spreading out the activity over several sessions. In a group setting, some students may struggle to focus. Students can be spread out so they have their own space, which would help minimize distractions.

Evaluation Plan: A pre-/postsurvey can be utilized to examine students' ability to name and share positive and difficult events of their life story and their future dreams and goals, as shown in the included example.

For each statement, please circle Yes or No.

1. I can name the positive events that have influenced my life.   Yes   No

2. I can name the negative events that have influenced my life.   Yes   No

3. I have told someone I trust about my life story, including the good   Yes   No
   and bad things that have happened to me.

4. I have shared with someone my future dreams.   Yes   No

5. I have set goals that will help me achieve my dreams.   Yes   No

6. I know what I can do today to work toward my goals.   Yes   No

---

MUSICAL QUESTIONS

James R. Huber and Diane J. Shea

*T*his is a brief, problem-solving activity in which students work together in small groups to generate a list of popular song titles that contain the word "why?" Details are listed below under instructions.

Modality: Music and Movement

ASCA National Model Domain: Personal/Social Domain

Deliver via: Group and/or classroom guidance

Age Level: Elementary, middle, and high school

Indications: Can be used to facilitate personal/group learning regarding getting acquainted, trust building, risk taking, feelings awareness, multicultural sensitivity, team building, social skills, coping with change, and problem solving.

Materials: Paper and pencil

Preparation: Room should allow for movement and time should allow for a minimum of 20 minutes (5 minutes for activity and 15 minutes for processing time).

Instructions:

1. Explain to students that this is a _____ (e.g., problem-solving, team-building) exercise.
2. Form small groups of four to five students, with enough space between the groups to enable them to work with some degree of privacy.
3. Repeat the following task to each group: "*Your mission is to work together and write down five popular song titles that contain the word 'why?' At least half of your group must know the song and at least one person should*

be prepared to sing the song title later, if needed, to prove it is a real song. You will have 3 minutes to complete the task."

Pause here to answer any questions, clarify the instructions, and/or repeat the rules. Once you believe all groups are ready, tell them to begin.

4. After 3 minutes, ask everyone to stop working, stay where they are, and begin processing with each group, sharing one song title at a time until all groups have declared all five song titles. When in doubt, ask a group member to sing the title as needed. Allow for duplicates and normalize any overlaps as evidence of a song's popularity versus "They stole our song!"

Suggested Modifications (for Special Needs Populations): Be aware of cultural differences in music and in the language in which the song is written. If titles are not in English, encourage students to process the universality of feelings even when the language is different.

Evaluation Plan: Gather some perception data based on age group and the purpose of the exercise. For example, for a high school team-building group:

1. How did your group go about solving the problem or completing the task?
2. How did you decide which songs would be accepted?
3. How did you determine who would write down the five song titles?
4. How did you handle any disagreements or different opinions?
5. How did you work on the task and still make it fun?
6. How did the time limit influence your problem solving?
7. Why do you think there are so many song titles that contain the word "why?"
8. What does this tell us about the importance of good questions?

STRESS IS PLAYED OUT: USING MUSIC TO DE-STRESS

Tamara J. Hinojosa and Suzanne D. Mudge

This activity is designed to be used in a group setting. The purpose of this group activity is to help students better understand stress and to use music as a way to alleviate stress symptoms. Although this activity can be modified, to fully help students engage with this activity, it should be conducted in a setting where students have access to a music library (e.g., computer lab or library with access to the Internet, music CDs, or MP3 players).

Modality: Music

ASCA National Model Domain: Academic, Career, Personal/Social
Deliver via: Group counseling

Age Level: Middle or high school

Indications: This small-group activity is designed to help students manage stress and deal effectively with the negative impact of emotional conflict and/or change.

Materials: A CD player or any type of device that plays music. Counselors can also use Internet music sources, such as Spotify, iTunes, or YouTube to play music.

Preparation: Have your own song selected that you will use as an example. Also, if conducting the group session in a computer lab, counselors should have the computers set up so that students can immediately begin searching for their own music.

Instructions:
1. If the group is being held in a computer lab, begin the session in a circle away from the computers (so that students are not distracted). Open the activity by defining stress and by helping group members understand that everyone experiences stress in different ways.
2. Facilitate a discussion about the triggers and symptoms each group member has when feeling stressed. This will help group members see how each member experiences stress differently.
3. Introduce the group to the concept that music is a tool that can be used to calm and/or motivate students during stressful times.
4. Share examples of songs that have helped you de-stress and discuss how and why these songs helped alleviate stress. It is ideal to play these songs for students.
5. Group members are then each instructed to select a song that helps them de-stress. If groups are held in a computer lab, students can use the Internet to find songs.
6. Once songs have been selected, facilitate a discussion about why each member selected her or his song. Additionally, the diversity of music selected can be acknowledged and appreciated. Questions that can help students elaborate on their music choice are as follows:
   a. *"I notice this song has a very fast pace (or slow pace); how does that make you feel?"*
   b. *"What do the lyrics in this song mean to you?"*
   c. *"What stands out about this song to you?"*
   d. *"What do you think about when you listen to this song?"*
7. At the end of the group session, group members will write down the title of the song and artist. Group leaders can make a CD or playlist (on iTunes, YouTube, etc.) for all group members. The CD/playlists can be distributed and discussed during the following group session.

Suggested Modifications (for Special Needs Populations): Not all counselors will have access to an Internet music library, so group members could also be assigned homework to find their songs in between group sessions. Once the students bring their songs to the group leaders, the leaders can then make a CD and play that CD in the following group session. If group leaders cannot make a CD, they can also create a playlist on YouTube and add all of their students to this YouTube playlist so that they have access to it.

Evaluation Plan: To evaluate the effectiveness of this intervention, you could have a follow-up session about de-stressing and ask students if they have been using their songs to alleviate stress.

IV �֎ Movement and Dance

8 ✠ Movement-/Dance-Based Interventions in the Academic Domain

CAKEWALK HIP HOP: DANCE YOUR WAY TO ACADEMIC SUCCESS

Katherine M. Hermann

*P*ositive time management skills promote positive study skills, and good study skills promote academic achievement. So, how can counselors impart this knowledge on students? With a Cakewalk Hip Hop! This activity incorporates a 10-minute dance party, that is, a Cakewalk Hip Hop, as a way to model to students how to structure their time, communicate with others, and persevere.

Modality: Movement/Dance

ASCA National Model Domain: Academics

Deliver via: Group counseling of classroom guidance

Age Level: Elementary school

Indications: Elementary school is frequently a time when students learn study habits and the concept of academic achievement. For some individuals, particularly those with behavioral concerns or possible conduct disorders, developing positive academic skills can be difficult. As such, the Cakewalk Hip Hop is a comprehensive exercise designed to promote awareness of time management, communication with peers and teachers, and discuss persistence in a way that is both fun and instructive.

Materials: Sound system with start/stop features and open dance space.

Preparation: Arrange a room with an open space and set up sound system equipment.

Instructions:

1. Because this activity requires some vulnerability, dancing in front of peers, beginning with a discussion that it is *okay to be silly* on the dance floor is important. Addressing respect and support may also help facilitate students' creative expression during the dance and discussions. Emphasize and reflect on the positive interactions you notice throughout the exercise using comments such as: *"You really helped one another out by . . . "* or, *"You do a nice job supporting each other's ideas when. . . . "*

2. Provide the following explanation of the activity to the group: *"The music will play for a total of 10 minutes. When the music is playing everyone has to dance, but when the music stops, everyone freezes without moving."*

   Before starting the music for the first time, discuss the idea of time-management and task-management skills with questions such as: *"What does it mean to manage time? When do you need to work and when do you need to play? What can you do to be most effective at both* (setting a timer, for example)? *How is this activity today a time management activity* (e.g., dance when the music plays, stop when the music stops)?"

3. Start the music. After it has played for a few minutes stop the song and say, *"Freeze."* While everyone is holding the dance pose, ask which students could use help to keep from falling or to stay in position.

   Select several students to ask a classmate for help. After the students have been assisted, let everyone relax (sitting down on the floor where they were dancing) and spend a few moments discussing communication skills, how to tell when one needs help, and how to ask for help (e.g., in a classroom raise your hands; at home, ask an adult). The following questions may be helpful in facilitating discussion: *"How did you know you needed help? How do you know whether you are 'hanging in the air' or in an uncomfortable situation when you are doing your schoolwork? What can you do when you are in this situation? Who will you ask? How can you ask in a way that gets you the help?"*

4. After processing communication and discussing how to ask for help, restart the music. Start and stop the music several times and let the students practice asking for help. Taking a few moments after everyone has been supported, introduce the topic of dependability. Use the following questions to help start the discussion: *"Was your classmate dependable? What does it mean for you to be dependable? How can you be dependable with your schoolwork* (e.g., turning homework in on time)?"

5. Start the music again. At this point students may begin to feel tired, so this is a good opportunity to introduce the idea of persistence when you are practicing time management. Questions that can facilitate this discussion might be: *"When do you have to be persistent with your schoolwork? Was it hard to start dancing again after we stopped? What can you do when you*

get tired of doing schoolwork? If you need to take a break, what can you do (e.g., set a timer to remind you to get back to work)?"

As you close the activity, review the concepts that have been discussed and how they relate to the activity: time management (e.g., sometimes we need to take a break, and sometimes we need to persevere even when we do not want to assign time for fun and time for schoolwork); asking for help (e.g., when we are tired or confused, we need to ask for help); and being dependable (e.g., do our best when someone needs help or we have a task to complete).

Suggested Modifications (for Special Needs Populations): Throughout this activity, a lot of discussion topics are presented; when working with younger students, it may be helpful to select only one or two areas for discussion and processing. Alternatively, if a group meets weekly, process a different content area each week during a Cakewalk Hip Hop. In addition, other topics can be introduced and processed, such as goal setting or maintaining a positive attitude. If a group member is unable to move freely around the room, encourage him or her to move to the music in any manner he or she is able from a seated position.

Evaluation Plan: The success of this activity can be evaluated based on discussion conversations. Indicators of a positive outcome would be students' ability to connect the dance experiences and ways to improve their academic habits and performance.

9 Movement-/Dance-Based Interventions in the Career Domain

OVERCOMING OBSTACLES: NAVIGATING THE ROAD TO CAREER SUCCESS

Sarah LaFont and Lindsey M. Nichols

This activity provides a way for students to explore situations, the self, support, and strategies (Schlossberg, 2011) to reach their career goals. The exercise can be used at any point during career exploration in which barriers—physical, emotional, or mental—become a challenge to developing identifiable goals. Using creative movement expression, students will describe their own stressors or obstacles in their career development and will move into identifying support as well as strategies. The focus of the activity is to stimulate greater self-awareness as well as to increase the mind–body relationship during a time of exploration and potential stress. Creative movement can "enable a person to cognitively process and overcome frightening events, feel one's physical self, analyze problems, find constructive solutions for everyday life, and improve one's body image and self-esteem" (Brauninger, 2010). The school counselor can provide a unique experience to students through which they can clarify what they need to reach their own goals, in this case focused on career, and strategize how to get there, using both internal and external resources.

Modality: Creative Movement

ASCA National Model Domain: Career

Deliver via: Group counseling, although can be adapted for individual or classroom guidance

Age Level: High school, although appropriate for use with any age group—modify the topic, focus, and processing questions to align with the students' developmental levels and stage of career exploration

Indications: This activity aims to focus primarily on setting career goals (American School Counselor Association [ASCA] C:A1.6), incorporating four secondary objectives: (a) understanding the importance of planning (ASCA C:A1.7); (b) understanding that work is an important and satisfying means of personal expression (ASCA C:C1.7); (c) demonstrating how interests, abilities, and achievements relate to achieving personal, social, educational, and career goals (ASCA C:C2.1); and (d) pursuing and developing competencies in areas of interest (ASCA C:A1.8). Please note that this exercise focus can be altered and adapted to fit other career-development competencies, as well as other competencies (see Modifications section).

Materials: Open space to move and explore, live or recorded music, notecards (three per participant), large sheets of easel or butcher paper (one per participant and several extra for group discussion), lined paper for everyone, markers, masking tape, pencils, and any art supplies as desired.

Preparation: Prepare an area set up for group discussion, with a large area to write where everyone can see; create a few of your own obstacle cards for pairs to use in order to help stimulate further learning and experiencing. These can be challenges that you know your students are experiencing. Example obstacles could include: *8 years of schooling, no money, parents, time, currently working a lot*, and so on. Prepare the last discussion section with questions specific to your group. Have a resource list prepared that students can go to for help.

Instructions:

Basic Activity Outline (60 minutes):
1. Warm-up circle (5 minutes)
2. Playing with the obstacle course (10 minutes)
3. Discussion/activity to identify challenges (15 minutes)
4. Re-creating the obstacle course with challenges (10 minutes)
5. Follow-up discussion and connecting the points (15 minutes)
6. Closing circle (5 minutes)

Please note that the times listed below are slightly different due to the nature of this specific example and possible variations.

Introducing the Activity (10 minutes):
Gather students together in a circle and let them know that today you will be using creative movement to explore career aspirations. Begin by asking students to participate in the career circle warm-up exercise, which is a fun and playful way for students to relax into their bodies. Ask everyone to pick a career that interests him or her and to give it a specific representative movement or a gesture. Everyone will then introduce him- or herself by name (even when they know each other) and demonstrate his or her career gesture. Demonstrate yours to the group to encourage both creativity and confidence. Ask the group to then repeat each person's name and copy his or her gesture. From this activity, begin a brief discussion about how students selected the various careers and movements (i.e., characteristics or qualities associated with this particular career);

explain that we can learn a lot from how we move. Explain also that with the following activity they will be using movement to think about career exploration and how to move around different obstacles or challenges they might encounter on their road to work. You will then discuss resources and strategies that can either support or hinder movement and the student's progress.

Creating Obstacles (10 minutes):
1. First, the students will learn to create obstacles. With soft music in the background, the counselor splits the group into pairs. Select a volunteer to assist you in demonstrating how one partner will serve as the obstacle creator—by using arms, hands, body, feet, and legs to mime or draw obstacles—to challenge the other partner, who will find ways to maneuver through the obstacles. The counselor will demonstrate both parts—the creator and the mover. Instruct the other partner to find a way to deal with the obstacle. Is it over, around, under, or through the middle? Where is there space for you? How do you maneuver around it?
2. Ask these questions to encourage student engagement:
   "Really watch your partner create the obstacles. See if you can remember the shapes, the details of what your partner is drawing, and then see if you can respond to those details. Let yourself be creative."
   "Try using different techniques. How many different ways can you get through? How many different body parts can you use?"
   "Notice what it feels like to move through this challenge. Are there movements that are easier or more difficult?"
   "Are your thoughts influencing your movements? What makes you try something or not?"
3. When the group is ready (or after 4 to 5 minutes), ask the partners to trade roles.
4. Gather back into one large group. Thank group members for their creativity and willingness to try out the activity. Let them know that you will be applying these skills to real-life challenges and adding to this structure in a few minutes.

Identify Career Goals (10 to 30 minutes, depending on artistic endeavors):
1. Ask students to spread out, finding their own space on the floor. Pass around the large easel paper, markers, and art supplies you may wish to use. Tell the students that you will be asking them a series of questions and then giving them a few minutes to respond on the paper. They can write words or phrases, as well as draw pictures or symbols—whatever comes to mind for them. Do let them know that their drawings will be shared with the group. Ask the following questions, pausing for a moment after each one:
   "If you could magically have any career in the world, what would it be?"
   "What would your obituary say about your career life?"
   "In terms of work, what would you most like to accomplish?"

"What would you like to be doing workwise in 5 years?"

"What gifts, skills, or talents do you have that you would most like to share?"

Give them an opportunity to add anything else pertaining to their career future. Give them a countdown of when they will be stopping, 5 minutes, 2 minutes, and 1 minute. Honor the time and dedication they put into their work.

2. Next, pass around notebook paper and pencils. Ask students to identify and write down what it might take to reach these goals using the following questions as prompts:

"What skills might be necessary to achieve your goals?"

"What does it look like to get from Point A to Point B? What steps or progression might be necessary to reach your dreams?"

"What will it take to reach your goals? What qualities do people have who reach their goals?"

Exploration of Career Goals and Obstacles (15 minutes):

1. Direct students to circle the things on their lists that feel like challenges (i.e., obstacles) they have encountered or anticipate encountering in reaching their goals. The counselor can give an example on a large paper in front of the room.

2. Next, give each student three index cards and ask them to write an obstacle on each card. Let the students know that these will be shared with their partner but not the entire class.

3. Ask students to get back into pairs. Have the partners tape their goal posters on the walls around the room in such a way that they will be spread out. Then, with a partner, demonstrate to the class what the obstacle course will now look like. One partner will share one of his or her own obstacle cards. Encourage him or her to describe the obstacle to his or her partner and to share why it feels like an obstacle. Describing these to the partner will not only give an opportunity to share concerns, but will also allow the partner an opportunity to be more creative when directing obstacles in the next section.

4. Instruct the partners who just listened to create the obstacles, focusing on the specific obstacle stated on the card. Again, to encourage creativity and embodiment, the counselor and a partner will demonstrate how the obstacle course will look. As before, one partner will be the obstacle creator, and the other will be moving through the obstacles. The creator will create the obstacle(s) that the partner wrote down, even showing the card while making the obstacle.

5. The pairs will be positioned across the room from their papers so that they are able to see and read their goals, as well as be able to "keep their eye on the goal." Their movement sequences can be done moving toward their goals.

6. Questions and coaching to facilitate the activity:

Encourage the mover to focus on his or her goal on the other side of the "barrier," keeping a peripheral eye on it as he or she moves through.

Remind students to embrace the obstacles. Each obstacle may affect the movement as one attempts to overcome it. Ask students, *"What kinds of effort or energy will overcoming each obstacle take?"*

"Notice how it feels to be confronted with the obstacle. How do you respond to it? Where do you feel it in your body? Does it cause you to want to use a certain movement?"

7. Have students rotate through the various obstacles. Honor their diligent work and creative expression. After 5 minutes or when the group is ready, switch roles, beginning with the other partner sharing his or her obstacles.

8. Last, the counselor can throw in a few obstacles that pertain to the focus of the lesson and this group of students. Ask the partners to again take turns moving through these.

Putting It All Together (20 minutes):

1. Bring the students back together for reflection and discussion, making class lists as necessary on large paper; ask the following questions as prompts:
   "What was the obstacle course like? What did you experience?
   What attributes did it take to move around the obstacles?
   How did your bodies and minds respond to the challenges?"
   Encourage students to make comparisons and explore what efforts, skills, or qualities were necessary to move through these difficult areas. Prompt them to consider what inner resources they have to help them. Make a list of the skills students mention that can help them navigate and achieve success. Be prepared to add the qualities of people who achieve their goals.

2. Next, ask students what resources and supports they have used or know about that can assist them in reaching their career goals (i.e. Department of Labor website, shadowing, etc.). Make a possibilities list. Be sure to include resources that may be helpful in addressing the specific challenges identified by your students.

3. Finally, begin the closing circle. This is a good time to allow students to share any concluding thoughts about the activity and for the counselor to review the lesson by saying:
   "Today, we identified career goals and work that would be important and meaningful to us. We identified ambitions that we would like to achieve in our fields of interest. Through creative play, we looked at challenges that we may experience in reaching these goals. During our discussion, we identified character qualities and the resources we have to help us through these places of struggle."
   To end the circle, ask the students if they would be willing to close their eyes. Ask them to imagine moving smoothly through the obstacles they identified today. Ask them to move from one point to the next with the skills they identified today (maybe list a couple) and into the goal or career they

envision. Have them imagine doing this work: *"What does the job look like and feel like? What does it feel like to be there?"* Ask students to hold this place of success. Give them a moment or two to reflect. Ask them to take a deep breath in . . . and out, knowing that this vision lives inside of them. Invite them to wiggle their fingers and slowly open their eyes. Thank them for their hard work and focus.

Suggested Modifications (for Special Needs Populations): This activity could be further emphasized following an interest inventory and career-exploration class and could be preceded by an action or goal-setting class. This exercise can be expanded into a focus on decision-making skills. Here, a more lengthy movement exploration and discussion could focus on how we make decisions and how we work through challenges. It could also explore the mind–body connection and include a lesson on how our beliefs affect us.

This exercise could become a regular activity, using the same form but exploring different topics. Or, it could be used the same way each time, as in a support-group setting. Students could use high-quality paper when printing their goals and be given ample time and supplies to express their goals artistically. Their artwork could remain on the walls and be showcased.

This exercise could be modified to fit into personal and social domains by looking at obstacles that hinder healthy self-esteem, peer relationships, and meaningful work, as well as obstacles that influence addictions. It could be used any time students are feeling blocks or challenges in accomplishing goals. Finally, this activity can be modified and adapted to the population with which you are working. Set developmentally appropriate goals and refine the activity to meet these needs, while still following the same format. For students with exceptionalities, the breadth of movement may be smaller, more contained, and in place rather than covering a linear distance.

Evaluation Plan: To evaluate the effectiveness of this intervention, you may use the following survey as a pre- and postassessment.

Students will complete this assessment as a pretest and as a posttest of their understanding of the concepts and process addressed during the activity Overcoming Obstacles.

1. Identify at least one future career goal.
2. Identify three obstacles/challenges you may encounter in reaching this goal.
   a.
   b.
   c.

3. Identify three external resources that are available to help you through these challenges.
   a.
   b.
   c.

4. Identify three internal qualities that can help you in reaching this goal.

   a.

   b.

   c.

REFERENCES

Brauninger, I. (2010). Dance movement therapy group intervention in stress treatment: A randomized controlled trial. *Arts in Psychotherapy, 39*(5), 443–450. doi:10.1016/j.aip.2012.07.002

Schlossberg, N. K. (2011). The challenge of change: The transition model and its applications. *Journal of Employment Counseling, 48*(4), 159–162.

10 Movement-/Dance-Based Interventions in the Personal/Social Domain

BALLOON WALK

Diane J. Shea and James R. Huber

This is an experiential activity in which students must learn to cooperate as a group to reach a finish line while walking with balloons between them. Details are listed below under the instructions.

Modality: Movement/Group exercise

ASCA National Model Domain: Personal/Social

Deliver via: Group counseling or classroom guidance

Age Level: Middle, high school

Indications: Can be used to facilitate personal/group learning regarding building trust, risk taking, being aware of feelings, team building, flexibility, and social skills

Materials: Balloons.

Preparations: Room should be arranged so that students can line up and walk a distance of approximately 20 feet.

Instructions:

1. Explain to students that this is an experiential exercise and that they should pay attention to their feelings throughout the activity.
2. Students should be divided into groups of four to five students (depending on whether this is a group or guidance lesson). There should be at least two groups, but this may vary.
3. Balloons should be blown up and one should be placed between each student in the single-file line.

4. In single file, students will walk as a group from the start line to the finish line while trying to keep the balloons from falling to the ground. If a balloon drops to the floor, this whole group of students must go back to the start line and begin again.

5. Process with the students what it felt like to have to rely on their group members to help them get to the finish line. Invite them to discuss the role they played in their group's progress.

Suggested Modifications: Depending on the size of the group(s), and size of the classroom, this exercise may be done in smaller groups.

Evaluation Plan: Gather perception data based on age group and purpose of exercise. For example, for a middle school friendship group:

1. How valuable was this exercise in terms of understanding how you feel about cooperating in a group?

   Not at all ___ A little ___ Somewhat valuable ___ Valuable ___ Very valuable ___

2. What did you learn about yourself in this exercise?

THE BANANA SPLIT

James R. Huber and Diane J. Shea

This is a brief group-building exercise in which students line up according to their favorite flavor of ice cream. Details are listed below under the instructions.

Modality: Movement

ASCA National Model Domain: Personal/Social

Deliver via: Group and/or classroom guidance

Age Level: Elementary, middle, high school

Indications: Can be used to facilitate personal/group learning regarding getting acquainted, trust building, risk taking, feeling awareness, multicultural sensitivity, team building, social skills, coping with change, personal space, and problem solving

Materials: None needed.

Preparations: Room should allow for movement and time should allow for a minimum of 20 minutes (5 minutes for activity and 15 minutes for processing time).

Instructions:

1. Explain to students that this is a _____ (e.g., trust-building, team-building) exercise.
2. Ask students to stand up, move to the front of the room, and form a single line from left to right across the open space.
3. Tell them to imagine a giant letter A on the left wall and a giant letter Z on the right wall, with an imaginary line on the floor connecting the two letters.
4. Now ask them to arrange themselves alphabetically along this imaginary line by the first letter of their favorite flavor of ice cream. For example, show them that students who like *chocolate* would stand more to the left side; those who like *strawberry* would be further to the right.
5. Encourage them to talk to each other as needed and to handle any duplicate flavors by standing together close to the same "letter" spot on the imaginary line.
6. Once they are arranged alphabetically, ask the students to listen carefully as each person states his or her name and declares proudly, "My favorite ice cream flavor is _____!" beginning with A, then B, and so on until all students have shared.
7. During this process, repeat each flavor for the group so everyone can hear it, offer positive comments about the preferences, show interest in each choice, and affirm both commonality and diversity of flavors.
8. After everyone has shared and before they return to their seats, summarize the group process and point out how they have just created a "giant banana split" by recognizing, accepting, respecting and appreciating individual differences and similarities. Embellish the collaborative "team moment" by asking them to imagine themselves each as a big scoop of ice cream on the world's largest banana, complete with whipped cream and chopped nuts!

Suggested Modifications (for Special Needs Populations): Change instructions to accommodate students who may be hearing, speech, and/or mobility impaired. Encourage students who may be lactose intolerant to name their favorite ice cream substitute.

Evaluation Plan: Gather some perception data based on age group and purpose of exercise. For example, for a junior high team-building group:

1. What did you learn about your own preferences related to others?
2. How did it feel to be the only _____ flavor? Why?
3. How did it feel to be one of several _____ flavors? Why?
4. What did you have to do as individuals to complete the exercise?
5. What did you have to do as a group to successfully accomplish the goal?
6. What does this activity tell us about team building?

BEING ATLAS: CARRYING THE WEIGHT OF THE WORLD

Charles E. Myers

*S*chool counselors can use this activity in individual, group, or class settings. The activity provides students with a concrete representation of the metaphorical weight they carry when holding onto negative emotions and experiences. School counselors may start by asking students to reflect on those emotions or experiences that may weigh them down, draining them of energy.

Modality: Movement and Physical Experience

ASCA National Model Domain: Personal/Social

Deliver via: Individual, group, or classroom guidance

Age Level: All grade levels

Indications: This activity is useful in increasing student awareness and acceptance of how suppressing negative emotions and experiences weighs them down and hinders their goal attainment and happiness. Additionally, this activity could easily be adapted to the academic domain by looking at all of the activities and responsibilities students are trying to balance and how the weight of those activities and responsibilities may hinder them from meeting their academic goals.

Materials: Book bag, rocks, and paint of different colors.

Preparation: First, collect round river rocks, about half the size of a fist. Paint the rocks in various bold colors. Next, write words on several rocks that relate to emotions and experiences that may interfere with student happiness and academic success (e.g., addiction, anger, anxiety, bullying, fear, guilt, hurt, loneliness, sadness, secrets, shame). It is important also to have rocks with no words that can be used to represent ideas generated from students. Describe these student-generated ideas in list or sentence format, as appropriate.

Instructions:
1. School counselor starts with a brief story about the titan Atlas (Roman & Roman, 2010, pp. 92–93) who carried the weight of the world on his shoulders.
2. School counselor invites student(s) to share negative emotions or experiences that may weigh a person down.
3. School counselor asks for a volunteer from the group or class to come up to the front of the room (or if individual counseling, invite student to do an experiment). Have the student put on the book bag and ask, *"How heavy does the book bag feel?"*
4. School counselor picks up a rock (either one with a word that the student[s] had shared or one that is blank) and says, *"These rocks are like our negative emotions and experiences; they weigh us down, keeping us from being happy and meeting our goals in life."*

5. School counselor then places the rock in the book bag, again checking in on how heavy the book bag feels. The school counselor can then talk about how one or two things may not weigh us down much and how we can normally shoulder this weight.

6. Then the school counselor begins to add more rocks, using a word that the student(s) had used when placing each rock into the book bag.

7. After several rocks are placed in the book bag, the school counselor asks about the weight again and then facilitates a conversation on how our negative emotions and experiences might prevent us from being happy or meeting our goals.

8. Finally, the school counselor facilitates a conversation on different ways to rid ourselves of our negative emotions and experiences and how that by doing so we free ourselves to be happier and successful.

Suggested Modifications (for Special Needs Populations): School counselors may modify their language to meet students' developmental level. For those students in wheelchairs or otherwise inhibited from wearing a book bag, school counselors may use a box or basket that these students can hold into which the rocks are placed.

Evaluation Plan: To evaluate the effectiveness of this intervention, school counselors may ask students to complete the following survey as a pre- and postassessment.

Students will complete this assessment as a pretest and as a posttest of their understanding of the concepts and materials addressed during the activity Being Atlas: Carrying the Weight of the World.

1. List three negative emotions or experiences.
   (a)
   (b)
   (c)

2. True or False?
   Negative emotions or experiences are best kept to ourselves.

3. List three things you want to accomplish.
   (a)
   (b)
   (c)

4. True or False?
   Talking about our negative emotions and experiences can help us meet our goals.

5. List three ways that you can let go of negative emotions or experiences.
   (a)
   (b)
   (c)

REFERENCE

Roman, L., & Roman, M. (2010). *Encyclopedia of Greek and Roman mythology*. New York, NY: Facts on File.

EMOTIONAL OBSTACLE COURSE

Eric Jett

The emotional obstacle course is an activity that provides the opportunity for exploration of the needs of safety, emotion, loss, and future. The obstacle course helps individuals to understand that the future is what guides us, and safety and kindness toward others are essential and influence other important skills that relate to safety, emotions, and loss. The obstacle course can be completed in a group setting or in a family-therapy environment, being adapted to meet the needs of the individuals participating.

Modality: Visual/Movement

ASCA National Model Domain: Personal/Social

Deliver Via: Group

Age Level: Elementary, middle, or high school

Indications: This activity is appropriate for individuals who struggle with emotional regulation and for emphasizing the importance of a support system. If an individual in the activity drops the ping-pong ball, a discussion can begin about what "happens" when our emotions run away from us. We have to stop, gather ourselves, and consider what we need to do next.

Materials: Two hula hoops or other obstacle course items, blindfold, ping-pong ball, plastic spoon, and a chair.

Preparation: Have all the needed materials present and ready for use. Participants in the group should be asked to take turns holding the hula hoops upright, with the hula hoop touching the floor so someone could crawl through the hoop.

Instructions:
1. Introduce the activity by asking students to consider and discuss how hard it can sometimes be to make decisions, and how emotions can be overwhelming. From this discussion explain that the ping-pong ball will represent our emotions, which have to be carried on the spoon through the obstacle course.
2. Explain that sometimes the best way to get through difficult decisions and to hang onto our emotions is to rely on our support system. This is a great opportunity to talk with the students about who is part of their support system and how they are able to use their support system to help them get through difficult times.

3. Ask two of the students to help hold the hula hoops and place them in different areas.

4. Explain that part of the obstacle course is to make it through each of the hula hoops without dropping the ping-pong ball and make it to the chair on the other side. Also explain that each student will be blindfolded on his or her journey through the obstacle course.

5. Let the students know that before they go through the obstacle course they have the option to walk through the obstacle course without the blindfold and to write down directions if they want. They can then let one of their peers read the directions to them. However, if they decide they do not want to write down the directions, then no one in the room can help them through the obstacle course. Provide students time to walk the obstacle course and write down their directions if they want to.

6. As each student takes his or her turn, blindfold the student and hand him or her the plastic spoon with the ping-pong ball. If the student chose to have a peer help, then the peer can begin to read the directions or tell him or her what steps to take through the obstacle course.

7. Most individuals will drop the ping-pong ball. When the first student drops the ping-pong ball it is a great opportunity to stop the activity for a second and discuss how our emotions can "run away" with us sometimes and how hard it can be to keep them under control. If the student has asked a peer to help, then the peer can give advice on how to find the ping-pong ball. If the student did not ask a peer for help then the counselor can suggest, *"If you need help finding your emotions, I'm sure someone will help you if you ask."* Allow the student to ask his or her peers for help finding the ping-pong ball. Once the ball is found, the student resumes the obstacle course until he or she is able to find the chair on the other side of the room.

8. Allow each of the students to go through the obstacle course. At the end, when everyone has had a chance to complete the exercise, encourage the students to discuss what it was like when their emotions "ran away" from them and what is was like asking their peers for help. If there were students who chose to go through the obstacle course without asking a peer to give them directions, the counselor can compare this to those who had directions by asking students to discuss what seemed the easier path: "with support" or "without support."

Areas for discussion include reactions to unplanned events. For instance, if the person wrote directions down and dropped the ping-pong ball, the person helping him or her can provide directions on where his or her emotions went. The key discussion is the importance of having a support system. Consider how difficult it would be to get through the obstacle course without any help. If the person did not write down directions, allow him or her to search for the ping-pong ball until he or she asks for help. Allow the group to help the individual out and then open up the group for discussion. What made the individual ask for help now compared to writing down directions before? Emphasis is placed on the need for us to ask for help, and that the knowledge that requiring help does not show weakness but rather strength because acknowledging the need for assistance from one's support system indicates self-awareness.

Suggested Modifications (for Special Needs Populations): Modify the language used based on the age level of the students. Be aware that some students may not want to be blindfolded for various reasons. If a student does not want to be blindfolded, then he or she may be elected to help hold the hula hoops or ready directions/provide support for other peers who are participating. The obstacle course can be adapted to the age level of the student. For younger students, you may choose to omit the hula hoops and possibly use something such as a stuffed animal for the student to have to walk around. For older students, middle school or high school level, the counselor might choose to increase the difficulty by using more than two hula hoops or incorporating other safe objects into the obstacle course. The course can be as creative as the counselor wants it to be.

Evaluation Plan: The following may be used to evaluate the effectiveness of the technique as a pre- and postassessment.

1. Who do you go to for help when you are angry or upset?
   a.
   b.
   c.
2. List three things you do to keep control of your emotions.
   a.
   b.
   c.
3. True or False? Everyone needs to ask for help sometimes.

EXERCISING OUR BODIES AND BRAINS

Sarah O. Kitchens and Amanda M. Evans

This activity is designed to work with a group or classroom of students while focusing specifically on students with sensory processing disorder (SPD). "A person with SPD finds it difficult to process and act upon information received through the senses, which creates challenges in performing countless everyday tasks. Motor clumsiness, behavioral problems, anxiety, depression, school failure, and other impacts may result if the disorder is not treated effectively" (SPDFoundation.net, 2014). Since SPD can impact the regulation of emotions and behaviors, classroom-guidance activity addresses the SPD student(s) who are in the mainstreamed classroom while providing a stimulating activity for all students.

Expressive Arts Category: Movement/Dance

ASCA National Model Domain: Personal/Social

Deliver Via: Group or classroom guidance

Age Level: Elementary

Materials: CD player/radio/computer with music of various tempos/rhythms; SPD tools: lap bags with rice (serve as weighted tools), sticky dough, dishwashing brushes, and so on.

Preparation: Have the materials ready for students.

Instructions:
1. Begin with exercising the students' bodies (a circuit-training system can be set up in which the students are divided into groups and engage in physical stimulation activities). Plan to spend about 10 minutes on this activity. Note: Students with SPD can meet their sensory needs during this exercise.
2. Students then transition into the "exercising the brains" intervention activity. Dance and movement are incorporated into this exercise.
   a. Discuss a variety of age-appropriate emotions (happy, sad, angry, scared, etc.). Ask the students when they feel the emotion, how their body responds to the emotion, and how they act out the emotion, and so on.
   b. Select a specific emotion that you will ask the students to express through dance; start the music and have students begin moving. Process the experience with a brief general discussion.
   c. Choose another emotion and repeat the activity as time allows.

Suggested Modifications: Younger children may need additional help exploring their emotions. Feeling cards that show specific emotions may also be used to encourage students to engage in the activity.

Evaluation Plan: Ask students to individually perform their favorite emotion/ dance and talk about how it feels to act out their emotions and how it felt to watch their classmates act out their emotions, too.

REFERENCE

The Sensory Processing Disorder Foundation. (2014). *About SPD*. Retrieved June 11, 2014, from http://www.spdfoundation.net/about-sensory-processing-disorder.html

---

GIVE ME A HAND!

James R. Huber and Diane J. Shea

*T*his is a brief "get acquainted" trust-building activity in which students greet each other with a nondominant hand shake. This helps them move out of their normal routine behavior to try on something new.

Modality: Interactive: Verbal and Movement

ASCA National Model Domain: Personal/Social

Deliver via: Group and/or classroom guidance

Age Level: Elementary, middle, high school

Indications: Can be used to facilitate personal/group learning regarding getting acquainted, trust building, risk taking, feeling awareness, multicultural sensitivity, team building, social skills, coping with change, and personal space.

Materials: None needed.

Preparation: Room should allow for movement and time should allow for a minimum of 20 minutes (5 minutes for activity and 15 minutes for processing time).

Instructions:

1. Explain to students that this is a _____ (e.g., trust-building, team-building) exercise.
2. Ask students to stand, move around the room, and greet each other as follows:
   a. Smile.
   b. Shake hands with the nondominant hand.
   c. Say, "Hello, my name is _____, and I'm not perfect."
3. After approximately 5 minutes, ask students to stop, stay where they are, and begin processing with questions relevant to the specific purpose of the group. Questions may include: *"How did you feel? What did you learn about coping with change? How did this help you get acquainted?"*

Suggested Modifications (for Special Needs Populations): Change instructions to accommodate students who may be hearing, speech, limb, and/or mobility impaired.

Evaluation Plan: Gather perception data based on age group and purpose of exercise. For example, for a fourth-grade team-building group:

1. How much did you enjoy this exercise?
   No fun ____ A little fun____ Some fun____ Fun ___ Lots of fun ____
2. Which team members did you get to know better?
3. What was the most interesting thing you learned?

JUST DANCE!

Amanda N. Byrd-Desnoyers and Jennifer Rhodes Wood

The student will learn to use music and movement to help reframe externalizing behaviors.

Modality: Movement/Dance

ASCA National Model Domain: Personal/Social

Deliver via: Individual, group, or classroom guidance

Age Level: Elementary, middle, or high school

Indications: This activity is appropriate for students learning to cope with feelings; it can be used for stress reduction and to reduce externalizing behaviors.

Materials: Paper, colored pencils/markers, MP3 or CD player, Music and Feeling Wheel handout, and open space for movement.

Preparation: Have a variety of music from across genres readily available and print out the Music and Feeling Wheel (see Figure 10.1 for a sample completed wheel and Figure 10.2 for the blank wheel).

Instructions:

1. Start with a discussion on feelings and behaviors. Discuss basic feelings with adolescents. Ask how they show they are sad, mad, bad, or glad. Ask them how others would say they show they are sad, mad, bad, or glad. Discuss how sometimes when they have these feelings their behaviors may cause problems with parents, teachers, or friends. Example: They feel mad because their teacher fussed at them, so when they come home from school, they are stomping, yelling, and "acting out."

2. Explain that all feelings are okay but that sometimes we need to "reset" or exchange our behaviors for different ones to keep from escalating a situation. Offer students an example: *"You are already in a bad mood from school, and when you get home you yell at mom so mom yells back and the situation escalates. Or maybe you are really excited because of something awesome that happened at school and you are a little hyper when you get home, but dad is tired from work so he doesn't immediately share your enthusiasm, and then it goes from being good to a battle between you and dad. Sometimes you need to pause. A way to do that is through movement and music. (You might even get your parents to join you with this one day!)"*

3. Ask, *"What is a feeling that leads to 'big' behavior (something that people KNOW you are feeling and may cause confrontation)?"*

4. Ask students to name some songs that represent this big feeling and to write them down on the Music and Feeling Wheel. If the student is struggling, show him or her a completed music wheel, with songs that you have available to play in the session.

5. Next, say, *"Okay, now that you have the song, we are going to dance to it."* If you do not have his or her song of choice available, ask the student to choose one from your song list.

6. Dance with the student.

7. Process the activity with the student using questions such as: *"How would you rate your change in mood/your excitability/etc. before the music and*

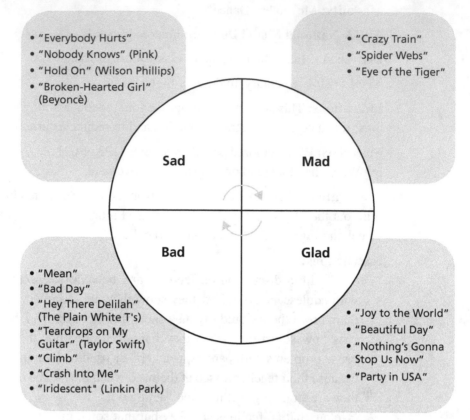

- "Everybody Hurts"
- "Nobody Knows" (Pink)
- "Hold On" (Wilson Phillips)
- "Broken-Hearted Girl" (Beyoncè)

- "Crazy Train"
- "Spider Webs"
- "Eye of the Tiger"

Sad

Mad

Bad

Glad

- "Mean"
- "Bad Day"
- "Hey There Delilah" (The Plain White T's)
- "Teardrops on My Guitar" (Taylor Swift)
- "Climb"
- "Crash Into Me"
- "Iridescent" (Linkin Park)

- "Joy to the World"
- "Beautiful Day"
- "Nothing's Gonna Stop Us Now"
- "Party in USA"

FIGURE 10.1 Completed Music and Feeling Wheel.

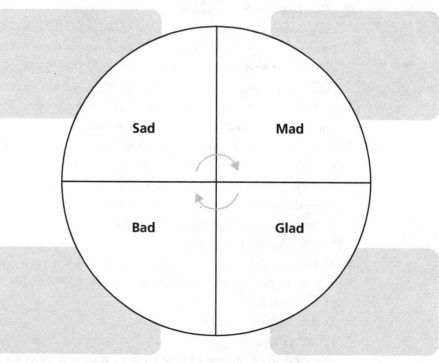

Sad

Mad

Bad

Glad

FIGURE 10.2 Blank Music and Feeling Wheel.

movement (same, better, worse)? How could you do this at home? Are there times when this could be beneficial? Are there times when this would not be appropriate? How could you get your caregiver to do this with you?"

MINDFUL MOVEMENTS

Tamara J. Hinojosa and Suzanne D. Mudge

*T*his activity should be conducted with a group in an area where group members have plenty of space to move around. The purpose of this group activity is to help clients alleviate stress by focusing their minds and slowing their stressful thought patterns.

Modality: Movement/Dance

ASCA National Model Domain: Personal/Social

Deliver via: Group counseling

Age Level: Middle or high school

Indications: This small-group activity is designed to help students manage stress and deal effectively with the negative impact of emotional conflict and/or change. Additionally, this activity could be used during physical education or dance courses. For example, exercise could be used for the group activity or music could be added and the focus could be on dance moves.

Materials: A large open space.

Preparation: Prior to conducting this activity, instruct students to wear comfortable clothing and shoes for this group session.

Instructions:
1. Begin the activity by facilitating a discussion about the triggers and symptoms of stress, with a focus on thought patterns and body sensations related to stress. Questions that can help members recognize stressful thought patterns and body sensations might include:
   a. *"How do you know when you are stressed? What kind of sensations do you have in your body (e.g., heart racing, tense shoulders, tense jaw, upset stomach, etc.)?"*
   b. *"What types of things are you doing when you have these physical reactions?"*
   c. *"What are you thinking during these times? What are you feeling?"*
2. Group leaders explain that the mind tends to race and to switch its focus among the past, present, and the future, which intensifies stress. However, keeping your brain focused on the present moment can alleviate stressful reactions, but can be very difficult to do. Explain that during this group session students will be challenged to stay in the present moment.

3. Rather than discussing the activity any further, group leaders will demonstrate a challenging movement and then ask group members to try to mimic this movement. Any range of movements can be used based on group members' motor functioning. For example:
   a. Balancing on one leg
   b. Yoga poses
   c. A complex dance movement
   d. Complex hand gestures

   It is important that the movement is challenging enough for group members so that they must deeply focus on their movements.

4. As group members attempt to mimic the movement, encourage them to take deep breaths and focus solely on the movement of their bodies.

5. After group members have attempted a specific movement, facilitate discussion to help group members explore the thoughts and feelings they had while trying to complete each movement. Students may begin recognizing that in order to complete the complex movements, they had to focus mind on body (and the present moment) and were unable to focus on any other thoughts.

6. Group members are then encouraged to identify other movements that they can use to focus their minds and calm their stress symptoms (e.g., dancing, swimming, martial arts, yoga, etc.). Invite group members to choose an activity to test out on their own from those that are shared in the group.

Suggested Modifications (for Special Needs Populations): This activity could be modified for students with all types of motor abilities by changing the movement types used in the session.

Evaluation Plan: Future group sessions could be conducted in which students share different movements (or physical activities) they have been using to alleviate stress symptoms. This would provide a tool for assessing student levels of stress-management development.

OFFICE BASKETBALL: TALK AND PLAY

Elizabeth Crawford and Jake J. Protivnak

This intervention is typically used as an introduction activity to build rapport with a student who is new to the school counselor. This intervention may be beneficial with a student who enjoys kinesthetic activity and may show resistance to a formal dialogue of questioning. Based on the client's responses, the counselor can determine what issues are important to discuss with the student (e.g., goals, social relationships, fears, attitudes). This general information about a student can be used as groundwork for later counseling sessions. The intervention can last anywhere from one to three counseling sessions. It is also able to be applied in a group setting to get to know members better.

Modality: Movement

ASCA National Model Domain: Personal/Social

Deliver via: Individual sessions

Age Level: Elementary, middle school

Indications: The frustration level of students can vary based on their ability to verbalize their answers or to shoot the basketball, thus this intervention can be highly diagnostic.

Materials: Trash can (or other type of large basket, or Nerf-type mini-basketball hoop), appropriate-sized "bouncy" ball, questions, whiteboard or paper and pencil to keep track of points.

Preparation: Set up the room prior to the student arriving in the office. The school counselor should generate a number of questions to ask the student and write them on small slips of paper and place them in an envelope. Place the trashcan (or other type of large basket) in one corner of the room.

Instructions:
1. The school counselor explains the activity to the student and asks for participation.
2. The school counselor pulls a question out of an envelope and reads it to the student.
   Sample discussion questions include:
   a. *"Who is your hero and why?"*
   b. *"Describe your family to me."*
   c. *"When are you the happiest?"*
   d. *"When are you the saddest?"*
   e. *"Who do you feel the closest to in your family?"*
   f. *"Describe some of your friends to me. What do you like to do with them?"*
   g. *"What is your favorite place to visit?"*
   h. *"What is your favorite food? What is your least favorite food?"*
   i. *"What is your favorite subject in school? Which subject is your least favorite?"*
   j. *"What job/career do you want to have when you grow up?"*
   k. *"What is something that worries you?"*
   l. *"How do you perform in school?"*
   m. *"What are the three words that describe you best?"*
   n. *"What do you like to do for fun?"*
   o. *"What is your favorite color and why?"*
   p. *"What is something that you do very well?"*

Each school counselor can generate his or her own list of questions based on the grade level of the student and his or her own perspective on how to direct the conversation.

3. The student answers the question, and the counselor can probe further if appropriate.

4. After answering, the student bounces or throws the ball into the trashcan. The student keeps track of the points. He or she gets one point for answering the question and another point if he or she makes the basket.

5. The counselor then answers the question after the student and repeats the process. The student continues to keep track of the points. (If the student is making all of the baskets, ask the student to move back a step from the basket each time he or she answers a question.)

6. The activity can be made more challenging by having the student shoot the ball over objects in the office.

7. At the end of the activity, discuss the activity with the student, asking what information he or she enjoyed sharing, what was difficult to share, and so on.

Suggested Modifications (for Special Needs Populations): It may be difficult for some students to verbally express themselves. These students can draw or write out answers to questions. In addition, some students may not possess the coordination to shoot the basketball. This activity can be modified by moving the student closer to the basket.

Evaluation Plan: An evaluation at the end of the activity could be a self-report from the student (when processing the activity with the student). Ask the student what he or she learned in the session and what he or she perceived the purpose to be.

POP GOES THE FEELING

Barb Wilson

In this activity, students process emotions through the act of inflating and popping balloons. This activity involves several physical actions; therefore, it is considered a "movement" activity. There are several adaptations to this activity, which can be modified to meet the needs of your student(s), as described below.

Modality: Music/Movement/Dance

ASCA National Model Domain: Academic, Career, Personal/Social

Deliver via: Small group, individual

Age Level: 3rd through 12th grade

Indications: This activity can be modified to meet the needs of nearly any group or individual. Some examples of presenting concerns appropriate for this group are physical aggression, anxiety, anger/hurt, bullying, friendship, social skills, career exploration, test preparation, academic support, and changing families.

Materials: Balloons of various colors and sizes, markers, pens, pencils, small pieces of paper.

Preparation: Depending on the activity, the school counselor may want to pre-write words on the papers. The counselor may also need to inflate a few balloons prior to the activity to assist students with special needs.

Instructions: The following directions are for an anger-management group or an individual with anger-management concerns. The activity can be modified according to the needs of your group or individual. Additionally, the school counselor may choose to write words directly on the balloon rather than on the pieces of paper. Modifications are listed in the directions.

1. Explain the activity to the student(s). Say, *"We will be talking about the things that make us angry. Feeling angry is a normal response in many situations, but it is important to understand what triggers this feeling. By understanding what upsets us, we can learn how to handle the situation early and more appropriately."*
2. Make the balloons and writing materials available (paper optional).
3. Ask the student(s) to think about what makes him or her upset (stressors). Offer some possible answers (i.e., getting in trouble, siblings). Ask the student(s) to write these answers either directly on the balloons or on small pieces of paper.
4. Inflate the balloons. If you have opted to use the small pieces of paper, place one piece of paper inside each balloon prior to inflating the balloon.
5. Ask the student to think about which of the responses is most upsetting. Then, have the student pop that balloon (use a pencil point, grab it with hands, or sit on it). Monitor for any safety concerns. If you have opted for the pieces of paper, ask the student(s) to select a balloon to pop, then read that piece of paper.
6. After each balloon is popped, discuss the word on or in that balloon. Help the student process what that stressor means to him or her, what typically happens during these times, and talk about healthy and safe responses to the stressor. For example, if the student selects a "bad grades" balloon, begin by defining "bad grade." Then, talk about how often this happens and in which class(es). Ask the student what has typically been his or her response during these moments (i.e., yell at teacher, shut down, self-harm). Discuss alternative, healthier, and/or appropriate responses.
7. If time permits, pop more than one balloon. Balloons can be saved for the next session.

Suggested Modifications (for Special Needs Populations): The school counselor may need to inflate the balloons for students with asthma or other breathing concerns. For students with safety concerns, pop the balloons through passive measures (i.e., sitting on the balloon).

Evaluation Plan: The included pre-/postassessment that follows may be used as a paper assessment or as a guide for discussion(s). Please modify to meet the needs of your student(s) and his or her presenting concerns.

1. On a scale of 1 to 5, where 1 is "extremely relaxed" and 5 is "extremely stressed," how would you rate your feelings right now?
2. Please name at least one feeling word.
3. Please describe at least one appropriate response to feeling angry.

SCRAMBLED FEELINGS

LaWanda Edwards and Sherrionda Heard-Crawford

Students will use this game to become aware of negative feelings and identify different ways to address the negative feelings.

Modality: Movement/Dance

ASCA National Model Domain: Personal/Social

Deliver via: Classroom guidance or group counseling

Age Groups: Middle and high school

Indications: Poor behavior, conflicts with others

Materials: Feeling cards, room large enough to play game, tape for index cards, one die for each playing board, and carpet/rug to serve as the game board. Due to the space needed for each game, plan to have only one pair of students playing at one time. If gym space is available, you can have more pairs playing, but you will need to prepare one set of 24 cards per pair and have one rug per set of cards.

Preparation: Write 12 words on two sets of index cards; when you finish you will have 24 cards. Example words include (1) Mad, (2) Embarrassed, (3) Sad, (4) Ashamed, (5) Confused, (6) Afraid, (7) Shy, (8) Tired, (9) Frustrated, (10) Unsure, (11) Powerless, and (12) Annoyed. Cards will last longer if you laminate them before playing the game.

You will be making four columns and six rows with the cards on the rug. Place the cards approximately 1 foot apart and tape them to the rug. Put the first 12 cards on the right side of the rug and then place the other 12 cards on the left side. The cards do not have to be in a particular order.

Instructions:

1. Opening—Begin the lesson by having a discussion about feelings and what happened to the students in the past that made them have these feelings. Discuss interactions with teachers, parents, friends, and so on, and how they

handle these feelings. After discussing situations and how they make them feel, identify ways that students should appropriately respond to these situations (e.g., being assertive, using "I" statements, using positive thinking, walking away, taking a break, taking deep breaths, asking for help, asking for clarity, etc.).

2. Tell students that they will be playing Scrambled Feelings and share the following directions.

   a. Choose a pair of students to play the game and choose a third student to act as "referee."

   b. The referee will roll the die for the players. The meaning of the numbers is as follows: 1 = move right arm, 2 = move right leg, 3 = move left arm, 4 = move left leg. If referee rolls 5 or 6, he or she should roll again. (You can also make up your own rules about the meaning of the die number.)

   c. Each player should start out with each foot on a different word.

   d. The referee will start the game by rolling a die and calling out which limb to move based on the roll.

   e. The team member on the game piece should move as directed by the referee to place a foot or hand on a feeling card on the rug.

   f. The referee reads the feeling on this card aloud, and the player is asked to share how he or she would address this negative feeling.

   g. The referee will be responsible for ensuring that each player identifies the feeling word and discusses how he or she would address this feeling.

   h. A player can only occupy one card with one limb. (The player cannot put a hand and a foot on the same card.)

   i. Players cannot share a card.

   j. When a player loses his or her balance or has his or her hand or foot slip off a card, the game ends and a new pair of students can begin the game.

3. To wrap-up the lesson, discuss the different negative feelings that were identified in the game and allow some of the students to identify ways that they would handle these feelings.

4. Complete "Ticket Out the Door" for evaluation.

Suggested Modifications (for Special Needs Populations): Counselors may partner special needs students with another student when playing the game; the referee should read the word on the cards for players.

Evaluation Plan: Use the following method to evaluate the activities' effectiveness:

Ticket Out the Door
Have students write down three different ways that they can handle negative feelings, or have one question with 5 to 10 multiple-choice answers and ask students to choose three of the answers to identify how they would handle negative

feelings. The counselor should then analyze the results and report how many students were able to identify at least three ways to handle negative feelings. (Example: 85% of the 200 sixth graders were able to identify three or more ways to handle negative feelings.)

STEPPING STONES

Jenny Wagstaff

Stepping Stones is an experiential exercise that is often used in challenge/rope course settings, but can be easily adapted to any indoor setting. Challenge/ropes course activities are often used in adventure-based counseling (ABC), which combines experiential activities with traditional methods of therapy. In particular, ABC is a natural fit in the group therapy setting because the combination of experiential learning activities (outdoor adventures and/or ropes course activities) with group-counseling practices fosters an environment in which participants receive immediate feedback about their behaviors, become more self-aware, and make changes as they see fit (Glass & Myers, 2001; Swank & Daire, 2010). Stepping Stones has emerged as an activity that stimulates insights around problem solving, strategy development, collaboration, teamwork, communication, mutual support, encouragement, and celebration.

Modality: Other—Experiential Counseling

ASCA National Model Domain: Personal/Social

Deliver via: Group counseling

Age Level: Middle or high school

Indications: Best used with groups focused on decision making, building self-esteem, taking personal responsibility, enhancing communication skills, and so on.

Materials: Carpet squares, manila file folders and/or bandanas, or similar square-shaped items. To determine the number of squares needed, count the number of participants and divide in half and add one. Example: 12 participants would equal 6 + 1, for a total of 7 squares. Also needed are two lengths of rope or tape to mark off opposite banks of the "pit of doom." The rope or tape needs to be 10 to 20 feet in length, depending on group size, and the distance from bank to bank should be between 25 and 40 feet depending on available space and group size.

Safety Considerations: If the stepping stones used are manila folders and the activity is being conducted on a cement or asphalt surface, caution the group to be careful as the paper may tear or slip when used.

This exercise has a very low injury risk factor and should be easy for most everyone to do. However, maintaining balance may be difficult for some participants so they should be encouraged to literally support each other during the exercise so no one is injured.

Special arrangements should be made for those who have a physical challenge, that is, those wearing a cast, in a wheelchair, and so on.

Instructions: The group needs to move across the "pit of doom" without anyone touching anything other than the resources provided (carpet squares, manila file folders, and/or bandanas, etc.) The pit of doom is full of people, places, and things that interfere with our ability to do our best. Themes could address boredom, peer pressure, emotions, communication, bullies, and so on.

The resources (carpet squares, bandanas, and/or manila file folders) represent the tools that are needed to successfully navigate the issue at hand (peer pressure, self-esteem, bullies, etc.) and must be utilized in accordance with the following rules:

1. Students can only move forward.
2. For the resource to function, someone must be touching it at all times. If a resource is ever untouched, it disappears.
3. The resources cannot slide/shuffle along the ground.

Before starting the exercise, ask the group to brainstorm and identify the resources necessary to successfully navigate the issue and explain that the carpet squares, bandanas, and/or manila file folders represent the resources they identified as a group. For example, if the group is addressing the issue of peer pressure, responses may be teachers, counselors, family members, friends, self-confidence, courage, belief, and so on. Remind the group that its task is to cross the pit of doom as an in-tact unit without falling in or losing any of the given resources.

Suggested Modifications (for Special Needs Populations): In general, this activity is appropriate for use with most groups who have the ability to function as a team. School counselors may need to modify the activity for those students who have a physical challenge, such as those wearing a cast, in a wheelchair, and so on.

Evaluation Plan: In line with Kolb's Experiential Learning Cycle (Kolb, 1984), it is critical to follow the model and process the experience as a group. The four processes that must be present include Concrete Experience (Feeling), Reflective Observation (Watching), Abstract Conceptualizations (Thinking), and Active Experimentation (Doing; please see http://www.simplypsychology. org/learning-kolb.html for an illustration of how this process has been conceptualized). For more information on this learning cycle, please see Kolb (1984). Debriefing or thinking and reflecting on the experience facilitates the learning cycle. The following are some debriefing questions that school counselors can ask at the end of the activity.

1. How do you think you did? Why?
2. How did it feel to fall into the pit of doom?
3. How did it feel to lose the resources that aid you in your journey?
4. What were your strengths and weaknesses?
5. What metaphors in relation to "doing our best" come to mind as a result of this activity?
6. What were the reasons for some of the penalties/consequences that occurred while doing the activity?
7. How do these consequences relate to the issue at hand?
8. What did you learn about yourself?
9. How does the experience you just had and what you learned from it relate to your personal journey?
10. While participating in this activity, I felt . . .
11. One thing I can change in my life to make it better would be . . .
12. What role did you play in the group?
13. Is this role consistent with how you typically behave in a group?

REFERENCES

Glass, J. S., & Myers, J. E. (2001). Combining the old and the new to help adolescents: Individual psychology and adventure-based counseling. *Journal of Mental Health Counseling 23*(2), 104–114.

Kolb, D. (1984). *Experiential learning: Experience as the source of learning and development.* Englewood Cliffs, NJ: Prentice Hall.

Swank, J. M., & Daire, A. P. (2010). Multiple family adventure-based therapy groups: An innovative integration of two approaches. *Family Journal: Counseling and Therapy for Couples and Families 18*(3), 241–247.

SHAKING MEDICINE: A GROUP INTERVENTION FOR AT-RISK YOUTH

Christine Abrahams

Shaking medicine is a healing dance that the Kalahari Bushmen use to dissolve psychological and interpersonal conflicts within their community. They cultivate the energy in their bodies and then shoot «arrows» to other tribe members by embracing and shaking them. This turns into a spontaneous movement for the individual and the group. Elements of these spontaneous movements are visible in present-day culture, such as davening among the Jews, and shaking among the St. Vincent shakers. The Quakers and Shakers used to shake until their communities put a stop to it because it looked to the larger community that this spontaneous movement was not inspired by their devotion to the divine, but rather to the devil. "Shaking" was also reintroduced to Japanese culture by Ikoko Osumi in the form of Seiki Jutsu, an individual practice.

Note: In order to use "Shaking Medicine" in a high school setting, I combined elements of Seiki Jutsu and the Bushmen's version. Because of my previous experience with using noncontact, noncompetitive martial arts, a form of choreographed movement to mitigate risk behaviors in adolescents, I wanted to use a similar population, but here I focus on spontaneous movement.

Expressive Art: Movement/Dance

ASCA National Model Domain: Personal/Social

Deliver via: Group

Age Level: High school (could be used with younger students)

Indications: This intervention is appropriate for at-risk youth, including those dealing with drug/alcohol use, divorced parents, discipline referrals, and low grade point average (GPA).

Materials: CD player or any device that can play music, African drumming CD, Internet access to show the students the Bushman dance (http://www.youtube .com/embed/YJdtsd_Cjro?rel=0 or http://www.youtube.com/watch?v=RWEQOG-VUsI&list=TLirtNq5Iy-vy2qijZR4aKpCvJ8hdRJtdx) and an example of Seiki Jutsu self-exercise, which is what the students will be doing: http://www.youtube .com/watch?v=J8GWHqa-Vu4. Explain that the woman demonstrating touches her eyes to let her body know that she will begin the Seiki practice. A good video of a Seiki Jutsu master activating Seiki in another is here: http://www.youtube. com/watch?v=QOJeaPA6MUU. These videos were not available at the time I ran these groups, but should be very helpful in teaching students what they are doing.

Preparation: Familiarize yourself with the movements of Seiki. You can get a good understanding of this through the Seiki self-exercise YouTube video noted above. Counselors should practice this themselves prior to using it with the group. Select between 8 and 10 students for the group and select those who display "at-risk" behaviors.

Instructions:
Meeting 1:
- Show and discuss the Kalahari Healing Dance and an example of Seiki Jutsu.
- Explain that the group will be using Seiki Jutsu with music.
- Explain that movement is helpful in getting students to de-stress and focus.
- Ask the group to try it by closing their eyes and letting the rhythm of the music move their bodies.
- Explain that one can simply move a finger or a toe or an eyebrow . . . encourage students to have fun with it. Have them do this for about 30 seconds to 1 minute.
- Work up to about 3 to 5 minutes as your group progresses.
- Tell them that you will start each group with this kind of movement.
- Proceed with the content/discussion for the type of group you are conducting.

The rest of the meetings will include time to move to music of your choice. You can also invite the students to bring in music that they think would be appropriate for Seiki Jutsu.

If the students are really comfortable with each other, and as the group progresses, you can suggest that they stand and move, and finally hold hands in a circle and move with the energy of the group.

Suggested Modifications (for Special Needs Populations): No modifications are necessary. All students move and on some level understand the value of it. Even if you have a person with paralysis, he or she can move parts of his or her face or head.

Evaluation Plan: I originally conducted my evaluation using two experimental groups and two control groups. The experimental groups received the "shaking" intervention and the control groups did not. I did a pre- and posttest using the Multi-Dimensional Self-Concept Scale (MDSCS) to measure the students' self-esteem and also look at discipline referrals. In my "shaking" groups, the students improved on the self-esteem scale, and although they still had discipline referrals, they had many fewer than my other two "at-risk" groups.

I constructed a School Connectedness Questionnaire and the results showed that the "shaking" group overall felt more connected to the school after the conclusion of the group.

Additionally, I looked at the GPAs of both groups, and the students in the "shaking" groups had a slight increase in their GPAs.

You can design an evaluation as I did or simply use some pre- and postassessments that you construct to measure what you are trying to achieve with these students.

STRIKE A POSE: EXPRESSING EMOTIONS THROUGH BODY POSTURES

Diane M. Dryja

The purpose of this activity is to therapeutically promote self-awareness, understanding of communication through body language, and ownership of feelings as well as gaining empathy toward what others may be feeling in different situations. This activity can be introduced in a variety of ways. It can be introduced using bibliotherapy and discussing feelings through appropriate children's literature. Say, for example, "What was Red Riding Hood feeling when. . . . Show me what that feeling would look like." It also may be introduced more directly. For instance, by asking the student, "If you couldn't use words or facial expressions and your body was the only tool you had to tell me, show me a pose of what anger—or fear, or sadness, or happiness—looks like." Another option is to use situational cards and ask the student to show what one might feel like if put into this situation (use situational cards).

Modality: Movement/Mind–Body/Physical Expression of Feelings

ASCA National Model Domain: Personal/Social

Deliver Via: Individual, small group, classroom guidance

Age Level: Elementary, middle, and high school

Indications: This activity is appropriate for students presenting with self-esteem issues, difficulty naming and identifying emotions, difficult peer relationships, and sibling rivalry concerns.

Materials: Appropriate grade-level literature, questions, or situational cards; a poster, handout, or short video clip of basic yoga postures could be used to help students think about ways they can move or position their bodies to express emotion.

Preparation: Preparation only involves assembling the necessary materials for the intervention.

Instructions:

1. After introducing students to basic poses, set the stage by stating the objectives for the activity: Self-awareness, communication through body language, understanding of students' own feelings and the feelings of others. Tap into prior knowledge by asking students what they already know about body language. State to the class that they will be able to better understand the actions and feelings of themselves and others through this awareness activity.

2. Model the activity for the class. As an example, you might say: *"Bobby borrowed his sister's skate board without asking permission. He broke the board and did not tell his sister that he broke it. The sister discovered the board."* Then ask a student to demonstrate a pose to express what Bobby's sister is feeling and then a pose to show how Bobby is feeling. The class holds up their cards to share how they think each is feeling. The class then discusses how the body language expressed the feelings and how the body language communicated a message to the other person.

3. Begin the activity by inviting a student to pick a story or an activity card. Ask a student to volunteer to be the poser. Have the students hold up their cards. The poser can then pick someone with the correct answer to express why they picked the feeling. Then have the poser pick someone who had a different feeling card and ask that student to express why he or she picked that emotion.

4. Play several rounds to make sure each student participates in some manner.

5. Close the lesson: Restate the objective. Lead a discussion about self-esteem, awareness, and empathy toward others as it relates to the lesson activities. Ask students if they have any questions or comments.

Suggested Modifications (for Special Needs Populations): Depending on the population, this could be adapted to be completely teacher directed, if necessary. Adaptations could also be made for physical limitations; for example, playing the game seated using the upper body only. A suggested small-group modification: Introduce as a charades-type game in which others in the group have to guess the emotion.

Evaluation Plan: The goals of this activity include raising self-awareness of one's own emotions as well as identifying the emotions that others are experiencing and expressing. This step can be achieved by having students demonstrate understanding of what they have learned in a variety of ways. Depending on the grade level, students may be asked to give verbal feedback; demonstrate an emotion by striking a pose; or write about a time when they misread someone's emotions or had some other type of miscommunication experience, or a time when they experienced clear open communication with someone.

V ❖ Expressive Writing/Poetry

11 ❖ Narrative/Expressive Writing Interventions in the Academic Domain

COLOR-CODED ELEMENTS

Edward F. Hudspeth and Glenda L. Hyer

*T*his intervention is designed to support the learning process of students of any age. This may be used with younger students having difficulty learning sentence structure or older students with developmental and learning disabilities. Being supportive of student learning is not only important to improving their grades, but also because it boosts their self-esteem. The intervention may be used with individuals, groups, or as a part of classroom guidance. With younger students or those having learning difficulties, the counselor may begin by assessing whether students know the basic parts of a sentence (i.e., subjects, verbs, adjectives, adverbs, etc.). Other sentence elements (e.g., pronouns, articles, direct and indirect objects, modifiers, etc.) may be added as students progress. Students may work individually or in dyads when doing this as a group or with classroom guidance.

Modality: Writing/Narrative, Visual Arts

ASCA National Model Domain: Academic or Personal/Social

Deliver via: Individual, group, or classroom guidance

Age Level: Elementary, middle, or high school (This may be utilized with any age group. Modify the intervention and words utilized to align with the students' developmental level, age, or learning ability.)

Indications: This may be used as a routine supportive measure for those having difficulty with sentence elements and structure. Though this intervention is primarily for educational purposes, it is easily adapted for personal/social issues. It is frequently used with students who will not communicate (e.g., selective mutism), have difficulty communicating (e.g., expressive language disorder), or are simply shy or resistant. By using previously created element cards, students are able to communicate and express themselves without speaking.

Materials: Coloring pencils, crayons, or markers; colored cardstock paper.

Preparation: Have art media out and available to all students. Prior to beginning, take sheets of cardstock paper (8.5 × 11) and cut each into four equal pieces. Also, have sheets of cardstock with examples of subjects on one color of paper, verbs on another, and so on, depending on the elements you are covering. This provides a color-coded, master list or summary of each sentence element. Make sure you have stacks of the smaller cards, equal in number and color, as to the color and number of elements presented on the master lists. Also, make sure that if your master list has 10 words you also have 10 smaller cards. For example, if you are using two master lists with subjects on green cardstock and verbs on red cardstock, make sure you also provide a stack of smaller green and red cardstock.

Instructions: Introduce the activity by saying, *"When you speak or write or read a sentence, do you know the parts of the sentence?"* Show/write an example of a simple sentence: "Cats drink cold milk." Identify the elements by pointing to each. Emphasize the basic order of sentence elements.

Intervention: The intervention begins by saying, *"A good way to remember each part of a sentence is to give it a color. Let's say subjects are green, verbs are red, adjectives are blue, and objects are yellow. If we can remember the color, we can remember the part. In front of you are colored sheets with the parts we've just mentioned."* Use the invitation/question, *"So, green is a _____, red is a _____, blue is an _____, and yellow is an _____."*

Using the words (emphasize *subject*) on the green sheet, put one *subject* on each of the smaller green cards. Repeat this for each word and then each sentence element utilized.

Next, repeat the invitation/question, *"So, green is a _____, red is a _____, blue is an _____, and yellow is an _____."*

Intervention Application: To apply this intervention, the counselor might say, *"I bet we can take our cards and make sentences. We may even be able to tell a story."* Invite students to create simple sentences. They may construct several sentences to tell a story. Offer help as needed. This intervention may be done on a weekly basis or more frequently, in an intensive format, as learning difficulties and the need for help are identified.

Suggested Modifications (for Special Needs Populations): The words utilized and number of sentence elements may need to be modified for different ages/ developmental levels. This intervention is particularly useful with younger learners, those beginning to have difficulties, and those with learning/developmental disabilities. The counselor may choose to start with more or fewer elements. The number of elements, to begin with, may be determined by the age, developmental level, and/or learning ability/need of each of the students involved.

Evaluation Plan: To evaluate the effectiveness of this intervention, you may use the attached survey as a pre- and postassessment. The primary goal of the intervention is to support learning of sentence elements and structure.

Students will complete this assessment as a pre- and postassessment of their understanding of the concepts addressed during the intervention. Questions 1 and 2 are appropriate for both pre- and postassessment; however, question 3 is solely for postassessment. The assessment may also indicate learning of sentence elements. For younger students, this may be done verbally.

1. What are some parts of a sentence?
   (a)
   (b)
   (c)
   (d)
2. What is the basic order of the parts of a sentence? Below, match the number with the word.
   1 Adjective
   2 Subject
   3 Object
   4 Verb
3. What color did we give?
   (a) Subjects _____
   (b) Verbs _____
   (c) Adjectives _____
   (d) Objects _____

IMAGINING A FUTURE ME

Erin N. Friedman and Benjamin P. Friedman

Students adopt identities, including those that relate to their future selves, at a relatively early age (Oyserman, 2001, 2013; Oyserman, Elmore, & Smith, 2012; Oyserman & James 2011). In a school setting this could involve imagining a future self who is a math whiz. On the other hand, future identities are not always positive. For instance, students can see themselves as a "stupid" student who has no chance at being successful in school. Counselors need to help students with negative future identities to identify the necessary steps to meet their goals to achieve self-identified positive outcomes in their lives. This process should include the development of specific strategies, exploring students' strengths, and making plans so that students have resources when difficulties occur; this is particularly critical for students who are from a low socioeconomic background (Oyserman, 2013; Oyserman, Johnson, & James, 2011). This activity is centered on improving students' views and feelings about their academic ability and giving them concrete strategies to use to achieve their academic goals. This activity can be used independently or in concert with the other activities mentioned below that will guide students through a process of understanding themselves as learners and uncovering any deep-seated beliefs they hold about themselves. Imagining a Future Me follows narrative therapy's outline for scaffolding information with children, starting with identifying the problem and moving to developing a plan of action and a new image of themselves (Ramey, Tarulli, Frijeters, & Fisher, 2009). This activity, and the related activities listed below, provide children an opportunity to examine how they view themselves and the school environment before transitioning into creative writing exercises that allow students to edit their "story" and the beliefs they hold about themselves as learners. This can facilitate an increased sense of agency, improved self-concept, and self-esteem by targeting the barriers preventing students from achieving their goals (Wilson, 2011). Counselors will be active in the process of helping students reflect on their experiences through both the provided process questions as well as by using creative writing as a means to get students to explore academic themes and attributes in their own lives. This activity can be used with psychoeducational groups or with students on an individual basis.

Modality: Creative Writing

ASCA National Model Domain: Academic and Personal/Social

Deliver via: Psychoeducational group (approximately six to eight students) or modified for individual counseling

Age Level: Middle school or early high school

Indications: Building self-esteem and academic self-concept through creative writing group reflection. Imagining a Future Me would work well in concert with Lyrics and My Life (see Chapter 5) and My (Gritty) Collage (later in this chapter) activities.

Materials: Folders for each student to place projects in spanning the entirety of the activity. Computer access, coloring and writing utensils, paper, and the student's folder containing his or her projects from previous lessons are needed for this activity.

Preparation: Students should be selected for this group because they have a diminished self-concept of themselves as learners. It is important that the interventions used are related to the same domain that the student is struggling with (Oyserman, Terry, & Bybee, 2002); therefore, activities have been shaped to target this particular population and domain.

Instructions: The activity is broken into different phases, with increasing levels of depth that the counselor can use with students to further explore their academic self-concept, self-esteem, and self-efficacy. Each phase of Imagining a Future Me will center on students writing their own stories and editing them to become the students they want to be through a scaffolded process of creative writing and group processing. Counselors should briefly reference related activities or conversations they have had with the student(s) related to self-concept prior to students working on the current activity; this will allow students to begin working the themes/revelations from previous weeks into their current work.

1. First-Phase Instructions: Begin the process of having students develop a well-established story about themselves, within an academic context, through creative writing. Help students identify which type of writing they wish to do. Writing should focus on a story students identify with specifically as students. Students may use any form of writing he or she is interested in (creative writing, poetry, graphic novel, theatrical play, writing their own song). The style of writing is flexible; the only requirement of this activity is that students develop a story arc explaining how they have encountered obstacles in the school or as a learner. This phase should focus on having the student write about who he or she is as a student and learner. The counselor can title the project, "[Student Name]: A _____ Learner," or a different general but applicable title. The counselor can help students map out the story of themselves as students, as they encounter an obstacle, and how they feel about and react to that obstacle (a story arc of themselves as a student or learner) through the provided writing prompt. A graphic organizer, which you can usually obtain through an instructional or curriculum coach in your school, may help students who are struggling with organizing their thinking and developing a story arc. Students should be given the opportunity to present this activity within the group.

■ **Writing Prompt:** Create a story in a school setting with you as the central character. What obstacles do you encounter during your day? How do you react to them? How do you feel about yourself in these situations?

First-Phase Process Questions: Ask, *"What was it like examining your story of a difficult experience in school from start to finish? What parts did you want to change the most? What are some good things you noticed in your storyline?"* For more in-depth exploration of academic self-concept themes, counselors can say: *"Think about who you would be if you could be anyone. What is stopping you? What can you do to change that?"*

2. Second Phase: In the second phase students will identify strategies they can use to overcome their obstacles in school with the support of the counselor and finish the writing activity. This will involve creatively ending their story with the successful achievement of the students' hopes and goals. New strategies can be self-identified or prompted by the counselor, who will challenge students to find ways to change their stories as they think about who they can become. Counselors should help develop students' sense of agency by having students think about their strengths and how they can incorporate them into their story. Students should be able to reflect on what these changes will allow them to accomplish. This activity will help build students' self-esteem by focusing on their strengths while helping them develop a sense of empowerment through the identification of concrete strategies they can use to accomplish their objectives.

Second-Phase Instructions: Counselors will continue the writing activity that students worked on during Phase 1, but give students individual feedback by asking how the story could be different. Make small challenges for them to try to incorporate into the story as well as encourage them to identify strategies of their own that they can try. The counselor should provide some feedback but also leave space for the students to make their own discoveries. Students may need help identifying their strengths and how they can incorporate that into strategies to overcome their barriers. Ask students to include a moment in the story when the changes they've made and the results of those changes are evident. Students should finish this phase with an in-depth concept of how they will achieve who they want to become with specific strategies to make that change happen.

▪ **Writing Prompt:** If you could be any type of student, in any class, what type would you want to be? Put yourself in that position and imagine what it would look like and feel like. Now, think about your current experience in the classroom. What is preventing you from getting to where you want to be? How could you overcome these obstacles?

Second-Phase Process Questions: Ask the students: *"What are some of your strengths? How have those strengths helped you? What are some changes you are excited about making?"*

Suggested Modifications (for Special Needs Populations): School counselors may modify their language to meet students' developmental level. Students with writing difficulties may be assisted by making lists of hopes and fears in a graphic organizer that can then be written about in story format. Additionally, students unable to write for themselves can dictate their story to a scribe (a trusted group mate or adult). If students are English Language Learners (ELL), allow them to complete the activities in the language in which they are most comfortable. The goal of the activity is to get students to explore their feelings about themselves so language is not a main concern. If time is available, the counselor could periodically check in with students to see how they are doing in the journey to become their ideal student. All activities can be shaped to do with individual students if that is more applicable to a particular student's needs.

Evaluation Plan: To evaluate the effectiveness of this intervention, school counselors may revisit this activity in the future. Students can assess for themselves whether they were able to achieve any of the hopes they had and avoid any of their fears. This can also take place through discussion with the counselor.

REFERENCES

Oyserman, D. (2013). Not just any path: Implications of identity-based motivation for disparities in school outcomes. *Economics of Education Review, 33,* 179–190.

Oyserman, D., Elmore, K., & Smith, G. (2012). Self, self-concept, and identity. In M. Leary & J. Tangney (Eds.), *Handbook of self and identity* (2nd ed., pp. 69–104). New York, NY: Guilford Press.

Oyserman, D., & James, L. (2011). Possible identities. In S. Schwartz, K. Luyckx, & V. Vignoles (Eds.), *Handbook of identity theory and research* (pp. 117–145). New York, NY: Springer-Verlag.

Oyserman, D., Johnson, E., & James, L. (2011). See the destination but not the path: Effects of socioeconomic disadvantage on school-focused possible self content and linked behavioral strategies. *Self and Identity*, *10*, 474–492.

Oyserman, D., Terry, K., & Bybee, D. (2002). A possible selves intervention to enhance school involvement. *Journal of Adolescence*, *25*, 313–326.

Ramey, H. L., Tarulli, D., Frijters, J. C., & Fisher, L. (2009). A sequential analysis of externalizing in narrative therapy with children. *Contemporary Family Therapy*, *31*, 262–279.

Wilson, T. D. (2011). *Redirect: The surprising new science of psychological change.* New York, NY: Little, Brown.

MY (GRITTY) COLLAGE

Erin N. Friedman and Benjamin P. Friedman

Students will create a combination collage and creative writing piece that will help them explore both their thoughts and feelings toward the obstacles they experience in school. They will then generate potential strategies for dealing with difficult experiences and brainstorm what outcomes might occur depending on their choices.

Modality: Creative Writing and Collage

ASCA National Model Domain: Academic and Personal/Social

Deliver via: Psychoeducational group (approximately six to eight students) or modified for individual counseling

Age Level: Middle school or early high school

Indications: Building self-esteem and academic self-concept through creative writing group reflection. My (Gritty) Collage would work well in concert with Imagining a Future Me (previous activity, this chapter) and Lyrics and My Life (see Chapter 5).

Materials: Bring in student-appropriate magazines or catalogs that can be cut up, poster board, glue, scissors and writing utensils.

Instructions: Students will cut out pictures from magazines or catalogs, or create a multipicture collage using their own illustrations, showing how they feel and how they have dealt with difficult experiences or obstacles in schools. Students should create images that reflect how they typically overcome their chosen obstacle (helpful or unhelpful strategies addressing things such as feelings about school, getting a poor grade on an assignment, etc.) as well as images of other ways they could approach coping with or overcoming that obstacle. Children should incorporate writing into this activity through speech bubbles, brief reflections, or a feature story or interview (such as those found in magazines). This activity can be especially effective for students who are not strong writers and those who enjoy expressing themselves creatively. Students should be given the opportunity to share their collages in a small-group setting.

Process Questions: Ask: *"What are some of the new strategies you explored? What did it feel like trying to make these changes? Did the changes feel possible?"*

Suggested Modifications: Counselors in schools with computer access for students may wish to use a photo-editing program (e.g., Preview, Adobe Photoshop) and images from the Internet instead of physical magazines for this activity. Search-engine preferences should then be changed to "Safe Search" options so that only appropriate images are given for students' search queries.

Evaluation Plan: "Grit" indicates persistence through difficulty over months and years to achieve one's goals (Duckworth, Peterson, Matthews, & Kelly, 2007). Since this process plays out over time and through many difficulties, reviewing the collages can be a source for reflection as well as hope. Students may revisit the collages as often as needed, adding new pages to represent new and important events.

REFERENCES

See "Imagining a Future Me" activity in this chapter for other references.

Duckworth, A. L., Peterson, C., Matthews, M. D., & Kelly, D. R. (2007). Grit: Perseverance and passion for long-term goals. *Journal of Personality and Social Psychology, 92*(6), 1087–1101.

THE PLAYBOOK

Amanda N. Byrd-Desnoyers

*T*his activity is designed to be used in individual counseling to help students set goals and make decisions. The counselor should ensure the student is interested in sports before proceeding, as this activity can be modified to reflect other team sports that use playbooks (basketball, soccer, rugby, etc.). The counselor should start the sessions on The Playbook by discussing decision making and goal setting. The football playbook will provide a tangible analogy for students to use to set a goal and create an action plan for achieving it.

Modality: Expressive Writing

ASCA National Model Domain: Academic, Personal/Social

Deliver via: Individual

Age Level: Middle or high school (modify the processing questions to align with students' developmental level)

Indications: Personal responsibility, decision making, academic concerns, goal setting

Materials: Dry erase board, markers (two colors), folder or notebook for student, demonstration playbook, football field diagram.

Preparation:

Football Knowledge

This activity requires some basic understanding of football and football play-books. There are great resources on the web that explain both. The key concept in this metaphor and related activity is that the touchdown is the end goal. The offensive is looking to make the goal and the defensive is trying to block it. In a football playbook, shapes represent plays that lead to the score, or block of the score (Figure 11.1). For the purpose of this activity, the playbook will focus on offensive or goal-making plays and should not become overly complicated.

Demonstration Playbook

Prepare a diagram of a football field on either a felt board or a dry erase board. If you have access to the Internet, you can use www .footballplaybookonline.com to create custom images. You can also print out copies of Figure 11.2.

Instructions:

1. Opening:

   A. Introduce the concept of the football playbook.

      a. Ask: *"When you get ready for a football game and for football practice, what do you do?"*

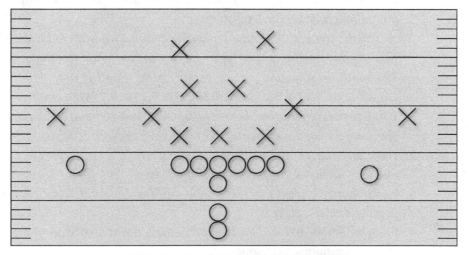

FIGURE 11.1 Football playbook basic design.

Source: www.footballplaybookonline.com

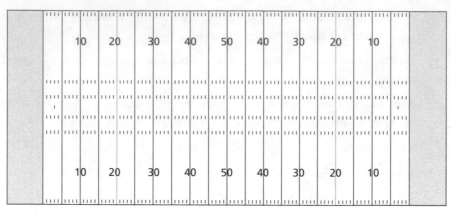

FIGURE 11.2 Blank football template.

Source: li16-138.members.linode.com/sportsdiagrams/images/gridiron-notes.pdf

      b. *"How does Coach know what to do?"*

      c. *"Do you have a set of instructions to follow through?"*

   B. Introduce the playbook.

      a. Tell the student: *"The playbook is the guide to help you make decisions on the field. What is the purpose of these decisions to achieve the goal of winning the game?"*

      b. *"When you are not playing football and you have to make decisions, what do you do? What plans do you have for achieving your goals?"*

2. Link the concept of decision making to football and the playbook.

   a. Ask: *"How can we take football and help use it to accomplish personal goals?"*

   b. *"Is there only one step that leads to the goal, or like in football are there several plays leading up to accomplishing it?"*

3. Review decision making and goal setting.

4. Link a realistic example to football and the playbook. An example is *Make a passing grade on an English test.*

   Tell the student: *"In these types of decisions, we want to be the offensive, running and making plays. We are trying to score. You are the quarterback. The touchdown means a C or better on the English test. What plays are we going to run? What is the defense going to do? What problems are you going to encounter along the way? How are you going to make the goal? Do you have a team or supports? Will you have to do a 'Hail Mary'?"*

5. Have the student create his or her own play for a small goal (e.g., *passing one test; no in-school suspensions for 1 week*).

6. Each offensive player is one of the student's supports (teachers, internet, parents, friends, etc.).

7. Each defensive player is a barrier to the student's success (time management, no supplies, no supports, etc.).

8. Follow up on the small goal progress and celebrate the goal (score).

9. Have the student plan incrementally larger goals and see how many tasks, like football, are a series of plays to get the score.

Suggested Modifications (for Special Needs Populations): School counselors may need to modify the language of the descriptions and the detail included in the goal planning based on students' developmental needs. This activity is geared toward student athletes and sports enthusiasts. Students may need more descriptive examples than "Xs" and "Os" depicted in an actual sports playbook. A school counselor may need to use pictures of the different players to make the example more concrete and less abstract.

Evaluation Plan: Question and Answer
1. What was your goal and did you achieve it?
2. What helped you achieve your goal? What kept you from achieving your goal?
3. What did you learn about goal setting? Decision making? Yourself?
4. If you were going to try to accomplish this goal again, what would you do differently? What would you not change about how you attempted to achieve your goal?
5. What do you think you've learned from this activity that can be applied in the future?

Additional Resources:
- http://football.about.com/cs/football101/a/bl_football101.htm
- http://www.ehow.com/how_6589328_understand-football-playbooks.html
- http://www.aolnews.com/2011/02/24/method-men-how-nfl-players-memorize-dizzying-playbooks/
- http://www.cyber-shack.net/cybercoach/htm/PDF/cc_o_i02.pdf
- http://www.nfl.com/rulebook/beginnersguidetofootball

REFERENCE

National Football League. (n.d.) *Rulebook: A beginner's guide to football.* Retrieved from http://www.nfl.com/rulebook/beginnersguidetofootball

12 Narrative/Expressive Writing Interventions in the Career Domain

CAREER STORY HAIKU

Katherine M. Hermann and Lauren R. Hasha

The Career Story Haiku is an opportunity for an individual or a small group of students to investigate future career paths using expressive writing. The activity enables students to explore and reflect on career opportunities, discover strengths and interests, and practice creative writing skills.

Modality: Poetry/Narrative/Expressive Writing

ASCA National Model Domain: Career

Deliver via: Group or individual counseling

Age Level: Middle or high school

Indications: This activity provides an opportunity for students to discover their talents and explore interests. Due to negative home environments, low self-confidence, or poor social skills, many adolescents find it challenging to recognize their individual strengths and how these strengths can be used to achieve long-term goals. By completing this task and collaborating with peers, students are able to experience feelings of success and reflect on their personal abilities. This activity can also help indicate those students who may need encouragement in cultivating career ideas and aspirations. It is a particularly good fit for students who are interested in creative writing.

Materials: Paper, pen/pencil, other art supplies (optional).

Preparation: Before implementing this activity, you may find it helpful to research haiku. In addition to being able to explain the structure and provide examples, having an understanding of the history of haiku may aid the counselor in engaging students and facilitating the activity. A good resource is found at http://www.poets.org/poetsorg/text/poetic-form-haiku.

Instructions:

1. Begin the activity with an exploration of career goals and aspirations. Ask students to consider things they currently enjoy, such as school subjects, extracurricular activities, and hobbies. After this reflection, ask students to develop a list of potential future careers. Questions such as the following may help explore both familiar and new possibilities:

   a. *"What are some of your interests/passions?"*

   b. *"What are some things at which you feel you excel?"*

   c. *"What is a career that includes these interests and/or strengths?"*

   d. *"Are there any other jobs that currently appeal to you?"*

   e. *"When was the first time you considered this career(s)?"*

   f. *"Is this your first career idea, or have you had others before? If so, what were they?"*

2. After students have chosen their possible career(s), invite them to share with the counselor and/or group. This gives them the opportunity to contribute ideas and further explore hopes and dreams in a supportive environment.

3. Next, provide students with an explanation of haiku as a form of Japanese poetry. Describe the general structure: a short poem comprised of seventeen syllables written in three lines. Traditionally, the first and last lines contain five syllables, while the second line has seven syllables. It may also be helpful to explain a syllable, as well as show examples of haiku, such as the following:

   I will be a nurse
   When I help others feel well
   I feel better too

   Teaching is my goal
   Helping people grow and learn
   People just like me

4. Once students have a clear understanding of haiku, ask them to create their own career haiku. They can write one haiku on multiple career goals, or they can write more than one haiku. Encourage them to include the following, in any order:

   a. One line describing and/or naming the career.

   b. One line describing what about the career is of interest to them or why they are passionate about the career.

   c. One line on their goal(s) regarding the career or what they will need to do to be successful in this career.

5. Invite students to share their haiku poems with the counselor and/or group.

6. As students share their poems, process the experience of reflecting on career goals, creating a haiku, and sharing with the counselor and/or group. Facilitators may find it helpful to ask questions such as:

a. *"What made you choose this career instead of another?"*
b. *"What strengths and/or talents did you discover about yourself through this activity?"*
c. *"How were you able to implement your strengths, interests, and talents into your career choice?"*

Suggested Modifications (for Special Needs Populations): If time permits, students could be asked to draw and/or paint a picture that corresponds with their haiku. This modification may also be used as an alternative if a student is intimidated by the process or unable to write a haiku. As some students may require additional guidance and direction, it is important for the counselor to be attentive to the age, ability, and interest of the students.

Evaluation Plan: To evaluate the effectiveness of this activity, facilitators may find it helpful to ask participants the following questions:

1. Did this activity help develop new career possibilities or to further investigate previously considered career choices?
2. Did you discover a talent of which you were formerly unaware?
3. Were you able to creatively explore current interests and strengths and utilize those to develop a future career plan?

13 Narrative/Expressive Writing Interventions in the Personal/Social Domain

BLUE GOODBYE

Barb Wilson

Termination is an important event when working with small groups, but is often overlooked in the planning and disbanding of groups. Bibliotherapy is a creative arts technique that can be employed by the counselor during the termination phase. The use of bibliotherapy can provide clients with opportunities to explore alternative feelings, perspectives, and actions. Bibliotherapy also facilitates a greater understanding of the world overall. This activity utilizes bibliotherapy to end a series of group sessions through the use of a story about moving on but leaving a piece of you behind.

Modality: Bibliotherapy, Visual Arts

ASCA National Model Domain: Personal/Social

Deliver via: Classroom guidance, small group

Age level: Elementary, middle, high school

Indications: When used as a classroom-guidance activity, this activity is best used when discussing transitions (i.e., graduation). This activity is appropriate for any small group as a part of the termination phase.

Materials: The book *One Small Blue Bead* by Byrd Baylor and Ronald Himler, blue beads, and thread for making a necklace or keychain (optional activity).

Preparation: No preparation is needed beyond acquiring the materials needed and having the group assembled in a comfortable setting. When sharing in a classroom-guidance setting, it may be helpful to include the classroom teacher as well, because he or she is part of the transition.

Instructions:

1. The counselor should welcome the group and introduce the activity, noting that it is designed to help the students through transitions.
2. Discuss "closure" and what that means for the group. Allow group members to process this idea of ending the group sessions.
3. Read the book *One Small Blue Bead* to the group.
4. Ask the group members to discuss their reactions to the story. Encourage group members to think about what elements of themselves they may have left in others. Also ask them to share what they learned in the group that they will take with them.
5. Distribute the blue beads, giving one bead to each person. Explain that the bead can be used however each individual feels appropriate. Some may make jewelry, some may make a key chain, and others may decide to put the bead in a special place.
6. Allow the group members to share final thoughts. It would be appropriate to ask each group member to say one word in closing that describes his or her experience with the group, asking him or her to focus on the positive things he or she will take away from the experience.
7. Thank them for their participation and encourage their continued reflections on what they leave behind and what they take with them.

Suggested Modifications (for Special Needs Populations): Some people are visual learners; be sure to show the pictures from the book.

Evaluation Plan: The school counselor should discuss and process the activity with the students at the conclusion of the lesson. A formal pre-/postassessment is not necessary, as this activity is focused on feelings and processing personal transitions, not acquiring knowledge.

REFERENCE

Baylor, B., & Himler, R. (1992). *One small blue bead* (2nd ed.). New York, NY: Scribner.

CAN YOU FEEL YOUR PERSONALITY?

Kelly Emelianchik-Key

This activity is used in group counseling with small (four to eight) and typically closed groups of students who know each other or who are looking to learn more about each other. This activity will assist group members in learning how to use all of their senses to understand other people's mood states and personalities. The group will be able to describe the parts of their own personalities and explore these parts of their personality through tactile senses, then through their visual senses. The counselor should start the group with a discussion about personality and the various types of personality. The students can reflect on the type of personality that they think they have and that others around them may have. For example, fun, mean, relaxed, happy, humorous, smart, caring, supportive, and so on. Students will then work together to learn and gain awareness about their personalities through tactile and visual senses.

Modality: Narrative and Tactile Arts

ASCA National Model Domain: Personal/Social

Deliver via: Group counseling

Age Level: Elementary, middle, or high school (Appropriate for use with any age group, 6 and up. Modifications would need to be made to the processing questions to align with the students' developmental level, insightfulness, and depth of sensory information.)

Indications: Could be used with small groups focused on getting to know each other and understanding differences, friendship groups that teach about appreciating all kinds of people, groups that help students understand and appreciate different personality types, and groups that help students to learn more about how others might view them.

Materials: Various small objects that will fit in an opaque bag. Objects with different textures, shapes, weights, and densities would be most effective. Some examples of appropriate objects are a paper clip, sand paper, shell, sponge, balloon, spoon, rock, tangerine, eraser, toothpick, and a ball of yarn.

Preparation: Place several items in an opaque bag. Items should be of all different textures. Items can be anything from around the home or office. For example, a sponge, piece of rubber, cookie cutter, sand paper, seashell, deflated balloon, box of matches, and so on. Make sure all items are small enough to fit in a bag and have something tactilely interesting about them. There should be double the amount of items as people in the group. Make sure that there is enough room in the bag for people to feel around and grab an object, but not to be able to peek into the bag.

Instructions: Introduce the activity by asking students to share about their personalities and how they view themselves. Then they can also explain how they think others might view them. From there, the leader of the group can explain that sometimes it is difficult to describe personalities and fully explain what a person is like; sometimes we can describe a person by using other senses, such as touch. There are many objects that are in the bag that will be passed around. Each object feels different. Take some time to feel some of the objects that are in the bag and pick out one object, without looking, that you think "feels" like your personality.

1. Have a group member feel around in the bag.
2. When he or she finds an item that he or she think fits, have the group member describe the feeling of the item, but not pull it out of the bag.

3. Tell him or her to only describe what he or she feels. For example, cold, hard, bumpy, smooth, or anything that they feel should be described in detail.

4. Then when he or she is done, talk about the description of the item and ask the group member to relate the feeling of the item to a part of his or her personality.

5. Tell the group member not to try to guess what the object is. Just rely on tactile senses.

6. After each group member has taken his or her turn, ask the other group members what they think of the description of the item and how the group members think that the item description fits with the personality of the group member who is "feeling" the object.

7. After they have done this, they can take the item out of the bag and hold onto it.

8. Ask the rest of the group members to follow the same steps above until each member has chosen an item and blindly described and related the item to his or her personality.

9. After each group member has gone, ask the group the following question, *"Now that you have all seen your items, how does your personality relate to the actual item's appearance, purpose, and/or function?"*

10. Have each group member take a turn.

11. After they have all spoken, ask the group if they would like to comment on anyone else's item and personality. For example, do they see any that fit really well, and how do they know? An example might be that if you have an eraser in the bag, the person might be flexible and easy going. They may also be open to admitting weakness or mistakes and quickly try to help people who are in need. An eraser's function is to clean up mistakes and make your written papers tidy, so you do not have to scribble. Is the person who picked it a helper? An eraser is also rough in areas where it has been used or worn down, but can be smooth in other areas. Does this relate to any areas of the person's life or personality?

12. You can ask the other group members if they can find any connection between the person's item and his or her personality, now that they can see the item.

13. After each person has gone through the series of questions about the objects that they have chosen and described them by tactile senses and visual senses, you can dump out the items that are left in the bag and ask the group members who may have struggled in their descriptions if they see any other items that might be a better fit.

   ■ If they choose a new item, make them describe why it is a better fit. Repeat the questions above that ask them to visually and tactilely describe the item in relationship to their personality.

■ If any group member keeps his or her item, check in with why they kept the item.

You can summarize to those who kept the original items and those who chose new ones, that if we truly "know" ourselves and our own personalities we can find the strength and relationship in anything. This goes for "knowing and understanding" other people as well. When we make an attempt to get to know someone, his or her personality, and how that person views him- or herself in the world, we can find their strengths with ease and be more accepting of the person.

Suggested Modifications (for Special Needs Populations): Counselors may need to modify the wording used in descriptions, processing questions, and directions provided to students to align with students' developmental level and cognitive ability. Counselors may also want to make sure each item is appropriate and safe for a group member based on the developmental level and age of group members. For example, do not utilize any objects too small that could be swallowed or anything that could be potentially hazardous if it is sharp. This activity is appropriate for use with most student groups and will be particularly helpful with students who respond positively to sensorial materials and activities. Students who have difficulty with fine motor skills and sensory processing may choose to observe the activity.

Evaluation Plan: To evaluate the effectiveness of this intervention, you could use a personality inventory pre- and postactivity to see whether the students self-report and score differently after examining, discussing, and processing the multiple facets of their personality with a group. Or you could do something simple, such as observe whether the students interact with each other differently and get along better in a group setting. I typically ask students to write a journal entry preactivity describing themselves in one paragraph. Then postactivity, I ask them to write another journal entry describing what they have learned about themselves from the activity and the group.

Activity Variations:
■ Use objects that are very fragrant and/or colorful.
■ Use fruits, small candles, or colorful candies (of varying tastes); anything that can be observed, smelled, and tasted.
■ Relate all of these senses and have them relate the items' taste, smell, and color to their personality or relationships with others. Modify the questions to align with the sense:

"How does that sour lemon candy relate to your personality? How does it taste? Can you identify times when you were bitter or sour to others? What caused you to behave in that manner? Can you identify times that you are sweet? What does that color yellow represent to you?"

THE COLLABORATIVE STORY

James R. Huber and Diane J. Shea

*T*his is a brief team-building/trust-building activity in which students collaborate to create a spontaneous story together.

Modality: Interactive: Verbal and Movement

ASCA National Model Domain: Personal/Social

Deliver via: Group and/or classroom guidance

Age Level: Elementary, middle, high school

Indications: Can be used to facilitate personal/group learning regarding getting acquainted, trust building, risk taking, feeling awareness, multicultural sensitivity, team building, social skills, coping with change, personal space, problem solving, and creativity.

Materials: None needed.

Preparation: Room should allow for movement and time should allow for a minimum of 20 minutes (5 minutes for activity and 15 minutes for processing time).

Instructions:

1. Explain to students that this is a _____ (e.g., trust building, team building) exercise.
2. Ask students to stand and form a circle in the center of the room.
3. Explain that the purpose of this activity is to enable them to work together to create a good story.
4. Tell them: *"All good stories have a beginning, a middle, and an ending."*
5. Designate one student to your left as "The Beginning" and one student to your right as "The Ending," and everyone else as "The Middle."
6. Ask them to listen carefully and follow these instructions to create their story:
   a. Only one person speaks at a time.
   b. The Beginning person starts by saying, "Once upon a time . . . "
   c. Each consecutive person (moving clockwise around the circle) moves the story forward by quickly adding a word or phrase or character or plot twist.
   d. Each person's contribution to the story should be quick, brief, and relevant to what the previous person said.
   e. When the story reaches The Ending person, he or she should give it a happy ending!
7. When everyone understands the process and is ready, ask the Beginning person to begin.

Suggested Modifications (for Special Needs Populations): Change instructions to accommodate students who may be hearing, speech, limb, and/or mobility impaired.

Evaluation Plan: Gather perception data based on age group and purpose of exercise. For example, for a high school team-building group:

1. What did you like/dislike about this process?
2. What feelings did you experience waiting for your turn to contribute to the story?
3. How important was it to listen carefully and pay attention to the developing story?
4. Which contributions seemed to make an unexpected impact on the story?
5. Why do you think the instructions asked you to be quick, brief, and relevant?
6. How did individual creativity enhance the collective creativity of the group?
7. What does this exercise demonstrate about the power of collaboration in reaching goals?

Once the students have processed the experience using the above questions, you can close by emphasizing that the story they just created (a) has never been told before and (b) would not be the same if any one of them had been missing!

EXPRESSING GRIEF THROUGH POETRY WRITING FOR SPANISH-SPEAKING STUDENTS

Katrina Cook

This activity is designed to be used when providing small-group counseling for adolescents who have experienced a loss. Students will read a poem by poet Gloria Velásquez, expressing her grief. English and Spanish versions of the poetry prompts are available, so the group is open to students whose primary language is either English or Spanish. Participants will hear the poet's expression of grief and will discuss their reactions to the poem. They will then be guided through a process of writing their own poem describing their personal grieving process.

Modality: Expressive Writing/Poetry

ASCA National Model Domain: Personal/Social

Delivery via: Group counseling

Age Level: Middle or high school

Indications: This activity is designed to facilitate group members' expression of grief or loss.

Materials: There are two different poems that could be appropriate for this activity. The first, "Zapatos Negros," is a poem about the death of the poet's brother in war. The second poem, "Despedida de Juan," is a poem about the death of the poet's father from illness. Decide which of these poems would be more appropriate for the group members. You may choose to use both poems if you believe both would be meaningful to your group members. There is a Spanish and an English version of each poem. Both poems can be found in Velásquez's 1997 book, *I Used to Be a Superwoman*, published by Arte Público Press. Additionally, the group facilitator will need markers, paper, pens, pencils, and highlighters.

Preparation: This activity would work best as one session in a series of sessions of a grief group. After selecting which of the Velásquez poems you will use, pass a Spanish and/or English version of it out to each student. Have enough copies of the poem for each of the participants. Also make pens, pencils, paper, and highlighters available for each student.

Instructions:

1. Ask a student to volunteer to read the poem out loud, or read it yourself. Encourage the students to highlight or make notes on their copy about anything that stands out to them as it is being read.

2. Ask students to discuss their reactions to the poem. Questions to facilitate the discussion about the impact of the poem include:

   a. *"What do you think this poem is about?"*

   b. *"What emotional reaction do you have to this poem?"*

   c. *"What are some words that the poet uses that indicate her feelings of grief?"*

   d. *"In the poem* 'Zapatos Negros' ('Black Shoes'), *the poet uses an ordinary object, such as shoes, to trace her memories and grief for her brother's death. What are some objects that remind you of your loved one who died?"*

   e. *"In the poem* 'Despedida de Juan' ('Farewell to Juan'), *the poet used the events of the day of her father's death as well as Memorial Day to trace her memories and grief for her father. What are some days or times that remind you of your loved one who died?"*

3. After the participants have finished discussing the poem(s), ask them to do a 5-minute sprint writing activity. Use the following instructions to get participants writing:

   a. *"Write for 5 minutes about the impact your grief is having on your life. You might start out, 'The way my grief is impacting my life. . . .' This is not a poem so do not worry about how it sounds, just get as many words on the paper as possible. Write as quickly as you can in English, Spanish, or both, and do not stop writing until time is called."*

4. Call time on the writing and ask the participants to put their pens down.

5. Invite participants to share a word, phrase, sentence, or their entire writing—whatever they feel most comfortable with revealing. Participants have the opportunity to pass if they want to.

6. Ask participants who were listening:
   a. *"What is your reaction to the work or phrase that [participant] just shared from his or her writing?"*
   b. *"What word or words stand out to you the most?"*
7. After everyone who wants to read has done so, give each student a marker and ask them to highlight any word or words in their writing that really stand out to them (these will usually be nouns, verbs, or adjectives). Encourage the participants to not highlight pronouns or words like "and."
8. Ask participants to write each of their highlighted words on a separate sheet of paper.
9. Ask participants to create a poem using primarily the words on the separate sheet of paper. They may add words if they need to for meaning, and they do not have to use every word in their poem.
10. Allow time for participants to write their poems.
11. Ask each participant to read as much of their poem as they would like. Participants have the option of passing if they want to.
12. As each participant reads his or her poem, ask the other participants to close their eyes and just take in the words of the poem.
13. Ask the listeners to share their reactions to the poem that was read. Questions to facilitate discussion include:
    a. *"What words or phrases speak to you the most?"*
    b. *"How is [participant's] experience similar to yours?"*

Suggested Modifications (for Special Needs Populations): Because both Spanish and English versions of these poems exist, this activity could work well with limited English-speaking students whose primary language is Spanish.

Evaluation Plan: The poems that the students create will indicate their ability to express their grief through the writing process.

REFERENCES

Adams, K. (2009, April). *Writing through troubled times: A journal mini-workshop.* Paper presented at the meeting of Chi Sigma Iota of Texas A&M University—Corpus Christi, Corpus Christi, TX.

Velásquez, G. (1997). Zapatos negros [Black shoes]. In *I used to be a superwoman* (pp. 94–97). Houston, TX: Arte Público Press.

Velásquez, G. (1997). Despedida de Juan [Farewell to Juan]. In *I used to be a superwoman* (pp. 106–109). Houston, TX: Arte Arte Público Press.

THE FORGET-ME-NOT BOOK OF REMINDERS DURING DEPLOYMENT

Laura S. Wheat and Peggy P. Whiting

This activity is designed to help older elementary-age children maintain their bonds with a parent or sibling who is deployed. It helps students ease some of the grief associated with separation as well as their fears for safety and stability during a disruptive time. Developmentally, students in the elementary age group need assistance with expressing their feelings in order to help continue the bond with the deployed loved one. It also helps them understand that they are not alone, and that they can not only seek support from their peers in the same situation, but that they can give this support as well. Students in small-group counseling will create memory books together using a variety of expressive materials. Later, the counselor will guide them to create pages based on the things they want to remember about their deployed loved one or things they want to be sure to tell or show the deployed loved one upon his or her return. Processing includes helping students see that although the individual books are very different, each student is missing a loved one who is deployed.

Modality: Writing/Poetry, Visual

ASCA National Model Domain: Personal/Social

Deliver via: Small-group counseling

Age Level: 4th and 5th grade

Indications: To be used with small groups of students affected by the military cycle of deployment, including children of National Guard and Reserve soldiers. The idea could also be modified only slightly for use with small groups of students whose loved one is incarcerated.

Materials: For the book itself, you need construction paper or cut-up colored butcher paper for the front and back covers, construction paper and white paper for inside pages, and yarn cut in 9.5- to 10-inch lengths and a hole punch for binding (or staples).

For later activities, you will need writing/drawing instruments such as crayons, markers, colored chalk, colored pencils, and so on; other decorative items that could be used to facilitate expression, for example, stickers, old magazines, pinking shears, and so on; glue sticks, and, optionally, a photo album digital voice recorder with labels (this can be found on the Internet).

Preparation: Before the session, have group members ask permission from a parent or guardian to bring a picture of their deployed loved one with them to group. On the day of the session, gather bookmaking materials in the center of the table or whatever space the group will be occupying. Be sure each group member has three to five sheets of white paper available.

Instructions:

1. Begin by asking for volunteers to share the picture of the deployed loved one and sharing how long he or she has been gone. Make connections between group members when appropriate (e.g., *"Lindsay, it looks like you and Jermaine both have a mom who has been gone for eight months."*) and help facilitate students' awareness that each of them is experiencing the same type of loss.

2. Explain that children often have many different feelings about and reactions to their loved one being gone, and give some examples, both positive and negative. For instance, sometimes children feel sad and worry about their loved one getting hurt or forgetting things about her or him, and sometimes children feel proud that their loved one is fighting for their country. The counselor then helps group members discuss the reactions they feel comfortable sharing.

3. Normalize group members' feelings and reactions, pointing out things members have in common and model giving support, reinforcing group members who support others. Then state that finding a way to cope with all the feelings that come up is important so that group members can concentrate while at school and do what needs to be done at home. One way to do this is by listening to each other and helping each other when one of us is having a hard time, and another way to do this is to make a special "forget-me-not" book to hold drawings, pictures, letters, and anything else group members might want to keep safe to show their loved one, such as report cards or special awards. The book can help them feel connected to their loved ones on any day, but particularly those days that are hardest. It also helps them learn that even though they are separated, they can continue the bond with their family member. Following are the steps in the bookmaking process:

   a. First, each group member picks out three to five sheets of paper for the inside pages of the book, and then a colorful piece of paper for the front and back covers. Instruct students to fold the papers in half crosswise so that they look like a book.

   b. Next, group members can punch holes in the middle of the book and thread yarn through the holes to bind the book, or they can staple along the spine of the book. The counselor may need to help group members complete this step.

   c. Finally, group members use glue sticks to attach the picture of their loved one to a page in the book if they have been given permission to do so. If there is time remaining, group members may use the various expressive materials available to personalize and decorate their book covers and the page on which they placed the picture.

4. When the bookmaking is completed, facilitate discussion among group members by asking questions such as, *"What kinds of things might you want to put in your book to help you remember your loved one?"* and *"How can we help each other when we're feeling down and missing our loved ones?"*

In subsequent sessions, you can facilitate additional expressive activities as ways to add to pages in the forget-me-not book. Possibilities include:

■ Have students draw a picture of their favorite memory with their deployed loved one and share the story with their fellow group members. Additionally, if some funding is available, use photo album voice recorders to help group members narrate the story of their favorite memory so that they can look at the book and listen to the story whenever they need it.

- Remind students that their deployed loved ones have special armor and other things they use as a shield to protect them. Ask students to create a "coping shield" of their own in which they list or draw strategies they use when they feel sad, angry, or worried about their loved one. Instruct them to leave a blank space. Ask group members to share some of the strategies they use, reinforcing appropriate strategies and helping the group devise alternatives to inappropriate strategies (such as "go play basketball" instead of "beat up my sister"). After everyone has shared what he or she chooses to share, group members can select one strategy someone else described and add it to their shield.
- Write a short poem or a letter to their loved one to let them know how they're doing.
- Prompt students to bring things to put into their books such as old insignia patches, ribbons, letters, photos, keepsakes, and so on, and encourage them to share the stories about these objects with the group.
- Ask students to bring artifacts of their own that they might want to include in the book to show their loved one upon his or her return. For instance, students might bring report cards, certificates, assignments, or tests on which they got a good grade, and so on.

Another possible variation of the memory book might be to decorate shoe boxes or cigar boxes to hold memorabilia rather than creating a book. By having a box, group members can decorate it according to their own preference and include items that might not fit in a flat book or that might easily fall out.

Suggested Modifications (for Special Needs Populations): Take care to assess the developmental needs and resources of each group member and adjust expectations about the activity accordingly. Students who have difficulty with fine motor skills may need the assistance of another group member (preferred) or the counselor when completing tasks associated with constructing the book (e.g., cutting out images or gluing things down with the glue stick). English for Speakers of Other Languages (ESOL) students may benefit from additional visual cues such as an example memory book or box. Instructions for each activity should be given in a simple, concrete, sequential manner so that students are not overwhelmed with too many instructions at any one time. More advanced or gifted students may be designated in advance as "buddies" for individualized assistance and encouragement to those with special needs.

Evaluation Plan: You may gather perception data about this activity by using the following as a pre- and posttest. If the forget-me-not book is used in other sessions of the group, the same assessment can be used in a modified format to reflect the individual goals of each session.

Please check the box to indicate whether you think each sentence is true for you:

STATEMENT	3 YES	2 NOT SURE	1 NO
1. I have ways to share what I'm thinking and feeling about my loved one with others.	□	□	□
2. I know more than three ways to let my loved one know important things about me even though he or she is away.	□	□	□
3. I know three other students who are going through the same thing as I am.	□	□	□
4. I feel understood about what I'm going through.	□	□	□
5. I know how to help a friend who is going through the same thing.	□	□	□

What else do you want to tell me about being in this group?

_____

"I LOVE BEING ME": BE THE AUTHOR OF YOUR OWN STORY

Cynthia B. Greer

This self-esteem and empowerment activity provides middle-school girls an opportunity to learn to be the author of their own story by telling and writing their own story/book/portfolio with a focus on psychological, academic, physical, and spiritual well-being. Through a person's story we begin to understand the person's worldview, her or his values, and priorities. The story gives voice to the person's experience. This activity provides an opportunity for students to give voice and appreciate their own stories, and learn not to be defined by their peers and/or popular culture. Reading and listening to others' stories can provide a mirror (identity) and a window to the world that provides an opportunity for insight and catharsis, which are the goals of culturally relevant bibliotherapy.

Modality: Culturally Relevant Bibliotherapy, Poetry/Narrative

ASCA national Model Domain: Personal/Social

Delivery via: Individual or growth group (six or fewer)

Age Level: 7th and 8th grade; however, the format can be adapted for any age group and demographic

Indications: This activity would be helpful for students who have been bullied, girls reaching adolescence who have questions about identity and are experiencing the impact of the influence of their peers and popular culture, and for girls of color in order to promote healthy identities.

Materials: Selected books/poems and other narratives, markers/pencils/pens, construction paper, scissors, hole punch, medium-sized index cards, and copies of the activity glossary:

Activity Glossary:
Attributes–qualities or characteristics of the person
Interpretation–your explanation of someone's words and /or feelings
Perception–your understanding of something or someone based on your own senses
Self-concept–how you believe other people see/view you
Self-image–how you see/view yourself

Preparation: Prepare a resource table with the art materials as well as copies of preselected culturally relevant books, poems, and other narratives that address the themes of academic/cognitive and emotional development, and physical and spiritual well-being. These narratives should tell the stories of young people who were dealing with issues about their own physical, cognitive, or spiritual differences and uniqueness. Appropriate passages from the books should be highlighted; autobiographies or lyrics from songs and other narratives can be used. Include books and narratives that are a part of the students' academic curriculum.

Instructions:

A. Introduction
   1. Provide students with an index card, pencil, and the glossary.
   2. Ask them to list five attributes/qualities that they like about themselves on one side of the index card.
   3. Ask them to list five adjectives that describe how they perceive themselves on the other side of the card.
   4. After 5 minutes, ask students about their comfort level and success in completing the listing exercise.
   5. Use their responses to provide a transition for you to explain that too often we listen to the criticisms of others or we compare ourselves to our peers and to people in popular culture, which may result in not having a healthy self-concept or self-image.
   6. Explain that it is important that we accept and love our "whole" selves and that we are more than our physical selves.

Let them know that the following activity will focus on reading about the experiences and feelings of other young people and how they were able to identify, appreciate, and grow to love their own strengths and abilities. The students will be told that they will have the opportunity to give voice to their own attributes by constructing their own stories.

B. Activity
   1. Send students to visit the resource table and choose a book with selected passages, poem, lyric of a song, or other narrative, and to take a few minutes and read their selection.
   2. Invite students to openly share and interpret what they have read and state whether they identified with the story/writer, and what they could learn from the writer's experience and story. Ask them to identify positive qualities and give their perception of the writer or characters, and specifically state how the person overcame obstacles or dealt with her or his challenges.
   3. Summarize what has been shared and let the students know that as students they have an opportunity to be the author of their own story. They can choose to write a narrative, poem, or rap; draw; or create some other artistic creation in response to one of the following questions or statements:

      "Describe and draw yourself. State what physical attributes you like about yourself and explain why. Write about and describe an obstacle that you have successfully overcome or a challenge you have dealt with. Explain how you dealt with the situation."

      "Describe your talents or skills (something you believe you do well), and discuss/explain your future educational goals."

      "Explain how you are a friend to someone and how you demonstrate that you care about others."

      "If you could change the world, what would you do and how?"

Remind students that their work will not be evaluated or assessed. Provide students with positive feedback about their responses and encourage other students to give positive feedback to their peers. When students have completed their sharing, ask students to respond to one last question, *"What do you love about yourself?"* Encourage students to respond to the other statements/questions in their own time in order to continue to construct their own book/portfolio.

Suggested Modifications (for Special Needs Populations): The design of this expressive arts intervention program is very flexible. Facilitators may need to give more support to some students as they are preparing their responses. The readings and narratives can be provided in an audio format. Students can also respond to the questions/statements through other expressive arts modalities.

Evaluation Plan: Ask the students to review the lists on their index cards and ask if there are attributes that they would add to or take off the list. This index card exercise serves as both a pretest and a posttest assessment.

The content of the students' stories or final products can also serve as an assessment tool or as the beginning of a portfolio. The students' ability to complete the reading and to participate in the reflection and discussion will demonstrate improvement in self-esteem and growth in their self-image and self-concept.

PERSONALIZED STRESS BALL

Joseph Graham, Neffisatu J. C. Dambo, and Saron N. LaMothe

*A*lthough experiencing stress is commonplace, stress can become overwhelming and interfere with one's life activities. The cathartic effect of squeezing stress balls is widely accepted (Abbott, Shanahan, & Neufeld, 2013). This activity serves the dual purpose of normalizing anger/stress/anxiety and of individualizing each participant's experience of anger/stress/anxiety. Creative arts interventions have been shown to reduce stress (Walsh, Martin, & Schmidt, 2004). The personalized stress ball serves as a reminder that although what provokes anger, stress, or anxiety may be beyond our control, we have power over how we react and control our emotions.

Modality: Expressive Writing, Expressive Arts, Experiential Activity

ASCA National Model Domain: Personal/Social

Deliver via: Individual or small-group activity

Age Level: Middle and high school

Indications: Participants with presenting concerns related to anger, stress, or anxiety.

Materials: Scissors (for group leader), sheet of paper, writing instrument, Play-Doh, white or light-colored balloons, and decorative materials (e.g., glitter glue, markers), if applicable.

Preparation: Have materials ready for students.

Instructions: We like to conduct this activity without informing the participants that we are making a stress ball; we wait until the balls are made to point out what they are. These directions are for anger-management groups, but this activity can be adapted for stress and anxiety as well.

1. Instruct participants to write down on a sheet of paper everything that they can think of that makes them angry. Say, *"Take a moment to think about what kinds of things or people make you angry and write down as many of them as possible on your paper."*
2. Ask participants to share what they have written (other participants might want to add to their lists) by saying, *"I'd like to invite each of you to please share your lists with the group."*
3. Reflect and process what the group members have shared. Sample questions include: *"Did you hear anything you'd like to add to your list?"* Or, *"What is it like looking at your list?"*
4. Ask participants to come up with one word that summarizes everything on their lists and write that word as large as possible on their sheet of paper.

5. Process the writing of the single word with the group. A sample question might include: *"How did you determine your word?"*
6. Instruct participants to shred the sheet of paper into the smallest pieces possible and make a pile. Say, *"Now, with your hands, tear up the paper into the smallest pieces you can and make a pile."*
7. Reflect what you observed as group members did this and process by asking questions like, *"What was it like tearing up your sheet?"*
8. Give each participant a container of Play-Doh and instruct students to flatten it (I enjoy smelling the aroma of Play-Doh, as it can bring up childhood memories). Instruct the group members by saying, *"Next, take out the Play-Doh and flatten it like a pancake."*
9. Instruct participants to use the Play-Doh to pick up every shred of paper; this usually requires several folding attempts, but it can be done. Say, *"Place the Play-Doh on top of your shredded paper and fold the paper into the Play-Doh. Don't worry; it will pick up all the pieces."*
10. Give each participant a balloon; instruct participants to put the Play-Doh inside; this usually is done in tandem. Say, *"Next, select a partner to help you put the Play-Doh into the balloon. Usually, one person will use his or her thumbs to open the balloon and the other will insert the Play-Doh."*
11. Instruct participants to shove the Play-Doh as far into the balloon as possible, tie off the end, and cut off the balloon tail that develops.
12. Reflect and process with questions like, *"What is it like holding all of your stressors in your hand?"* and/or *"When do you see yourself using your stress ball?"*
13. Instruct participants to decorate their balloon in any fashion they desire. (Optional)

Suggested Modifications (for Special Needs Populations): None.

Evaluation Plan: A pre- and posttest will be given to assess the students' ability to identify emotions, rank their level of stress, and report coping strategies.

Pre- and Posttest Processing Questions
1. What emotions do people experience?
2. What situations cause stress?
3. Rate your stress level (1 being the lowest and 10 the highest).
4. Rate your knowledge of coping skills (1 being the lowest and 10 the highest).
5. List your current coping strategies.

Additional Processing Questions
6. What is it like seeing all the things that make you angry right in front of you?
7. What are some of the things you all have in common?
8. How did you determine your one word?

9. What is it like to hold all the things that make you angry in the palm of your hand?
10. What do you think is the purpose of this activity?
11. How will you use today's activity for the rest of the week?

REFERENCES

Abbott, K. A., Shanahan, M. J., & Neufeld, R. W. J. (2013). Artistic tasks outperform nonartistic tasks for stress reduction. *Art Therapy: Journal of the American Art Therapy Association, 30*(2), 71–78. doi:10.1080/07421656.2013.787214

Walsh, S. M., Martin, S. C., & Schmidt, L. A. (2004). Testing the efficacy of a creative-arts intervention with family caregivers of patients with cancer. *Journal of Nursing Scholarship, 36*(3), 214–219. doi:10.1111/j.1547-5069.2004.04040.x

STRENGTHS SCRABBLE

Amanda N. Siemsen

*T*his activity consists of students brainstorming positive attributes and/or strengths about themselves and creating a visual representation of these adjectives. Students will write their names and create a visual "Scrabble board" of their positive attributes. In order to do this, each word has to share a letter with another word. All of these adjectives are then linked together to the student's name in a visual representation of his or her strengths. On completion, students can hang this visual piece inside of their lockers to serve as a reminder of their strengths in the future.

Modality: Narrative

ASCA National Model Domain: Personal/Social

Deliver via: Individual or classroom guidance

Age Level: Middle or high school

Indications: This activity can be useful for students who have low self-esteem.

Materials: Scratch paper, card stock, colored markers, fine-tip black markers, pencils, list of positive adjectives, and tape.

Preparation: Provide each student with one piece of scratch paper and one piece of cardstock or regular paper that has a large table printed on it. You can use the table function in your word processing program to create a blank table as large as needed. In the example (Figure 13.1), an 11 × 11 cell table was used. Display the list of positive adjectives on a presentation board.

Instructions:
1. Instruct students to think about their own positive attributes and strengths.
2. Instruct students to create a list of positive adjectives describing themselves. If students have a difficult time listing positive attributes, help them brainstorm or provide a couple of attributes that you recognize in him or her.

				A	W	E	S	O	M	E
				M			P			
	L			A	B	L	E			
	O	P	E	N			C			
	V			D	A	R	I	N	G	
	I			A			A			
	N						L			
	G	I	V	I	N	G				

FIGURE 13.1 Strengths Scrabble example using the name "Amanda."

3. On a practice sheet of paper, have students organize adjectives so that each word shares a letter with one other word (see Figure 13.1). Have students print their name first and then find adjectives that they can connect to the name or to other adjectives as shown in the example.
4. Have students copy their board onto card stock using a colored marker for the name and a black marker for the adjectives.
5. Encourage students to hang these in their lockers as a reminder of their strengths on bad days.

Suggested Modifications (for Special Needs Populations): The positive adjectives provided to the client should be developmentally appropriate. If the client is unable to manually create the visual representation, a computer program may be utilized to generate the illustration after the student provides the words he or she would like to use to describe him- or herself.

Evaluation Plan: The counselor can discuss and process the activity with the students after the activity by inviting students to give examples of how they exhibit each trait.

THE TRUST TUBE

Kevin A. Fall

*T*his activity is designed for psychoeducational groups and can be facilitated in small groups (six to eight) or larger class settings (15 to 20). The focus of the activity is to help adolescents reconceptualize their *perspectives and beliefs about trust, both how to recover from a betrayal or hurt and how to actively build trust in any relationship. Often, this activity is preceded by a discussion of what trust means (a group definition exercise), followed by a discussion of times when they feel trust has been broken, by themselves as well as others. This discussion will provide the group with a universal sense of what it feels like when we have been hurt and when we hurt others. This shared feeling of hurt naturally leads to a wondering about how one can recover from the pain.*

Modality: Narrative

ASCA Model Domain Name: Personal/Social

Deliver via: Group counseling

Age level: Middle or high school; the abstract concepts are a bit too difficult for younger students to grasp.

Indications: This activity is ideal for any psychoeducational group that deals with life skills. It can also be used in relationship-focused groups or leadership programs.

Materials: A writing surface, preferably something that can be saved and referenced in later groups; large pieces of paper, such as the large "Post-It" easel pads work well, as they can be saved and placed on a door or wall for later use; alternatively, a whiteboard could be used.

Preparation: No real preparation is needed other than placing three large pieces of paper on the wall for writing purposes.

Instructions:

1. This activity is introduced after the group has discussed the definition of trust and has had an opportunity to share experiences of times when each member has had trust "broken," either through their own behaviors or by others. Some examples of group members' experiences may include: *My boyfriend cheated on me by going out with another girl behind my back. It hurt because I felt like I wasn't as good as the other person. I lost a boyfriend and a friend that day.* Or, *I lied to my parents about a party I went to and they found out. My mom said she was disappointed in me and that it was going to take a lot to win the trust back. It's been 6 weeks and she still doesn't trust me.*

2. The group leader links these experiences and identifies some common themes that occur when trust is negatively impacted in relationships, such as *feelings of sadness, inferiority, confusion, and anger; a sense of lack of control over how to fix the relationship;* or *a fear of getting hurt again.*

3. After noting these common themes, offer an overview of the traditional model of viewing trust: a vase. The following sample dialogue is a typical method for introducing the traditional model:

    "The way we typically view trust in relationships is like a vase. When we form a relationship with someone and trust develops, it's like we buy a fancy

vase and we are happy we have it and we place it up on a shelf to admire. When someone in the relationship, you or the other person, does something to hurt the trust in the relationship, what happens to the vase?" (The group will respond with "the vase gets knocked and broken.") *"Yes, the vase is knocked off the shelf and breaks on the floor. We even have that symbolism in our language about trust. We say, 'He broke my trust,' like it's a break-able object. Once the trust vase is broken, who is responsible for putting it back together?"* (The group will answer, "The person who knocked it off.") *"Right, in this model, the person who broke the trust is responsible for put-ting it back together. What does the person who was hurt do?"* (The group will answer with some variation of, "They wait for the person to prove they are trustworthy again.") *"Yes, the person who was hurt will sit back, with his or her arms crossed, and wait for the person to fix the vase. This is one problem with the vase model; it puts you, as the hurt person, in a passive role, where you are just waiting for the other person to fix the relationship issue. There is another common problem with the vase model. How do you know the vase is repaired?"* (The group will struggle with this question and will typically give an answer along the lines of, "You'll just know it in your gut.") *"That's the second problem with this model. It's very difficult to know when the trust is reestablished. Even if you glue a vase back together, what can you always see?"* (The group will answer, "The cracks.") *"Yes, in this model, no matter what the other person does to repair the trust, the hurt person will always be aware of the cracks. You can probably think of times when you've been hurt an vd how difficult it is to forgive. That struggle is an example of you looking at the cracks in the vase. Part of that issue is related to the difficulty of forgiveness, but a lot of it has to do with the nature of the vase model and how, when hurt, you are put in the position of merely waiting and assessing. Although the vase model is common, I am not sure it's the best model for dealing with trust issues. What we need is a better model. Would you like to see a better model?"* (Hopefully the group will say, "Yes!")

4. With the vase model for comparison, the Trust Tube can be presented as an alternative model for trust. Have three areas of writing space. This can be done on a wide whiteboard, or have three large sheets of paper affixed to the wall. Label one sheet, "When I trust, I. . . ." Label the other sheet, "When I don't trust, I. . . . " Work first with the sheet labeled, "When I trust, I. . . . " On this sheet, list all of the actions and attitudes people display when they trust someone. Group members have listed items such as "feel close to them," "tell them my secrets," "spend time with them," "share stuff with them," and "let my guard down" as examples of attitudes or behaviors they display when they trust someone. Try to fill up the entire column. If you get stuck, push the members to think about how someone would know if they trusted them. How would they act? How would they feel?

5. Next, complete the paper labeled, "When I don't trust, I. . . ." Under this column, list the attitudes and behaviors people display when they do not trust someone. Examples could be "am angry," "yell," "ask lots of questions," "get jealous," and "shut others out." Try to fill up the entire column. If the group struggles with this list, encourage them to think about how someone would know that they did not trust them. How would they act? How would they feel?

Here is an example list from a group of 14-year-olds.

When I trust, I. . . .	When I don't trust, I. . . .
Hang out with them	Ask lots of questions
Share money and food	Don't tell them deep stuff
Tell them my secrets	Am cold to them
Feel free to show emotions	Feel on edge, snap at them more
Am relaxed around them	Talk behind their back
Let them around my boyfriend	Always think they are up to something
Am cool with them doing their own thing	I really watch them closely, to see if they'll mess up

6. On the third sheet, draw a picture of a cylindrical tube. This is the "trust tube." The trust tube has a hole in the top and a rubber stopper on the bottom. The tube is a symbol of a relationship because a relationship is the container that holds trust. The liquid that fills up the tube would represent the amount or level of trust currently in your relationship. To demonstrate the fluid nature of the model, ask the group, *"What would you say about a relationship that has the tube mostly filled up with liquid?"* (The group will answer, "It has a lot of trust.") What would you say about a relationship with just a little liquid in it? (The group will answer, "It doesn't have much trust."). Propose to the group that the tube model is a more accurate model of how trust works in a relationship. In relationships, trust really is rarely broken. More accurately, in every relationship, one's "trust level" will vary. There will be times when the relationship feels more full of trust than others. When someone does something to hurt the relationship, it has the effect of temporarily removing the stopper and draining the trust liquid out of the tube. When someone does something good in the relationship, it adds trust to the tube, increasing the felt amount of trust in the relationship. Once the group understands how the tube works in relationships, return to the previous lists.

7. Ask the group to examine the answers on the previous two lists. Ask the group, *"Of the two lists, which set of behaviors and attitudes would have the highest chance of increasing trust in your relationship? Which set would add liquid to the tube?"* If the group answers, "The 'when I trust' list," they are on target. Behaving in open, kind, noncontrolling ways and feeling good

about a relationship almost always adds liquid to the tube (builds trust). Ask the group, *"Of the two lists, which set of behaviors and attitudes would have the highest chance of decreasing trust in a relationship?"* If the group answers, "The 'when I don't trust' list," they are on the right track. Even when trust is high, behaviors such as yelling and attitudes that come from jealousy will pull the stopper and let the trust drain out of the trust tube.

8. At this point, the group should understand the basic workings of the trust tube and how it describes the process of trust growth and loss in relationships, and how it differs from the vase model. Before moving on, make sure the members understand that there is a collection of behaviors and attitudes that build trust and a set that diminishes trust in the relationship. Next, present some conclusions about the model.

9. State that one of the most interesting observations about the model is how, when most of us need to build trust the most (when we do not trust someone, when there is less liquid in the tube), we do two very ineffective things:

   a. We make it the other person's responsibility to build the trust ("You have to earn my trust"). This is the basic philosophy of the vase model. Within the trust tube model, it would be like someone did something to pull the stopper and drain the trust (talked about me behind my back) and then we wait passively for the other person to refill the trust. With the tube, we need to understand that we can be active in refilling the tube and our behaviors will impact the level of trust, regardless of who created the initial problem. This is a position of empowerment because it is active and does not rely on other people to create change.

   b. When we experience low trust in a relationship, we tend to think, feel, and behave in ways that actually *decrease* trust in our relationships, as demonstrated by the behaviors and attitudes listed in the "When I don't trust, I. . . . " list. When you withdraw from another person, or adopt a suspicious attitude toward him or her, it actively decreases the trust in the relationship. By choosing this set of behaviors, we sabotage our relationships when we need trust the most.

10. In most groups, these two points will take the members by surprise. This confusion is due to the prevailing vase philosophy, which dictates that, when you are hurt, you should protect yourself and wait for the other person to fix it. The trust tube points out that if a person waits, an opportunity to build trust is wasted. Even worse, "protecting oneself" almost always means participating in behaviors and attitudes that drain trust from the relationship. In practice, the combination of these two elements could mean that even if the other person consistently tries to add trust to the tube, if the other person is draining the trust, the relationship will always feel less than trustworthy. These concepts will lead to some interesting dialogue within the group.

11. In closing, plan to leave the members with some final thoughts. Say: *"The fact of the matter is, although you might be hurt by another person, if you*

choose to stay and work on the relationship, then you are also responsible for filling the tube (building trust). The simple rule to remember from this exercise is as follows: If you are not actively creating trust, then you are pulling the stopper of your relationship tube and actively working to decrease trust. *Trust is an important aspect in our relationships, and the better we are at building trust, the better we will be in relating to each other."*

Over the next few weeks, group members can be encouraged to examine their role in building trust in any relationship. They can use the group to discuss and process new ways of creating trust and learn from others in the group about different obstacles and pathways to trust.

Suggested Modifications (for Special Needs Populations): Counselors are encouraged to consider the age and developmental level of the group members when explaining and processing this exercise. This activity can be integrated into many different types of psychoeducational groups and can be applied to any relationship (friends, parents, intimate, etc.).

Evaluation Plan: To assess the impact of this activity, each member can fill out his or her own "When I trust, I. . . . " and "When I don't trust, I. . . . " lists. Group members can also answer the following process questions: Describe one of your relationships through the lens of the vase model. Now process that relationship through the trust tube. The trust tube emphasizes proactivity and accountability in trust building. What does that mean to you?

WHO AM I?

Kanessa Miller Doss

S tudents of all ages struggle with their overall self-image and concepts of self-worth. This activity is designed to aid students in developing positive attitudes toward their unique characteristics through expressive writing. Students will create these literary works to identify personal strengths and assets, increase self-awareness, and/or resolve intrapersonal conflict.

Modality: Expressive Writing/Poetry

ASCA National Model Domain: Personal/Social

Deliver via: Individual, group, or classroom guidance

Age Level: Upper elementary, middle, or high school

Indications: This activity can be used as a self-awareness exercise with any student, especially individual/group counseling settings with individuals exhibiting issues such as low self-esteem, intrapersonal conflict, and identity issues.

Materials: Pencil, paper, and copies of the poem included in the Instructions.

Preparation: Provide examples of poems and quotes that promote positive self-images to share.

Instructions:

1. Ask the participants to define *self-awareness, self-image, self-worth*, and *self-esteem*.
2. Using open-ended questions, facilitate a discussion of the importance of self-awareness, self-image, self-worth, and self-esteem.
3. Generate a list of ways that people develop a negative self-image.
4. Generate a list of ways that individuals develop a positive self-image.
5. Read aloud the poem below:

   Who Am I?

   Kanessa Miller Doss

   I have two feet, two hands, and two eyes and most importantly a bright
      mind,
   I can add, subtract, multiply, and divide.
   I write stories, songs, and poems that intrigue. I can even skip, jump rope,
      and run.
   My favorite color is pink splashed with a bit of green.
   I construct fantasies of the future me and all that I can grow up to be.
   I believe I can choose any career in time: a lawyer, a doctor, an astronaut,
      or maybe a talking mime.
   I love to bake, but hate to rake.
   Did I mention I am great at eating cake?
   I love to read. I love to sing. I love ice cream. I hate green beans.
   I am like no other person you see. I am perfectly and uniquely designed
      to be me!
   I am a swimmer that swims like a fish.
   I am a dreamer with only one wish: To be the BEST me I can be!
   Watch out and you'll see!

6. Instruct the students to write a poem, short story, or essay, about the following as it relates to them:
   a. Special characteristics (i.e., fiery red hair)
   b. Likes and dislikes
   c. Strengths and weaknesses
   d. Goals and aspirations (i.e., planning to be a doctor)
   Remind the students that their piece does not have to rhyme.
7. Invite students to share their creative writing project within a small or large
   group (unless it is an individual counseling session) and discuss the items
   that make them unique.

Suggested Modifications (for Special Needs Populations): This activity should
be adjusted to the individual ability of the students and include age-appropriate

tasks. The length of the poem may be shortened or lengthened (gifted) appropriately. Facilitators may also encourage the use of metered rhythm instead of blank verse for gifted students.

Evaluation Plan: The session should be evaluated through questions and answers that relate to the definition and importance of self-awareness, self-image, self-worth, and self-esteem. The facilitator should review the techniques described as methods for developing positive and negative self-images.

VI ❖ Drama

14 Drama-Based Interventions in the Academic Domain

ALBERT ELLIS'S ABCs THE DRAMA WAY

Jennifer L. Marshall and Trey Fitch

Albert Ellis developed Rational Emotive Behavioral Therapy (REBT; Ellis & Harper, 1975), which relates that it is not the events in our lives that cause us angst, but the beliefs centering on those events. When events occur that affect an individual's belief, that belief in turn affects one's emotions and behaviors, rationally or irrationally. For example: A student who is average at math is given a pop quiz on some math problems. Immediately this student states to him- or herself, "I can't do this; I am going to fail" (irrational thoughts and beliefs). The belief is that since the student is average at math, he or she will never be able to do well on an exam. This belief then may cause the student to become anxious (emotions) and sick to his or her stomach, which leads to the student not putting full effort into the test (behavior) and thus getting a bad grade (consequence).

If this student were to learn about REBT and the ABCs, then he or she could change the irrational thinking into more rational thinking. The ABCs are a way to teach students about how their beliefs affect their cognitions and behaviors.

A = Activating event
B = Belief about the event
C = Consequences that result from the belief around the event
D = Disputing thoughts/beliefs about the event
E = Effect of the disputing thought/belief

In this activity, students will role play the ABCs above using an event that has occurred recently within their lives. To begin the group an ice breaker will be completed that will help the students become more comfortable with group as well as the other group members. Students will then be taught what the ABCs are through the handout (see Appendix A).

After the students have applied the ABCs to an event on paper, the group leader will ask the students to do a brief warm-up, which involves a short dramatic enactment that will prepare them for the main group activity involving a group member's issue (which they have applied to the ABCs on the handout in an earlier activity) that the student is struggling with in his or her life.

After the group reenacts a member's issue, then another member will be asked to volunteer his or her issue to be enacted with the application of the ABCs. After four or five individuals have gone, the group leader will lead a discussion of the ABCs and the impact they can have on the students' lives when they apply them to irrational thoughts and/or beliefs.

Modality: Drama

ASCA National Model Domain: Academic or Personal/Social

Deliver via: Group

Age Level: High school

Indications: Anxiety and stress management

Materials: None required, but since this is a drama enactment the students and/or leader can bring in props. An example of a prop would be making large cardboard signs with A = Activating event, B = Belief about the event, C = Consequences that result from the belief around the event, D = Disputing thoughts/beliefs about the event, and E = Effect of the disputing thought/belief. When the students enact the issue, other group members could volunteer to hold up the A-B-C-D-E signs as they are being discussed by the central student whose issue is being enacted, or the group leader could have members give feedback involving the A-B-C-D-E, especially focusing on the D (Disputing beliefs) and the E (Effects). Another idea is that other props could be used such as different hats to represent each different letter A-B-C-D-E.

Preparation:
a. The leader will need to be familiar with Albert Ellis's ABCs (see description of the activity).
b. If the leader decides to make any props for the A-B-C-D-E, then these need to be made before the group or the leader could have the members of the group make them as they are discussing Albert Ellis's ABCs.
c. Copies of the handout need to be made for the group members.
d. Copies of the discussion questions need to be made for the group members.

Instructions:
1. Ice breaker: The ice breaker can be any activity that gets the students talking and familiar with each other.
   a. Some suggestions for ice breakers can be found at http://www.icebreakers.ws

b. One ice breaker that is commonly used is the ball toss: A soft stress ball is brought to group. The group leader then explains to the group that they will begin the ball toss by stating their names when they are tossed the ball. The leader states his own name and then tosses the ball to a group member, who then states her own name and the leader's name. She then tosses the ball to another group member who follows the same pattern of stating one's own name and the name of the person who has just tossed him the ball. This continues until all members have received the ball. Example:

a. Jennifer decides to toss the ball to James.

b. James states his name and states Jennifer's name, then tosses the ball to Sylvia.

c. Sylvia states her name and James's name and tosses the ball to Leah.

2. Next, use the handout (Appendix A) to explain the ABC model. (The explanation is on the handout.)

3. The leader will tell the group that *"drama and acting will be used to learn how to improve how the group members think about events that happen to them."*

4. The leader will then relate the following: *"There is an achievement test that you will be taking soon and you are anxious about the math portion of the test. In the past you have not done as well as you have wanted on your math tests in class or on the practice math achievement tests so you start saying to yourself, 'I will not do very well on the math part of the achievement test. I haven't done well in class or on the practice tests so I know I won't do well on the math portion.'"*

If the latter is not appropriate to the group, then describe an activity or event that is appropriate. For example, a school dance/prom could be pending, or create a scenario such as "your friend ignored you all week." Then have each group member fill in the worksheet (Appendix A) using that stressful event and apply the ABCs to the event described.

5. Next is the introductory activity. This activity is designed to help prepare for the ABC drama role. After the students have discussed the math achievement test example (**activating event [A]**) on paper, then the leader will relate the following:

"Now we will act out the event above using the ABCs. I will need a volunteer. Alright, we have our volunteer; now I would like you to try to put yourself in the position described earlier involving the math achievement test (or the other scenario the leader decided on). [Volunteer's name], *please describe your **thoughts and beliefs (B)** about taking the math achievement test based on the scenario. Please feel free to describe additional feelings and beliefs that weren't mentioned.*

"Now I would like [Volunteer's name], *with the help of the group members, to relate the **consequences (C)** that might occur if one continues to have the negative-irrational thoughts and beliefs.*

"Now I would like [Volunteer's name], *with the help of the group members, to relate some* **disputing beliefs (D)** *that might be helpful to combat the negative-irrational thoughts and beliefs expressed earlier.*

"Now I would like [Volunteer's name], *with the help of the group members, to relate the* **effects (E)** *that might occur after one has used the disputing beliefs to combat the negative-irrational thoughts and beliefs expressed about the math achievement test."*

6. After the students have completed the introductory activity, the group leader will relate to the students, *"Please write down on the handout a stressful event/activity* **(activating event [A])** *that you have been going through"* (Appendix A).

   After the students have written down this stressful event, the group leader relates,

   "Now apply the event that you have written down to the ABCs on the handout" (Appendix A).

7. Then the leader says, *"I need a volunteer who is willing to verbally share his or her activity as well as act it out with other group members.*

   "Now we will act out [Volunteer's name's] *event using the ABCs.* [Volunteer's name], *please describe the* **activating event**." If you are using props, then you will also ask for a volunteer to hold the "**A**" sign.

8. Next the leader says, "[Volunteer's name], *please describe a stressful activating event to the group."* After the group member describes the activating event, then relate the following, *"I need to have some individuals volunteer who are willing to play people related to the event. I also need group members to volunteer to represent the beliefs and emotional consequences. Pretend that you are on a stage and that you will announce the beliefs and emotional consequences as an actor would.*

   "For example, once the event is acted out, then the 'Belief' role will state the negative beliefs about the event. This person is usually in the background and is similar to a narrator of a play. Then the person with the 'Consequence' role will state how this makes him or her feel."

   If you are using props, then you will also ask for a volunteer to hold the "**C**" sign next to the "**A**" and "**B**" sign.

   "Also I would like a volunteer to state some **disputing beliefs (D)** *that he or she thinks might be helpful to combat the negative-irrational thoughts and beliefs expressed earlier. This person is also in the background and speaks after the 'Consequence' role is done."*

   If you are using props, then you will also ask for a volunteer to hold the "**D**" sign next to the "**A**," "**B**," and "**C**" sign.

   "Now I would like the volunteer to relate the effects (E) that he or she thinks might occur after one has used the disputing beliefs to combat the negative-irrational thoughts."

If you are using props, then you will also ask for a volunteer to hold the "**E**" sign next to the "**A**," "**B**," and "**C**" sign.

The group leader might also ask the other group members not participating for their thoughts and feelings in response to what has been said.

9. After the first volunteer group member has discussed and enacted his or her ABCs, then ask for another volunteer and follow the directions for number 8 again. The group leader may choose to do this with as many members as time allows.

10. After the volunteers have discussed and enacted their ABCs, use the handout in Appendix B to have a final discussion of the activity.

Suggested Modifications (for Special Needs Populations): In a school setting most students who need special accommodations will have those outlined in an Individualized Education Plan (IEP). The counselor should become familiar with IEPs for any of the group members and make adjustments as needed. Examples of accommodations for this group could include having someone read the handouts to the group member, providing an interpreter if needed, or a student with a cognitive disability could be paired with another student.

Evaluation Plan: A 5-item true/false assessment (Appendix C) will be given to the members of the group at the end of the session to help the group leader measure what has been learned during the activity.

REFERENCES

Ellis, A., & Ellis, D. J. (2011). *Rational emotional behavioral therapy: Theories of psychotherapy series*. Washington, DC: American Psychological Association.

Ellis, A., & Harper, R. A. (1975). A guide to rationale living (3rd ed.). Chatsworth, CA: Wilshire Book Company.

Icebreakers, Ice Breakers, Ice Breaker Games. (n.d.). *Icebreakers.ws*. Retrieved from http://www.icebreakers.ws

Appendix A: Albert Ellis's ABCs Handout

1. You will be asked to think of an event that has occurred. This event can be something in the past, present, or future, about which you had/have negative thoughts and feelings. For example: A student who is average at math is given a pop quiz on some math problems. Immediately, this student states to him- or herself, "I can't do this; I am going to fail." (These are irrational thoughts or thoughts that are negatively directed toward the student.) This student's belief is that since he or she is average at math, he or she will **NEVER** be able to do well on an exam. This **belief** may then cause the student to become anxious (emotions) and sick to his or her stomach, which leads to the student not putting his or her full effort into the test (behavior)

and thus getting a bad grade (consequence). Let's apply the ABCs to the above event:

A = Activating event: pop quiz in math.

B = Belief about the event: "I can't do this; I am going to fail." This student's belief is that since he or she is average at math then he or she will **NEVER** be able to do well on an exam.

C = Consequences that result from the belief around the event: Student becomes anxious (emotions) and sick to his or her stomach, which leads to the student not putting full effort into the test (behavior) and thus getting a bad grade (consequence).

D = Disputing thoughts/beliefs about the event: Student changes the irrational thinking to more rational thinking: "I can do this. I am going to get a good grade, but even if I don't it is not the end of the world."

E = Effect of the disputing thought/belief: Student believes that he or she will do well and concentrates on the pop quiz, which in turn leads to a passing grade.

2. Think of an event that has occurred about which you have/had negative thoughts or feelings.

3. Describe the event below in some detail. (This will be the A, activating event.)

4. Apply the ABCs to the event:

A = Activating event (refer to number 4 above)

B = Belief about the event

C = Consequences that result from the belief around the event

D = Disputing thoughts/beliefs about the event

E = Effect of the disputing thought/belief (Effects may not occur immediately when you write them down, but after some time, practice, and belief then you will begin to see the effects of the disputing thought/belief.)

Appendix B: Final Discussion Questions Handout

"Now that we have discussed and enacted many of the members' ABCs I want to review what the ABCs are again, and discuss how you might apply them to future issues."

The following are questions to use for discussion.

1. Describe Albert Ellis's ABCDEs.
2. What did you learn from doing the activity involving the ABCs?
3. Briefly describe another event that could be applicable to the ABCs.
4. Describe some irrational thoughts and beliefs.
5. Now replace those irrational thoughts and beliefs with rational thoughts and beliefs.
6. Describe how those rational thoughts and beliefs apply to the ABCs.
7. How might you apply the ABCs in the future?

Appendix C: Evaluation

This is a five-question TRUE/FALSE assessment over what was discussed in group today.

Please circle either True or False below after you read each statement.

1. True or False   The ABCs represent the following:
   A= Activating Event
   B = Belief
   C = Consequence
   D = Disputing belief
   E = Effect of the disputing belief

2. True or False   Feeling sick to your stomach after thinking I am going to fail a test is an example of a consequence.

3. True or False   You don't have the control to change your irrational thoughts and beliefs to rational thoughts and beliefs.

4. True or False   Events are more important than our attitude about them.

5. True or False   Using the ABCs helps you create more helpful thoughts about problems.

DOING SOMETHING DIFFERENT

Laura Bruneau

This simple prop intervention can be used in a variety of delivery systems, including individual counseling, small-group counseling, and classroom guidance. Based on the solution-focused concept of "doing something different," this intervention facilitates student understanding of how behaviors influence thoughts and feelings about situations. Using a prop, such as a handheld game controller, provides greater impact by (a) encouraging self-reflection and (b) making the discussion more memorable for the student.

Modality: Drama

ASCA National Model Domain: Academic or Personal/Social

Deliver via: Individual, group, or classroom guidance

Age Level: Elementary, middle, or high school (Appropriate for use with any grade level when examples and follow-up processing questions match students' developmental level.)

Indications: Could be used for a variety of concerns, including but not limited to: making friends, earning better grades, relating with parents, taking personal responsibility, and so on. In particular, it works well for students who feel "stuck" in a situation and have difficulty considering alternative solutions.

Materials: Handheld game controller (e.g., for PlayStation, Xbox, GameCube).

Preparation: None

Instructions:

1. Introduce the intervention by explaining that the student will be trying something new. This will help to pique the student's interest and raise the expectation that something different is going to happen.

2. Begin with a general dialogue about video games, such as favorite games. Introduce the handheld game controller by asking the student to explain how it works. For example, the student can show you a series of moves used when navigating a video game (e.g., with a PlayStation controller, a student may hold down the "X" and the "O" button simultaneously to produce an action, such as jumping). This brief warm-up phase creates a dialogue between you and the student (or between students), allowing rapport to be developed. For example, you can learn about video games the student enjoys and the student can take pride in teaching the school counselor something new.

3. Shift into the following dialogue with the student:

   School counselor: *"Imagine you are playing a game in which you have to successfully complete levels in order to win the game. In one of these levels, you had to jump over a canyon in order to finish the level. Let's say you hold the 'X' and 'O' buttons at the same time to jump over the canyon, but this doesn't work. Instead, you fall into the canyon. What would you do on your next attempt? Would you try the same combination again?"*

   Student: *"No, that would be silly. It didn't work the first time. I would do something different."*

   School counselor: *"Just to clarify, you would do a new or different move, something that would allow you to be successful or to get what you really want?"*

   Student: *"Yes!"*

   School counselor: *"Great! So, let me ask you this: How is doing the same moves over and over again in your own life working out for you? For example, you want to make new friends but you don't want to put yourself out there to meet new people."*

   Student: *"Oh, I never thought of it that way. I guess it's really not working out that well."*

   School counselor: *"Sometimes people get stuck in patterns of behavior. It can happen to anyone, especially when things feel hard or difficult. However, when people are stuck, they might end up doing the same things over and over again, while expecting different results. How does that fit for you?"*

Student: *"It makes sense. So, if I don't do something different, things might not ever change?"*

School counselor: *"Maybe, maybe not. We really can't predict the future. But sometimes when people try new or different ways of behaving, this can help them feel more hopeful and better about the situation. A small change may lead to a bigger one. Let's focus this back to you and your desire to make new friends. Going back to the video game example, what moves do you seem to be choosing to do over and over again in your own life?"*

Student: *"Well, as you said, I really want to make new friends but I expect others to come up and approach me. Because they don't, I usually just feel worse."*

School counselor: *"So, this move doesn't seem to be working for you. What could you do differently?"*

Student: *"Well, I guess I could try to start a conversation with someone. . . ."*

4. After further discussion (and feedback from other students if done in a group or classroom-guidance lesson), have the student develop a game plan for the next week or an appropriate time frame. Encourage students to consider alterative behaviors that will help them get what they really want. A specific, measurable, achievable, relevant, and time-bound (SMART) goal can be developed, for example, "During this next week, I will talk to one new person in class at least once a day and document what happened in a journal that will be shared with my school counselor."

Suggested Modifications: Another popular analogy used to explain the concept of *doing something different* is a car being stuck in the snow/mud and spinning its wheels over and over again. The vocabulary used to explain and process the concept may need to be modified depending on student developmental level and experience. In addition, the school counselor can use a variety of video game examples to explain the point, depending on gender, age, and interests, as shaped by the initial student–school counselor dialogue. This activity is appropriate for most students and may be especially helpful for those who respond well to imagery, as well as those who have an interest in video games.

Evaluation Plan: To evaluate the effectiveness of this intervention, inquire about the student's initial reaction to the prop intervention. For example, a scaling question can be used to assess the student's level of motivation in *doing something different*, for example, "On a scale of 1 to 5, with 1 being you don't think this will work and 5 being that you are ready to try this as soon as you leave here today, how would you rate yourself?" Looking at the long-term impact, you can follow up on the SMART goals developed each week and use a contingency management chart to monitor progress.

15 Drama-Based Interventions in the Career Domain

A CAREER FOR ME?

Lacey Ricks and Elizabeth Hancock

This activity is designed to be utilized in the working phase of small school counseling groups aimed at career exploration and development with adolescents. Providing a creative atmosphere, this activity encourages adolescents to explore, develop, and articulate career goals during single or multiple group sessions.

Modality: Narrative/Drama

ASCA National Model Domain: Career

Deliver via: Group counseling

Age Level: High school (10th to 12th grades)

Indications: Effective for adolescents unsure of career plans or goals; those who lack focus or motivation in discussing career plans; or those who are considering applying for college, trade school, or pursuing another field of study.

Materials: Paper, writing instruments, stickers, glitter, markers, or other materials to use for decoration of product; access to *Occupational Outlook Handbook* or Occupational Information Network (requires Internet access).

Preparation: Prior to beginning the group, discuss confidentiality requirements with group participants. Establish group rules that emphasize respect and consideration for all group members. Screen group members to ensure appropriate placement within the group. (For example, students with no career direction in mind should be placed in a group together, students with beginning career goals should be placed in a group together, etc.). Locate the *Occupational Outlook Handbook* (Bureau of Labor Statistics, 2014; http://www.bls.gov/ooh/) and *O*NET Resource Center* (n.d.; http://www.onetonline.org/) using the Internet or other published materials.

Instructions:

1. Introduce the activity by asking students to write a poem, short story, or song about their current stage of career development/exploration. The facilitator may need to assist students with a brief introduction or explanation of this activity. During the beginning stages of career exploration, students should be encouraged to look at their interests, strengths, experience, the variety of career fields that exist, and to think outside of the box.

2. Once group members have completed their expressive piece, the group facilitator should lead the group in a discussion of what their expressive piece means to them. Additionally, students should be asked to hold on to their expressive piece for future use.

   Example Processing Questions:
   a. *"What type of anxiety or stress is felt when trying to pick a career?"*
   b. *"How do you feel when parents, teachers, or others ask you about what you want to do?"*
   c. *"What does it mean to select a career (or major/college) because someone wants you to?"*
   d. *"What ideas do you have for yourself for your future?"*

3. The group facilitator should introduce concepts related to career exploration. These should include: interests, strengths, and experience/prior knowledge.

4. Ask group members to define what the following terms mean to them: *career, job, work,* and *money*. Have the group select one member to write down the definitions that the group comes up with.

   Example Processing Questions:
   a. *"What does having a career mean to you?"*
   b. *"What does work mean to you?"*
   c. *"What is more important, money or happiness?"*
   d. *"What does it mean to select a career for money rather than what you really want to do?"*

5. Ask group members to identify three careers of interest to them. The students should be reminded to consider their interests, strengths, experience/prior knowledge, the variety of career fields that exist, and to think outside of the box.

6. Once all group members have identified careers of interest, provide the group members with access to the *Occupational Outlook Handbook* (Bureau of Labor Statistics, 2014) and *O*NET* (n.d.). Encourage participants to read through and share careers that are interesting to them. While exploring careers, participants should note the nature of the work, education requirements, and salary/earnings.

7. Once group members have completed investigating careers of interest, they should be allowed to act out the researched careers for the group members.

8. Group members will guess the careers that are being acted out (using charades, miming, or short one-person skit) by other group members.

9. The group facilitator should lead the group in a discussion of the careers that are acted out, remembering to encourage the students to be respectful of one another.

10. Once all group members have participated, allow participants to re-read the material for any additional careers that may be of interest. (Steps 6 to 9 may be repeated as many times as desired.)

11. Upon completion of reading or acting, group members are asked to write an expressive piece, such as a poem, song, or short story, describing what they have learned. This may be decorated using the optional materials provided.

12. Group members should take turns reading their expressive pieces to the group.

13. Upon completion of the activity, group facilitators should process the experience with the group.

   Example Processing Questions:
   a. *"What was it like exploring careers that are of interest to you?"*
   b. *"What was it like listening to the different careers that interest other group members?"*
   c. *"Why is it important to identify our own strengths and interests versus relying on what others report?"*

Suggested Modifications (for Special Needs Populations): Materials may be adapted to allow for use and participation by individuals with disabilities. This may include a large-screen reader when accessing the Internet, or larger-size pens or pencils. Additionally, the facilitator may consider reading or explaining the careers listed/explored in the *Occupational Outlook Handbook* (Bureau of Labor Statistics, 2014) and Occupational Information Network (n.d.).

Evaluation Plan: To evaluate this intervention, the facilitator may compare the first expressive piece to the second expressive piece. Also, a questionnaire is included that may be used pre- and postintervention as an assessment or to identify students in need of additional career exploration.

Students may complete this survey as a pre- and postactivity assessment of their current knowledge and state of career exploration.

1. Define the following terms:
   a. Career
   b. Job
2. Do you have a career in mind for yourself?
3. What do your parents, teachers, or guardians think you should do for a career?
4. Do you agree with this? Why or why not?
5. List your five top strengths:
   a.
   b.
   c.

    d.

    e.

6. List your three favorite activities (that may lead to a career):

    a.

    b.

    c.

7. List three careers that you are (seriously) interested in:

    a.

    b.

    c.

8. Do you plan to go to college, trade school, or complete other advanced education? What will you study?

REFERENCES

Bureau of Labor Statistics. (2014). Occupational outlook handbook. Retrieved June 11, 2014, from http://www.bls.gov/ooh

O*NET Resource Center. (n.d.). Retrieved June 11, 2014, from http://www.onetcenter.org

16 ✻ Drama-Based Interventions in the Personal/Social Domain

ELVIS BLINDFOLD MAZE

Diane J. Shea and James R. Huber

*T*his is a trust-building activity in which students take turns being a "blindfolded" follower and the leader. Details are listed below under the instructions.

Modality: Narrative/Drama

ASCA National Model Domain: Personal/Social

Deliver via: Group and/or classroom guidance

Age Level: Middle, high school

Indications: Can be used to facilitate personal/group learning regarding building trust, becoming a leader, risk taking, being aware of feelings, team building, and social skills

Materials: Blindfolds, a simple maze drawn on paper (e.g., Elvis trying to get to Graceland, a dog trying to get to a bone, etc.), pencils.

Preparations: Room should be arranged so that students sit at a table or desk in pairs facing one another.

Instructions:
1. Explain to students that this is a _____ (e.g., trust-building, team-building) exercise.
2. In each dyad, have one of the students be the leader and the other wear the blindfold.
3. Place the maze on the desk in front of the blindfolded student.
4. Instruct the leader to give the pencil to her or his partner and place it at the beginning of the maze.
5. The leader then has the task of verbally directing the partner through the maze without touching his or her hand.
6. Once the partner gets to the end of the maze, the pair switches roles.

7. When all students have completed both roles, ask students to process the experience. *"What did it feel like to try to lead the person through the maze? What did it feel like to have to trust the leader to get you through the maze?"*

Suggested Modifications: Depending on the age of the students, the maze may be made more or less complex.

Evaluation Plan: Gather perception data based on age group and purpose of exercise. For example, for a high school leadership-building group:

1. How valuable was this exercise in terms of having a responsibility of leading another?
   Not at all _____ A little _____ Somewhat valuable _____Valuable _____ Very valuable _____
2. Did you learn anything about yourself in this exercise?

I SEE YOUR TRUE COLORS

Magdalena M. Furniss

*T*his activity is designed to be used in a group counseling setting. Students *"show their true colors" by selecting a piece of colorful fabric from a varied collection and then sharing and exploring their feelings with fellow group members. This activity reinforces some of the key principles of group therapy: universality ("I am not alone"), altruism (sharing one's strengths and helping other group members), development of socialization techniques (in a safe and supportive setting), and group cohesiveness (a sense of belonging). At the same time, this experiential activity allows participants to get in touch with their feelings by tracking their emotional responses and locating the emotion in their bodies during the course of the session.*

Modality: Drama Therapy

ASCA National Model Domain: Personal/Social

Deliver via: Group counseling

Age Level: Elementary, middle, or high school

Indications: Appropriate to use as an ice breaker during the forming stage of a group or at any time in the beginning of the session in an abbreviated form.

Materials: Large pieces of fabric ("scarves"), about 3 in. Ü 3 in., in a wide variety of colors and textures (e.g., solid colors, sheer, patterned, lacy, multicultural prints); you need at least twice as many scarves as students in the group; a large bag to contain the scarves.

Preparation: Place the scarves in a loose pile in the center of the circle or any other easily accessible place in the room.

Instructions:

1. Invite the students to choose a scarf based on the color and/or texture that appeals to them and that reflects what they are feeling today.
2. After students choose their scarves, ask them to sit in a circle.
3. Invite the students to hold their scarves or drape them on their bodies in a way that will communicate to other group members what they are feeling today. Remind students to avoid assigning their own values and meanings to the colors and textures.
4. The students are then invited to share their rationale for their choices and the meaning they have assigned the color and texture. For example, a student may say: "I chose red and I put it over my head because I'm feeling very angry with someone." Or: "I chose green because I'm feeling hopeful that I did well on a science test this morning."

   Sample questions to ask to facilitate sharing and foster universality and group cohesiveness include: *"Is anyone else feeling hopeful today? I see you draped the yellow scarf over your shoulders. What feeling are you trying to show us? Everyone in the group chose a different color and we are holding them in different ways. What does that make you think? Where in your body do you feel hope, anger, excitement, and so on?"*

5. Ask the students to *transform their feeling*, if they wish to, by changing the way they are holding their scarves and to track their emotions in the process. Prompts may include: *"How can you transform the feeling you are experiencing right now? What can you do with your scarf to show that? Where do you feel it in your body now? What was it like for you to transform your feeling?"*

6. Encourage students to try more than one type of transformation (e.g., hide, release, or transfer the scarf to another person), in order to experience a variety of resulting emotional responses.

7. Conclude the session by processing with the students what it was like to transform their feelings, where in their bodies they felt it before and after, and what emotional responses were elicited by the transformation.

Suggested Modifications (for Special Needs Populations): Modify language to match the developmental level of the student. For students who have limited language skills, this activity can focus on nonverbal expression facilitated by the counselor.

Evaluation Plan: The counselor may evaluate the effectiveness of this activity using a handout that features a chart of feelings, colors, places in the body where the feelings are located, transformation types, and resulting responses (see Figure 16.1). The chart may be simplified for younger students.

Feeling	Color	Where in the Body?	Transformation	Where in the Body?

FIGURE 16.1 "I See Your True Colors" assessment chart for students.

IMAGINE YOURSELF AS A HOUSE

Magdalena M. Furniss

*T*his activity is designed to be used in an individual counseling setting. Through the metaphor of the house as self, the student is guided to explore his or her self-concept, ideas about relating to others, and desire for change. This activity may also be useful in exploring the client's cultural background and beliefs. Both the completed structure and the process of constructing the house are considered during the session.

Modality: Drama

ASCA National Model Domain: Personal/Social

Deliver via: Individual counseling

Age Level: Elementary, middle, or high school

Indications: Appropriate to use with students presenting with issues related to limited self-awareness, social competency, and self-esteem, as well as experiencing an interpersonal or familial conflict.

Materials: A large selection of LEGO® blocks (or similar) in multiple colors and shapes, preferably including elements such as doors, windows, fences, flat base pieces, and other architectural elements; a camera for taking a photograph of the house.

Preparation: Place a flat bin of blocks on a cleared flat surface such as a table or floor.

Instructions:

1. Invite the student to build a house out of the blocks and explain that the house may be realistic or imaginary. A time limit is specified and should be about half of the session.

2. As the student builds, reflect the student's process through neutral comments (e.g., "*You're putting a roof on the house.*") and refrain from evaluative comments (e.g., "*Good job making the roof so strong!*"). Observe the student's behavior, noting whether the student was excited, comfortable, hesitant, nervous, picky, random, and so on, during the building process.

3. Keep track of time and gently remind the student how much time is left to finish building.

4. Invite the student to speak as the house: "*If you were this house, what would you say about yourself?*" For example, "I am a house. I am surrounded by a fence so nobody gets near." If the student is not comfortable speaking as the house in first person, invite him or her to simply speak about the house, noting details and purposes of the different elements. Sample questions to facilitate the student's self-discovery and potential for change may include: "*I see you placed a tall fence around the house. What's the fence for? As a person, how do you keep people away and how do you let them in? What would it be like for you to make a gate in the fence? There is a lightning rod on the roof. How does it work? As a person, do you ever feel like lightning hit you? What is that like and how do you deal with it? Who lives inside the house? What is the mood inside the house right now? Does it change and, if so, how? Where is this house located? Are there other houses nearby? What kind of landscape do you imagine around it?*"

5. Process with the student the behavior you observed during the building process. For example, if the student was hesitant in choosing blocks, you can say, "*I noticed you seemed unsure what blocks to choose.*" Allow the student to elaborate.

6. Conclude the session by asking questions about what it was like for the student to make a house out of blocks and to speak as the house or about it. What aspects of the activity were comfortable and fun? What felt uncomfortable?

7. If feasible, the house can be saved for another session and the construction and exploration can continue. If the blocks are needed for other students, the counselor offers a camera to the student to take a photograph of the house before it is taken apart, or takes a photograph him- or herself. The photograph can be printed for the student and the discussion can continue during the next session.

8. Younger students may quickly get attached to the house they built and become sad about taking it apart. Process with the student the feelings that emerge about dismantling the house.

Suggested Modifications (for Special Needs Populations): The counselor may need to modify the language to match the developmental level of the student. Larger blocks such as DUPLO® blocks (or similar) may be used with students who have difficulty with fine motor skills. For students who have limited language skills, this activity can focus on nonverbal expression facilitated by the counselor.

Evaluation Plan: The counselor may evaluate the effectiveness of this activity using a handout containing the following questions, which are focused on the student's positive discoveries and desire to change.

Student Handout
1. What did you learn about yourself when you were building a house out of blocks?
2. What are some of your strengths?
3. How are you unique?
4. What would you like to change about yourself?

LABELS ARE FOR CANS, NOT FOR PEOPLE

Sandra Logan and Tori Charette

The intent of this activity is to increase student awareness of the weight of first impressions and assumptions. By having students wear stereotypical labels and interact with one another according to the labels assigned, they can become aware of the consequences of accepting the connotation of such assumptions.

Modality: Role-Play/Drama

ASCA National Model Domain: Personal/Social

Deliver via: Classroom guidance, in 40 to 45 minutes (one class period)

Age Level: Middle school

Indications: Useful with students needing to grow in their multicultural awareness, openness to difference, and acceptance of stereotypes

Materials: Headbands with labels; at least four cans of soup or other nonperishable products.

Preparation: Prior to the lesson, prepare headbands with labels of stereotypical roles. Select those most appropriate to your student population, or make up your own:

■ Cheerleader
■ Class President
■ Preppy
■ Dork/Dweeb
■ Loner

- Teacher's Pet
- Jock
- Video Gamer
- Player
- Rich Kid
- Poor Kid
- Goth/Punk/Alternative
- Ditzy Girl/Airhead
- Class Treasurer
- Social Butterfly
- American Idol
- Smarty Pants
- Gangster

Instructions:

1. Begin the lesson with a brief 5-minute discussion on how our words affect each other. Ask students to volunteer with words that we use to describe one another. Write the words from the brainstorming on the board. Identify whether each of the words written offer a positive or negative connotation.
2. Ask for student volunteers. Although four students would suffice, six to eight is ideal.
3. Attach headbands to volunteers. Be sure that students are not aware of the label on the headband that they are wearing.
4. Inform student volunteers that they are a part of a role-play scenario in which they are being asked to plan a school dance. They are to respond to one another according to the role identified on the other person's headband.
5. Allow students 10 to 15 minutes to role-play the scenario. As needed, provide some facilitation to group members who may be struggling. An alternative would be to give students 2 to 3 minutes to interact, then ask them to switch to another student. This will allow students to see a variety of reactions to the label they are wearing.
6. Once time has elapsed, wrap up the role-play and have student volunteers stand at the front of the classroom facing their peers.
7. Ask student volunteers about their experience of participating in the role-play.
8. Individually, ask student volunteers to guess what label is written on their headbands according to how the group responded to them. Allow other classmates to guess as well.
9. Wrap up the lesson with a brief discussion on the need to respect diversity and to not simply view people by labels imposed by others. Use the canned products to visually represent the ideas of the lesson.
10. Upon conclusion of the lesson, ask students to write a brief paper about a time in which they felt like they were treated according to a label imposed by another person.

Suggested Modifications (for Special Needs Populations): It may be necessary to use more developmentally appropriate terms, or to spend additional time providing explanations of the meaning of the different stereotypical roles. Describing the difference between positive and negative connotations of words may be helpful. The definition of *connotation*, according to Merriam-Webster.com (n.d.): "The suggesting of a meaning by a word apart from the thing it explicitly names or describes." For example, *loser* implies a negative connotation. On the other hand, *social butterfly* typically alludes to a positive connotation.

Evaluation Plan: Students will be asked to write a brief narrative about a time in which they were treated according to a label. Assessment will include whether students can identify a particular scenario in their life, as well as identify the feelings associated with that label (positive or negative connation).

REFERENCE

Merriam-Webster. (n.d.). "Connotation." Retrieved from http://www.merriam-webster.com/dictionary/connotation

---

MY SUPERHERO STRENGTH

Lacey Ricks and Elizabeth Hancock

*T*his activity is to be used in the termination phase of school counseling groups aimed at personal/social development of adolescents. This activity provides a fun and creative outlet for adolescents to articulate positive personal traits that they possess and can bring to current/future friendships.

Modality: Drama

ASCA National Model Domain: Personal/Social

Deliver via: Group

Age Level: 4th to 6th grade, but may be modified for younger and older age groups

Indications: This activity is designed for students experiencing difficulty making or maintaining friendships.

Materials: For this activity, students will need paper, pens, and pencils to describe their personal strengths. Additionally, construction paper, fabric, markers, glitter, string, scissors, glue, and other creative materials can be provided to the students to design their superhero costumes.

Preparation: Prior to beginning the group, discuss confidentiality requirements with group participants. Establish group rules that emphasize respect and consideration for all group members. Screen group members to ensure appropriate placement within the group. Identify superhero examples and the personal strengths they possess (superheroes can be traditional superheroes, famous individuals, or personal acquaintances of group members) to illustrate the activity to group members.

Instructions:

1. Facilitators should help group members define what it means to be a "superhero." Discuss the traits of a good superhero. Listed below are potential processing questions for superhero discussion:

   a. *"What is a 'superhero'?"*
   b. *"Do all 'superheroes' have to have super-human strength?"*
   c. *"What makes a person a 'superhero'?"*
   d. *"Who are some people that we all know who are 'superheroes'?"*
   e. *"What types of traits/characteristics do these people possess?"*

2. Once group members understand the concept of "superhero," they should be encouraged to discuss a person in their life whom they see as a superhero and what makes that person a superhero to them.

3. After group members can articulate what a superhero is and identify a person whom they consider to be a superhero, they should be allowed to work individually to invent their superhero descriptions.

4. While students work to invent their superhero descriptions, the facilitator should instruct group members to identify a superhero name for themselves, a description of their superhero strengths, and a plan for acting out these strengths to the group. The facilitator may want to encourage the students to be creative when thinking of their name and how to describe their strengths.

5. Once group members complete their superhero description, they should be allowed to use the creative materials provided (fabric, construction paper, etc.) to design their own superhero costume.

6. Once group members have completed their superhero description and superhero costume, they should be allowed to individually act out to the group their superhero strength.

7. Group members will guess the traits/characteristics that are being acted out by other group members.

8. Once group members have identified the traits/characteristics of the superhero acting out his or her persona, the individual should be allowed to discuss his or her superhero name and why his or her traits/characteristics are "super."

9. Group members should take turns acting out their superhero personas until all group members have had a chance to share with the group.

10. Upon completion of the activity, group facilitators should process the experience with the group. Below is a list of potential processing questions:

    a. *"What was it like identifying your 'superhero' strengths?"*
    b. *"How can these strengths help you make/maintain friendships?"*
    c. *"Did you notice any similarities among group members?"*
    d. *"How can we all be 'superheroes'?"*
    e. *"Why is it important to identify our personal strengths?"*

Suggested Modifications (for Special Needs Populations): The group facilitator may modify materials to be understood for group members and provide additional information, support, and explanation of terms to the group. Additionally, accommodations need to be made to adhere to each student's Individualized Education Plan or 504 Plan.

Evaluation Plan: Pre- and posttests can be used to assess students' understanding of the material. A sample assessment is included that can be given to participants before and after group participation.

Please answer your agreement level with the following questions using the responses listed below the question:

1. I am a good friend.
   Strongly Agree   Agree   Disagree   Strongly Disagree

2. I can identify positive qualities that I can bring to my friendships.
   Strongly Agree   Agree   Disagree   Strongly Disagree

3. I can identify qualities I want in a friend.
   Strongly Agree   Agree   Disagree   Strongly Disagree

4. I understand the qualities that make a good friend.
   Strongly Agree   Agree   Disagree   Strongly Disagree

Please answer the following two questions based on your experience:

5. List three positive qualities that you have:
   a. _____
   b. _____
   c. _____

6. List three positive qualities you want in a friend:
   a. _____
   b. _____
   c. _____

USING YOUR WORDS AGAINST BULLIES

Imelda N. Bratton

This activity is intended for use during classroom guidance. It discusses situations such as bullying and peer conflict that typically occur in life. Additionally, the counselor will demonstrate a way that children can verbalize their feelings appropriately. Children can role-play the response during the presentation so they may know how to respond when they are in similar situations.

Modality: Drama

ASCA National Model Domain: Personal/Social

Deliver via: Classroom guidance

Age level: Elementary

Indications: Can be used as a way to teach students how to respond appropriately to situations that they do not like. This is an easy-to-remember response that can be integrated as part of a campus-wide plan for positive behavior and empowerment development. This activity can be adapted to specific issues that a class or school is experiencing.

Materials: Pictures of various bully situations and a book that has a conflict situation, such as *King of the Playground* or *Bullies Never Win.*

Preparation: To help stimulate students' focus on the activity, have images ready to show at the beginning of the lesson. Provide ample room for student volunteers to role-play after reading the book.

Instructions:

1. Introduce the lesson by showing several pictures of bully or conflict situations (such as arguing over a toy, pushing in line, hitting, etc.). Ask students if they have ever been in similar situations. Have them briefly describe how it felt. Discuss how most students have times when they do not like what is happening to them, for example if a friend pushes them or when a classmate tells them to do something they do not want to do.

2. Read the story to the class. Throughout the book talk about what is going on and how the characters feel when they are in bullying situations or have issues they do not like. Model empathy for the character who feels bad to promote empathy development in students.

3. Suggested questions to explore during and after reading the book:

   ■ *"How do you think the character felt during the bully situation or issue he or she experienced?"*
   ■ *"How do you feel when you have a conflict with someone else?"*
   ■ *"How do you feel when you see someone else having a conflict?"*
   ■ *"What do you do when you have a conflict with someone else?"*
   ■ *"How does it usually turn out?"*
   ■ *"What do you think is the best thing to do when you see someone else having a conflict?"*

4. Let students know you will show them an easy way to tell others to leave them alone when they do not like what is happening. Show them by standing up, lifting your hand with a flat palm facing out (as if you were saying "stop" with your hand), and using a firm voice say the words: *"Please stop it, I don't like it."*

5. Discuss with the students that by saying these words they can tell someone else what they are feeling and they can tell the other person to stop what he or she is doing. Tell students that they do not have to use ugly words to tell someone to stop. These words are nice, but they are also powerful. Have the class practice saying these words all together at the same time so they may try it out and begin to feel comfortable.

6. Select a student to role-play a situation, such as pushing. The counselor will pretend to push the student and have the student use the words, "Please stop it, I don't like that," in response. Never allow the student to role-play being a bad guy; it is too much fun, and you do not want to encourage negative behaviors. Select several students and repeat various situations to model the response.

7. Tell students that sometimes they may see classmates having conflicts with each other. For example, they may see one classmate saying ugly words to another classmate. Let them know that they can use the words, "Please stop it, I don't like that," to others when they see someone being hurt by someone else. This helps empower students who are bystanders during bully situations.

8. To review the lesson, have a few students describe something they learned during the lesson. End the lesson by having the class repeat the words, "Please stop it, I don't like that," all together.

Suggested Modifications (for Special Needs Populations): Students with limited speech abilities may use the hand signal and shake their heads to indicate "no."

Evaluation Plan: The school counselor may evaluate the effectiveness of this activity by observing how students interact after the lesson is taught. It may be necessary to intervene during a conflictual interaction between students to help redirect and remind the students how to use these words, "Please stop that, I don't like it." Additionally, the school counselor can check in with the class and teacher to see how they are using their words and the effect it has had on classroom behavior.

REFERENCES

Cuyler, M., & Howard, A. (2009). *Bullies never win*. New York, NY: Simon & Schuster.

Naylor, P. R. (1994). *King of the playground*. New York, NY: Simon & Schuster.

VII ❈ Other Modes of Creative Expression

17 ✤ Creative Interventions in the Academic Domain

SAND TRAY FOR SPECIAL NEEDS GROUPS

Suneetha B. Manyam

The purpose of this technique is to develop and refine social skills through expressive sand tray technique among children with special needs or children in general. Children and adolescents, especially with special needs, often have difficulty in expressing their thoughts, emotions, and experiences verbally. This activity helps them to convey their feelings and thoughts in a safe and creative way. In addition, sand tray therapy also provides them with a positive outlet for their pent-up emotions and channels their energy in a positive way. Through group sand tray technique, children with special needs will have an opportunity to interact with their peers and vent in a safe and playful environment. The duration of the activity may range from 1 to 1.5 hours and the technique can be utilized in small-group, family, or individual counseling settings. Sand tray groups can be conducted in a play therapy room, counselor's office, or any art/sand tray room at the school. According to Kalff (1993), sand tray provides a medium of expression through nonverbal imagery. Group sand tray technique not only facilitates students' manifestations of their unconscious totality, but also enhances prosocial skills through sharing and articulation of their sand tray worlds. The counselor should encourage the children to work in dyads or triads to collect the miniatures from the cabinets while building the individual sand trays for 30 minutes. Then, the counselor will ask the students to share their sand tray world to the whole group. The counselor will then process the content by facilitating a discussion via asking reflective questions and drawing themes from the children's participation.

Modality: Expressive Art and Imaginary Play

ASCA National Model Domain: Academic and Personal/Social

Deliver via: Group and/or individual counseling

Age Level: Elementary, middle, and high school (Appropriate for use with any age group as long as you provide age-appropriate miniatures and toys based on the individual's developmental level.)

Indications: Activity can be used with small groups in which the focus is developing prosocial and friendship skills; encouraging children's nonverbal expression of thoughts and feelings in a creative way; motivating children with special needs to vent their pent-up emotions through a positive outlet; developing networks of cooperation, sharing, and support; building articulation and listening skills; taking personal responsibility and decision making

Materials: The sand trays are plastic boot box trays filled with play sand from any home improvement store. The base of the boot box measures approximately 13"L × 6"W × 5"D. You will also need three big working tables, six chairs, six bamboo baskets for collecting miniatures, and six small or medium dry paint brushes for clean-up of the sand. Miniatures for building in the sand trays include, but are not limited to, small buildings, people, animals (wild, domestic, farm, ocean etc.), fencing, landscape items (trees, rocks, etc.), stones, monuments, transportation (cars, planes, motorcycles, etc.), sea shells, and various characters from life and fantasy.

Preparation: Have the sand trays set out on tables arranged in such a fashion that students are in close proximity to one another but with one sand tray in front of each chair. Also nearby, have a basket to retrieve items and a dry paint brush for smoothing the sand after building the sand tray.

Instructions: Group members should be selected based on similar developmental levels and, ideally, each group should complete the 1.5-hour activity once a week for 4 to 6 weeks.

1. Introduction to sand trays: Introduce the activity by asking students to choose a partner to work with at each table. There will be two students placed at each table with individual sand trays.
2. Explaining the rules: Explain or write the three important rules on the black board or on the poster board. They are (a) only two members at a time can gather items from the cabinet of miniatures; (b) build in your own sand tray—you cannot place or remove the items from others' sand trays without their permission; and (c) be respectful of others.
3. Instructions to "build a world" in your own sand tray: Invite the students to construct a *sand world* in their individual trays. Children can talk with their partner or peers while constructing the world. This may facilitate cooperation and sharing among them. Be a passive observer during this process and answer children's questions if any arise.
4. Building time: Inform the students that the maximum time allotted for constructing the sand world is 30 minutes. If they complete the task early, they may help their partner if he or she permits.

5. Sharing time: Invite the students to share their worlds one by one with the whole group for the next 30 minutes. All of the children should listen to what others are sharing and should be allowed to ask appropriate questions to either their peers or you.

6. Process time: The main purpose of this is to encourage discussion among the students. You will lead this discussion using open-ended questions to process the themes that emerged from the sand worlds for the next 15 minutes. These questions may include the following: *"What do you think/feel about . . .? How did you do that? What would happen if you . . .? What else could you do? What was the best part? What was the difficult part?"*

7. Clean-up and wrap-up: In the next 10 minutes, ask the students to clean up their sand trays by placing the miniatures and sand trays in the cabinets. They can use the baskets to carry the materials from the table to the cabinets. Children will be instructed to clean the extra sand on the tables by smoothing it with the dry paint brush. In the final 5 minutes, summarize the major themes that emerged from the session and encourage the students to apply the prosocial skills that they learned regarding respect, turn taking, personal responsibility, and so on, to their daily lives.

Suggested Modifications (for Special Needs Populations): Counselors can use this technique within individual or family sessions. If it is a family session, the family members can be passive observers or can coconstruct the sand worlds by helping their special needs students. You may also choose a specific theme and ask the students to construct their sand worlds based on that theme. Another variation would be to ask two or three students to construct a part of a big sand tray. This requires mastery of a specific level of prosocial skill building like cooperation and sharing. It may also require constant monitoring and supervision from the counselor while the students are building a shared sand world. Teacher–student sand trays can also be constructed in a similar way to encourage rapport building among them. This technique may be helpful for any age groups that enjoy nonverbal expression as well as who respond positively to sensory and imaginary materials. This activity can be particularly helpful for the students who have experienced trauma or severe abuse; are dealing with grief and loss; or display impulsive, aggressive behavioral issues.

Evaluation Plan: Teachers, parents, family members, school administrators, and children with special needs can be interviewed or surveyed before and after a series of sand tray counseling sessions to evaluate the effectiveness of this technique in terms of their social skills and expression of thoughts and emotions.

REFERENCE

Kalff, M. (1993). Twenty points to be considered in the interpretation of a sandplay. *Journal of Sandplay Therapy, 2*(2), 17–35.

18 ❋ Creative Interventions in the Career Domain

GARDEN OF CARE

Michael Paz and Dee C. Ray

The Garden of Care is a school intervention in which the counselor facilitates small groups of children in the creation and maintenance of a flower or vegetable garden. The purpose of the Garden of Care is to teach students to nurture a living organism, develop a sense of responsibility, learn to work with others to accomplish a task, and cultivate a sense of community. Additionally, taking care of plants is a unique opportunity to teach children about environmental awareness. This activity is designed to be implemented with small groups, but individual discussions may also be held with each student. Students who show aggressive behaviors toward others or who struggle to socialize appropriately with their same-aged peers will benefit from interacting with the other students who are also participating in taking care of a plant. Through individual and group weekly meetings, the school counselor will create an environment in which students will feel safe to share, discuss, and process what they have learned from their experience of taking care of their garden.

Modality: Horticultural Therapy

ASCA Domain: Career or Personal/Social

Deliver via: Small-group counseling

Age Level: 3rd, 4th, and 5th grade

Indications: This activity is indicated for students who struggle with impulsivity or self-control, exhibit aggressive behaviors and may be labeled as bullies, and have difficulty socializing appropriately with their same-aged peers.

Materials: Seeds for easy–to-grow vegetables such as tomatoes, potatoes, or carrots or annuals such as sunflowers, tall zinnias, or cosmos; potting soil;

signposts to mark plants; small, plastic pots or cups; 6 × 6 ft. garden plot; water; sufficient light; and small garden tools such as hand trowel, gloves, and so on.

Preparation:
1. Buy or solicit donations for the materials.
2. Prepare garden plot. An ideal plot is 6 × 6 ft. However, plots can be larger or smaller. Large tubs can also be used as garden plots, but holes will need to be drilled into the bottom for drainage. Each group will need its own plot.
3. Grouping. Organize groups of up to five students from 3rd, 4th, or 5th grade to participate in the Garden of Care.
4. Intervention. Each group of no more than five students will participate in a 6- to 8-week intervention, during which they will plant seeds and will be responsible for the care of the plants.

Instructions:

Meet with each group once a week for 30 minutes. During each 30-minute meeting, build a relationship with the students and use group-counseling skills to foster understanding and acceptance between the students who are participating in the Garden of Care. You will also process each student's experience of taking care of another living organism.

Week 1:
1. Meet with the group of students and introduce the Garden of Care activity by showing them the materials they will be using. Goals will be introduced and may include:
   a. Responsibility
   b. Care for another living organism
   c. Learning to work with others
2. Share pictures of gardens and discuss with students what can grow in gardens.
3. Introduce what is needed to grow a garden: soil, light, water, care.
4. Students will discuss what they as people need to grow, just like plants and vegetables.
5. Students decide what they want their garden to look like and what kinds of plants they would like to grow.

Week 2:
1. Ask each child to select seeds for one type of plant. The students will read the seed packets for directions. Facilitate discussion about what each student needs to grow his or her plant.
2. Students will list on a board or large sheet of paper the responsibilities needed to take care of the plants, such as (a) planting, (b) watering, (c) observing growth, and (d) weeding or trimming.
3. Students will plant seeds in a garden plot or may start seeds in cups if desired.
4. Students will place signposts for each of the plants in the garden.

5. Students will decide which tasks from the list of responsibilities each member will take for the week.
6. Provide supervision and assist students when necessary as they follow recommended directions on the seed packet. The number of weeks that will be needed to have a seedling sprout will depend on the type of seed that is used. Some suggestions to consider when planting the seeds are:
   a. Maintain even moisture in the soil so that seeds germinate properly.
   b. Exposure to adequate light is essential.
   c. Keep seedlings warm (70°F to 74°F).
   d. Have students check soil daily to keep it from drying out.

Week 3 through Week 8 (depending on how fast the seedlings grow):
1. During each group session, the students discuss how tasks were conducted and if each member met his or her responsibilities. They will also decide upon different task assignments each week. If responsibilities are not met, the counselor facilitates that discussion between group members.
2. Process with the students what they are experiencing as the plant grows or if it happens to not be growing. Engage the students in age-appropriate discussions about what they are experiencing and the feelings they have as they take care of their individual plants. Some suggestions for ways to engage students in discussions are: What have you noticed in your plant since the last week that we met? How has it been for you to take care of the plant over the last week? What have you learned about taking care of plants? About yourself?
3. If a plant does not grow, group members will brainstorm on how to help nurture the plant or discuss the need for planting a new seed.

Final Week:
1. Each student takes a picture of his or her plants/garden him- or herself.
2. Facilitate discussion of how the garden has helped students and what they have learned.
3. Ask students to make a list of what they learned in the garden that they can now apply every day in school.

Suggested Modifications (for Special Needs Populations): Any student with a physical disability may be partnered with a student who is also invited to participate in the Garden of Care. Students who have severe emotional disabilities will need additional energy and understanding from the counselor. Recruiting parent or other volunteers could be helpful in offering additional support for special needs students.

Evaluation Plan: The list developed at the final meeting of how group members will apply what they learned from the Garden of Care to how they function in school each day serves as the postevaluation for this intervention. The counselor can keep a copy of these lists and check with students periodically to see if they are still able to apply what they learned. Additionally, because the goals of the Garden of Care include increased understanding and nurturing of others, counselors can use behavioral instruments completed by teachers or parents to measure change from the beginning of the intervention to the end.

EXPLORING OCCUPATIONS THROUGH SAND TRAY AND MINIATURES

Varunee Faii Sangganjanavanich

The purpose of this intervention is to facilitate career development of elementary school students through the use of sand tray and miniatures. This intervention is suitable for their career developmental need— occupational information gathering. This intervention is conducted in a small-group format (six to eight students) where the counselor uses sand tray and miniatures to promote students' knowledge and understanding of different occupational information. A group environment not only makes this intervention informative, but also fun and interactive.

Modality: Other (sand tray)

ASCA National Model Domain: Career

Deliver via: Group

Age Level: Elementary school

Indications: This intervention can be used with all elementary school students, with a wide range of academic potential, as every student can benefit from learning more about occupational information. For some students, school counselors may notice that they appear to have less knowledge and understanding of occupational information than expected for their developmental level (e.g., if a student is unable to identity whether a white coat is associated with a physician), whereas for others, it is obvious that their development is higher than expected (e.g., a student is able to describe what a physician does and identify other objects associated with being a physician). Through group interaction, learning takes place.

Materials:

▪ **Sand trays:** Blue plastic trays with 12- to 16-inch diameters are preferred. Each tray should be two-thirds filled with sand. The number of trays depends on the number of students in a group (six to eight students).

▪ **Miniatures:** Diversity of presentation (e.g., race, age, gender, accessibility, cultural, occupational items), not quantity, of miniatures is important. The counselor may also consider having more quantities for common items that students may be likely to use (e.g., people, vehicles, trees).

▪ **Table or shelf:** A table or shelf is used to display all miniatures. The decision whether to use a table or shelf depends on the counselor's preference and convenience.

▪ **Water (optional):** Water can be provided for students to form the sand.

Preparation: All miniatures should be displayed and visible to all students. Regardless of using a table or shelf, students should be able to access all miniatures without any assistance from the counselor and without presenting any safety concerns or causing physical injuries. There is no restriction on how to place each miniature; however, miniatures that appear to be in the same category (e.g., people, household, animal, nature, creative, mystical categories) should be grouped and displayed in the same location.

Sand trays should be placed in a circle with at least 2 to 3 feet between trays to prevent distractions, yet provide closeness among students. Sand trays could be placed on the table or floor depending on the room arrangement. Distance between the table or shelf and tray placement should be approximately 6 to 7 feet so it is further away from the circle, yet close enough for students to make necessary trips to obtain more miniatures.

Instructions:

1. Building the Tray. First, the counselor asks all students to select one occupation of special interest and to keep the occupation choice to themselves. Once everybody silently identifies an occupation, the counselor asks students to use the miniatures to create their perceptions of the occupation in the sand tray by saying, *"Please use the miniatures to tell me what you know about the occupation you select. You can walk to the table and take up to 10 miniatures. You can make multiple trips to the table if you can't carry all of your choices at once. It is important that everyone is quiet during this activity. I will sit here quietly when you are setting up your trays. You have 15 minutes to complete your tray, and after that we will go around and share our trays with the group."*

2. Processing the Tray. Once students have completed their trays, the counselor asks students to take turns and share what they have created with the group by saying, *"You have 5 minutes to tell us about the occupation you chose and everything you know about it."* There is no restriction concerning who should share first and sharing should be on a voluntary basis. When a student finishes describing the occupation, the counselor asks the rest of the group, *"Does anyone have anything to add to what [student name] just shared with us?"* or *"Any questions at all?"* This provides an opportunity for students to create an interactive learning environment in which they all learn from each other. The counselor can also introduce new and/or additional factual information about occupations following each student presentation as appropriate in order to further their learning and interaction. For example, *"Tonya said a firefighter helped people out of their houses and office buildings when there was a fire. Jimmy agreed with Tonya and said he once watched his dad, who is a firefighter, doing that. I also know that firefighters help rescue people during tornados and floods too. They usually help rescue people who are in danger or emergency situations."*

3. Writing About the Tray. Lastly, the counselor distributes My Today's Discovery worksheet to students. Students are asked to write down the name of the

occupation that they chose when they created the tray and also the name of the occupation presented by the person who sat to their right. Students have 5 minutes to complete the worksheet. The counselor will collect the worksheets after the end of the activity.

Suggested Modifications (for Special Needs Populations): When working with students who are easily distracted by others, very aggressive, or extremely shy, school counselors may consider reducing the number of group members or conducting this intervention in an individual or triadic format. In addition, it is also important for the counselors to attend to cultural differences among students that may emerge during the activity (e.g., different views, knowledge, and understanding of the same occupation in different socioeconomic status and/or geographical locations).

Evaluation Plan: The goal of this intervention is for the students to learn about occupational information. To evaluate the effectiveness of this intervention, school counselors may utilize multiple assessment methods. First, counselors may conduct an observation during the intervention to assess the extent to which students can verbalize and narrate their knowledge and understanding of the occupations (e.g., only describe a duty versus multiple duties of a sheriff). Second, counselors may also review each student's My Today's Discovery worksheet to assess to what extent they can articulately demonstrate their knowledge and understanding of the occupations in writing.

About Me

Today, I chose to talk about _____

_____.

A _____ does many things,
including:

(1)

(2)

(3)

About a Person Next to Me

I also learned about _____ from a person who sat
next to me.

A _____ does many things, including:

(1)

(2)

(3)

Note:

19 ❈ Creative Interventions in the Personal/Social Domain

CONFLICT GARDEN: USING EXPRESSIVE ARTS TO ADDRESS CONFLICT WITH ADOLESCENTS

Nancy L. A. Forth, Corie Schoeneberg, Atsuko Seto, and Penny Dahlen

Since each student brings his or her own unique qualities and characteristics, it is essential that professional school counselors have an extensive repertoire of techniques to meet their students' needs. Using expressive arts is one intervention that can be used to help clients explore themselves in relation to others (Rubin, 1999), and since adolescents typically think abstractly (Utley & Garza, 2011), the use of the arts creates a more familiar, more accepting, and less threatening counseling environment for this population (Riley, 2003), resulting in an open engagement of self-reflection.

The Conflict Garden is an expressive group-counseling approach in which students, who are struggling in their relationships with their families, create a metaphor for their family of origin in order to gain insight into their current conflict as well as potential resolutions. This metaphor serves as an externalization that allows group members to separate themselves from their problems (Gladding, 2011), and offers a new way to view and experience what may be occurring within the individual as well as the family. During the process portion of the session, group members experience an increased self-awareness, find their own meanings (White & Epston, 1990), and discover new ways to think about what may be happening with those within their personal family system. This activity may also be used as a gateway to exploration of other relational conflicts and patterns that the adolescent may be experiencing outside of his or her family. The Conflict Garden technique is experiential and creative, using objects naturally found in nature, providing an environment that appears to be safer, more playful, and nonjudgmental to students.

Modality: Floral Arrangement

ASCA National Model Domain: Personal/Social

Deliver via: Group counseling (working stage)

Age Level: Middle or high school

Indications: Could be used with small groups focused on exploring family of origin, peer relationships, building support networks, and taking personal responsibility.

Materials: A variety of fresh flowers (in varying stages of development) that differ in size, shape, color, scent, and texture; other objects such as weeds (nontoxic to avoid health problems), leather leaf, small twigs, pebbles, pinecones, sea shells, and small pieces of bark; 12" disposable plastic plates; floral foam (for fresh flowers); floral moss; floral pins; hot glue gun and glue sticks; scissors; and index cards. If there are no safety concerns, scissors are also made available to members during the activity so objects can be cut as needed.

Preparation: Prior to the session, assemble an arrangement foundation for each group member using the following steps:

1. Cut floral foam into a 4"cube.
2. Hot glue floral foam to disposable plastic plate.
3. Soak floral moss in water.
4. Attach pieces of moss to cover floral foam using floral pins.
5. Lay out all flowers and objects on a large table.
6. Write names of each flower/object on index cards and place next to object.

Instructions: It is important to note that prior to this session you should have already discussed confidentiality and other ground rules necessary for the group members to feel safe in the session.

1. Introduce the activity to the members by addressing the importance of understanding oneself within the context of the family.
2. Invite each group member to choose a flower or object that represents him- or herself and place it into the floral foam or on the plate.
3. Follow this with an invitation to students to choose flowers or objects to represent each member of their family of origin and place these items into their arrangements. As each individual perceives *family* differently, members are welcome to identify *family members* based on their own definition. For example, the option of including alternative parental figures (i.e., grandparents, adoptive parents, and relatives) may be considered by some adolescents who have no contact with their biological parents. Additionally, some individuals value their pets and consider them as part of their family. It is important to emphasize that there is no right or wrong way to create the arrangement, and each group member's honesty and openness are encouraged.

Process: After all group members have created their arrangements, invite members to take time to explain what items they chose for themselves and their family members, along with the rationale for their choices. Remaining group members are encouraged to listen to the member who is sharing his or her arrangement. During this process, provide observational comments and probing questions that facilitate further reflection of the member. For example (Figure 19.1), one group member may have a rose representing a younger sister, which is placed next to her parents (two carnations), while placing a pinecone representing herself on the corner of the arrangement, away from the rest of her family. In using an observational comment, you may state, "*I noticed that you placed yourself away from the rest of your family. I wonder how you make sense out of that.*" An example of processing questions may include, "*As you look at you (pinecone) and your sister (rose), what comes to your mind about the roles each of you play in your family?*" or "*How do you see your relationship with your parents and how does it affect you?*" It is crucial to assist while challenging group members to explore meanings associated with their arrangements. Also, bear in mind that while you may ask various questions to encourage the client's creative mind, you should attempt to "interpret" the arrangement for the group member.

After each group member has finished sharing the meanings for his or her arrangement, invite members to express comments as well as personal reflections from this experience. While doing so, it is important to remind the group

FIGURE 19.1 Example of a Conflict Garden arrangement.

not to criticize or judge others' arrangements, but rather share how comments from others contributed to prompting their understanding of their own relationships with others.

At this point in the processing phase, it is important to facilitate possible here-and-now conflicts or relationship patterns that might be occurring within the group. Sometimes conflict that happens outside the group can parallel an existing problem within the group. For example, the group member who placed her pinecone in the corner of her arrangement may be isolated within the group as well. The group can serve as a safe place to provide and receive feedback about one's own patterns and also to begin practicing and experiencing a new way of being. These significant moments in the group that address here-and-now issues provide the soil for growth to occur in self-awareness, conflict resolution, and relationship patterns that occur outside the group as well, including within the group members' families of origin (Melnick & Fall, 2008).

As the final processing question, ask members to share what they plan to do with the arrangement. This allows for further process, as well as serving as an informal assessment of each group member. In using this technique, some group members are known to do various things with their arrangements, such as displaying them in places of prominence, rearranging them in a way that represents the family relationships they would like to have, discarding the arrangement, and/or the entire group working together to create one arrangement.

Considerations: Use of expressive arts in therapy has received increased attention in the counseling field. While professionals embrace various creative interventions, several points need to be taken into consideration. It is important that you be cognizant of clients' backgrounds and are able to modify the structure of an activity in order to maximize the therapeutic impact on each individual. Second, when exploring family-of-origin issues, encourage group members to include extended family members only when these individuals reside with them. Professional school counselors must also consider cultural values practiced by clients (Gladding, 2011). For example, not including extended family members can be culturally insensitive to clients who are from collectivist cultures with emphasis on strong family ties. Therefore, during the screening of clients, counselors should take note of the client's family history, cultural background, age, and current living environment.

When employing the expressive arts in sessions, counselors must allow clients to share their own stories (Gladding, 2011) and interpret their design from their own perspective. Professional school counselors may offer their own wonderings with an attempt to encourage adolescents to engage in deeper self-reflection. However, doing so may increase member defensiveness, threaten his or her ego, or give him or her a reason to withdraw from the session prematurely (Riley, 2003). It is essential that your comments are based on observation or probing of the client's comments instead of the counselor's personal interpretation of the arrangement.

Expressive arts can be a powerful tool to help clients tap into deeper feelings and thoughts. For clients at any age, such process is intense and can be overwhelming, especially when exploring painful life events (Gladding, 2010) that have negatively affected family dynamics. Not only may clients experience strong emotions during the session, but they may also identify different emotions as they observe changes in their floral arrangement. Therefore, you should be sensitive and prepared to facilitate a wide range of emotionally oriented conversations during the group as well as provide the members with concrete tools (i.e., journaling or individual counseling) for processing postsession feelings.

When working with clients who are at high risk for self-harm and/or violent behaviors, counselors may consider not using floral pins to hold the moss, since pins could be used for self-mutilation. For the same reason, caution should be used when allowing the clients to use scissors. Therefore, review clients' behavioral history in order to rule out this likelihood. You will also need to inquire about any allergies to flowers and other objects used for the activity.

Finally, from an ethical standpoint, the American Counseling Association's established Code of Ethics (2005), as well as the American School Counselor Association's Ethical Standards for School Counselors (2010), state that counselors must be aware of and practice only within their professional competency (Standard C.2.a. & C.2.b.; Standard E.1a.). When counselors are not properly trained to process intense emotions provoked through artwork and assess the client's artwork appropriately, ethical concerns pertaining to professional competency and do no harm need to be examined (1998). In addition, Hammond and Gantt (1998) recommend that counselors have the knowledge and skills to document clients' artwork in accordance with the policies of the agency where they are employed. Seeking consultation and supervision from appropriate professionals, as well as receiving additional training pertaining to the subject area, will be beneficial to those who are interested in increasing their competency as well as becoming familiar with guidelines developed by the American Art Therapy Association.

When considering expressive art therapy methods as creative interventions, a few crucial points may be offered. First, many counselors don't believe that they have permission to be creative primarily because traditional counseling training and education focuses more exclusively on talk therapy (Jacobs, 1992). To be creative may mean to be more unconventional, and thus requires courage to incorporate various nontalk-centered techniques to promote a client's growth. Therefore, nurturing one's own creativity may allow the counselor to become more effective in utilizing a variety of arts and other experiential activities in their work with adolescents.

Second, creativity is often explained using an abstract format, and few counseling theories actually explain the use of creativity in a constructive manner (Carson & Becker, 2003). In order to use creative interventions to foster the client's ongoing change process, it is essential to have a clear sense of how its concept is integrated into one's theoretical orientation (Jacob, 1992). Doing so may avoid the danger of using creative activity as a quick fix that appears to be fun and exciting but lacks a therapeutic means in helping clients break through their impasse and gain new insight.

Suggested Modifications (for Special Needs Populations): This intervention could be adapted for an individual counseling session, but the counselor should be aware that goals of the activity must also be adjusted since the benefits of a group setting will be eliminated.

Evaluation Plan: Group members self-report during the processing phase of this intervention. Self-awareness and relational insight generally lead naturally to the client generating his or her own personal goals as an end result. Follow up with group members and provide support regarding the goals generated as a result of this activity.

REFERENCES

American Counseling Association. (2005). *ACA code of ethics and standards of practice.* Alexandria, VA: Author.

American School Counselor Association. (2010). *Ethical standards for school counselors.* Alexandria, VA: Author.

Carson, D. K., & Becker, K. W. (2003). *Creativity in psychotherapy: Reaching new heights with individuals, couples, and families.* Binghamton, NY: Haworth Press.

Gladding, S. T. (2011). *The creative arts in counseling.* (4th ed.). Alexandria, VA: American Counseling Association.

Gladding, S. T., & Wallace, M. D. (2010). The potency and power of counseling stories. *Journal of Creativity in Mental Health, 5*(1), 15–24.

Hammond, L. C., & Gantt, L. (1998). Using art in counseling: Ethical considerations. *Journal of Counseling and Development, 76*(3), 271–276.

Jacobs, E. (1992). *Creative counseling techniques: An illustrated guide.* Odessa, FL: Psychological Assessment Resources.

Melnik, J., & Fall, M. (2008). A Gestalt approach to group supervision. *Counselor Education and Supervision, 48*(1). 48–60.

Riley, S. (2003). Using art therapy to address adolescent depression. In C. A. Malchiodi (Ed.), *Handbook of art therapy* (pp. 220–228). New York, NY: Guilford Press.

Rubin, J. A. (1999). *Art therapy: An introduction.* Philadelphia, PA: Brunner/Mazel.

Utley, A., & Garza, Y. (2011). The therapeutic use of journaling with adolescents. *Journal of Creativity in Mental Health. 6*(1), 29–41.

White, M., & Epston, D. (1990). *Narrative means to therapeutic ends.* New York, NY: W. W. Norton.

A CUP OF COMMUNITY

Kylie P. Dotson-Blake and Allison Crowe

This activity is designed to be utilized in small-group counseling. It facilitates student understanding of how their communities of support influence how well they are able to grow and develop. The counselor should start the discussion by asking the students to reflect on what types of supports help to facilitate their growth and what types of people they have in their community. Students will work together as a group to build a strong community foundation in which to plant small seeds.

Modality: Other—Horticulture

ASCA National Model Domain: Personal/Social

Deliver via: Group counseling

Age Level: Elementary, middle, or high school (Appropriate for use with any age group—modify the processing questions to align with the students' developmental level.)

Indications: Could be used with small groups focused on friendship, building networks of support, taking personal responsibility, or decision making.

Materials: Three small clear glass bowls, a cup of pebbles, a cup of potting soil, a cup of shredded paper, a cup of M&Ms, a few markers, a small amount of water (1/3 cup or so), and seeds (one for each member of the group).

Preparation: Place the three bowls in the center of a table with the cup of M&Ms, the cup of paper, and the cup of potting soil each placed beside one of the bowls. Each student should have one seed and two or three pebbles.

Instructions: Introduce the activity by asking students to consider and discuss how the community we surround ourselves with impacts our growth and development. From this discussion, explain that with this activity the seeds will represent the students and the substrates will represent different types of community choices. Discuss how the community foundation we build can either support or hinder the seeds' and the students' growth. For each type of material, discuss how well it fulfills three characteristics of a strong community: (a) provides a firm foundation for growth, (b) provides challenges to help community members grow strong, and (c) gives community members space to explore paths and interests.

Explore each type of material that is available to choose as a community for the seeds.

Shredded Paper Substrate
1. The school counselor picks up the shredded paper cup and pours it into the first glass bowl, explaining that the first community choice for the seeds is the shredded paper and encouraging the students to discuss the benefits and limitations of the paper for the seeds' growth.
2. Questions to ask to facilitate the discussion of the benefits and limitations posed by the shredded paper substrate for the seeds' growth:
   - *"Let's explore what benefits the shredded paper offers the seeds. For example, it offers a soft place to lay, cushioned and comfortable; protection from the direct sun; and a way to hold water close to the seed for easy access."*

▪ If this is the type of community that the students select for the seeds, ask: *"How will it impact the seeds? In what ways does the paper limit the seeds?"* (Limitations: The paper does not offer a strong footing for the seeds to put down powerful roots. The paper may hold too much water too close to the seeds and cause them to rot. The paper doesn't provide the challenge of growing up through a tighter substrate that gives the plant a strong stem to stand tall, supported by powerful roots. When the plant starts to develop flowers or bear fruit, the plant's roots will not be able to hold the plant upright in the shredded paper.) *"How well does this fulfill the three characteristics of a strong community, which are: (a) provides a firm foundation for growth, (b) provides challenges to help community members grow strong, and (c) gives community members space to explore paths and interests?"*

▪ *"How might a community for each of you be like the paper for the seeds? Sometimes we might be soft and comfortable, with the resources we need close at hand (like the water in the paper), but if we don't face the challenge of reaching out and stretching ourselves to get what we need, we can't develop the strong core and roots that allow us to be our best, most successful selves. In order to bear fruit (or flowers) for our community, we have to build a strong foundation for ourselves."*

M&Ms Substrate

1. The counselor picks up the M&Ms cup and pours it into the second glass bowl, explaining that the second community choice for the seeds is the M&Ms and encouraging the students to discuss the benefits and limitations of the candy for the seeds' growth.

2. Questions to ask to facilitate the discussion:

    ▪ *"Let's explore what the M&Ms offer to our seeds. This substrate is certainly the prettiest and sweetest. In fact, some of you probably want to dive into this community right now. Though the M&Ms are sweet and colorful, what other benefits does this substrate offer to our little seeds? The M&Ms provide the seeds with a larger, denser community to grow through; this community doesn't smother the seeds with resources like the paper did with the water and it does force the seeds to grow up and through, allowing the seeds to develop a strong core and deeper roots than the paper."*

    ▪ *"This community also has limitations though; the main one being that it is not long-lasting. Though the substrate might not melt in your mouth, it will decay over time and the seeds will be left sitting on the bottom of the plastic cup in a soupy, sugary mess. How well do the M&Ms fulfill the three characteristics of a strong community, which are: (a) provides a firm foundation for growth, (b) provides challenges to help community members grow strong, and (c) gives community members space to explore paths and interests?"*

▪ *"As a young citizen, what characteristics of the M&M substrate do you see in some of the community choices you have for yourself? Are there folks who are fun and cool to hang out with, people who expect you to pull your own weight, but in the long run who are not much concerned about your growth or success? Think about the people who are around for the fun, but when the real work gets going might not hang around to help. These folks are like the M&M community—available at the beginning, when things are fun and colorful, but over time this community falls away. If you don't have a strong foundation community built up around you, you may be left with just the soupy sugar."*

Potting Soil Substrate

1. The school counselor picks up the potting soil cup and pours about half of it into the third glass bowl, explaining that the third community choice for the seeds is the soil and encouraging the students to discuss the benefits and limitations of the soil for the seeds' growth.

2. Questions to ask to facilitate the discussion:

   ▪ *"As we initially look at the potting soil, what differences do we notice between it and the paper and the M&Ms?"* (Example responses: It is denser than the paper, it has more fine particles than the M&Ms, and it might have little balls of fertilizer.) *"Let's explore the benefits that this substrate has for our seeds. It provides stability for the roots, and it will hold the water to allow the seeds and plant to access that resource. It is thick/dense enough that the plant will have to work hard to reach the surface, allowing it to develop a strong trunk and providing support for heavy fruit and flowers."*

   ▪ *"Let's explore potential limitations. It is possible to pack the soil so tightly around the seed that the roots have trouble growing and the plant becomes locked and unable to branch out and grow. How well does the soil fulfill the three characteristics of a strong community, which are: (a) provides a firm foundation for growth, (b) provides challenges to help community members grow strong, and (c) gives community members space to explore paths and interests?"*

   ▪ *"As students and young citizens growing in your community, what would be some community characteristics that are similar to the soil?"* (Examples: Supportive and providing a good foundation for putting down roots, but also providing necessary challenges to help you develop a strong core and sense of self to support growth.)

After considering the three community types, allow students to choose the type they feel would be best for supporting the growth of their seeds. Then turn the discussion to the pebbles. Explain that the pebbles are meant to represent the very special people in each student's community. These people can be described as the ones who are always there for the student and who also give the student the space he or she needs to grow. For the small seeds and plants, tell students that the pebbles will serve to create airy spaces in the soil to ensure that the roots do not get compacted. Have each student write the name of any special person he or she would like to include on the pebbles with a marker. Then have the students embed the pebbles in the soil. Ask the students to push them down toward the bottom of the glass dish. A pencil works well for pushing them in if students do not wish to put their hands in the soil. Make sure there is a layer of soil fully covering all of the pebbles. Then ask the students to lay the seeds in the bowl on the soil and cover them with a final layer of soil. Pour a small amount of water across the top of the planted seeds.

Finally, wrap up by using the following processing questions. This is a good time to allow the students to eat the M&Ms, but have wipes available for students to clean their hands if they have placed their hands in the soil:

- ▪ *"Today we discussed community and the differences between building a strong, positive community for oneself and a community that doesn't truly support one's growth. As a person who is actively engaged in building your community, what are three characteristics you think are important for a good community?"*

- ▪ *"As we explored the different materials, we noticed that some materials had qualities that seemed positive at first, for example, the paper held the water close to the seed and the candy was sweet and pretty, but if we got too much of these "positives" they could keep the seeds from growing. Let's think about some of the things in our lives that we like and enjoy, but if we get too much of can keep us from growing our best."*

- ▪ As an extension for middle school and high school students, the reflection questions may focus on the student's impact on the community: Say, *"As we nestled the seeds into their community, one thing we might have noticed was how the seeds became part of the community. They are not separate and isolated from their community. This is true for each of you, too; you are critical parts of your community. What strengths do you bring to your community? How does your growth positively impact your community? When the little seeds sprout and grow, they'll provide flowers that bring beauty to their community—describe what you hope to contribute to your community as you grow."*

Suggested Modifications (for Special Needs Populations): School counselors may need to modify the language used in descriptions of the materials to align congruently with students' developmental levels. This activity is appropriate for use with most student groups and will be particularly helpful with students who respond positively to sensorial materials and activities. Students who have difficulty with fine motor skills may be encouraged to direct a partner or counselor in creating their layers in the cup.

Evaluation Plan: To evaluate the effectiveness of this intervention, you may use the attached survey as a pre- and postassessment.

Students will complete this assessment as a pretest and as a posttest of their understanding of the concepts and materials addressed during the activity.

1. List three characteristics of strong communities:
   (a)
   (b)
   (c)
2. True or False?
   Providing support and encouraging a person to work toward his or her goals helps him or her to grow and be successful.
3. True or False?
   As a community member, you have an impact on your community.
4. List three personal characteristics you have that you believe help to make you a good community member.
   (a)
   (b)
   (c)

THE MANY FEELINGS OF NATURE

Tori Charette and Sandra Logan

The intent of this intervention is to help children express their feelings through photographs that they take of nature. Because it can be difficult to teach children about emotions and feeling words with just books or facial expressions, this activity provides an alternative expression for addressing one's emotions. Students use digital cameras to take pictures of things in the environment that resonate with their identification of a variety of feelings. Students will receive a personalized book of feelings at the conclusion of the activity.

Modality: Photography

ASCA National Model Domain: Personal/Social

Deliver via: Small-group counseling

Age Level: Middle/upper elementary, grades 3 to 6

Indications: This activity would be suitable for any students who are presenting difficulty in identifying and/or managing their emotions.

Materials: Cameras (disposable or electronic), construction paper, markers, glue and a printer, white board (or poster paper, chalkboard, or PowerPoint slide).

Preparation: Prescreen a small group of students who would benefit from working with identifying and handling emotions; have a clear plan of what outdoor locations you will use with the group; provide students with a list of feeling words that they can use to guide their photographic work. These may include: *angry, depressed, excited, upset, frustrated, gleeful, stressed,* or *exhausted.*

Instructions:

1. Begin by inviting students to introduce themselves to the group.
2. Allow students to brainstorm feeling words. Come up with about 12 to 15 different feeling words and write these on a whiteboard or type them on the slide so that they are highly visible for the students during the brainstorming session.
3. After the word brainstorm, explain to students how the activity is going to unfold. Inform them that they will go outside and use cameras to take five pictures of things in nature that remind them of feelings. Let the students know that they may use the words on the board as examples.
4. Establish rules for the students using the photographic equipment. The rules can include, but are not limited to:
   a. All devices must stay in your hands.
   b. You may not switch camera devices with another person.
   c. You are allowed to take a maximum of 15 pictures.
   d. You are only allowed to take pictures of things in nature, not of people or yourself.
5. Pass out cameras or picture-taking devices (iPads, smartphones, etc.). Explain to students how to use the devices.
6. Lead the students to the area that you have decided to use for the group. Show students where they are allowed to go. For instance, from one tree to another tree is the boundary that they must stay within. Review the rules for the photographs.
7. Give students 20 minutes to complete picture-taking activity. Provide supervision.
8. After 20 minutes, collect the cameras and lead the group back to the classroom/office.
9. When students have returned to their seats, process the activity with them. Ask questions such as:

   a. *"What did you enjoy about this activity?"*
   b. *"What did you notice about nature that you hadn't noticed before?"*
   c. *"What was difficult about this activity?"*
   d. *"What did you learn about yourself while we were outside?"*
   e. *"What would you do differently next time?"*

10. In a follow-up session, have pictures printed for students to make a "Feelings of Nature" book. Print all of the pictures on regular 8.5" × 11" paper, leaving space for students to write about each emotion on the paper. Bind

or staple all of each student's pictures together and create a booklet. Allow students 20 minutes during the second group to write about each picture in their booklets.

Suggested Modifications (for Special Needs Populations): Students with physical needs may pair up with another student to take pictures if their fine or gross motor skills do not allow them to use the camera devices. Students with intellectual disabilities, such as reading or developmental disabilities, may be given picture cues of certain emotions to match with nature.

For English for Speakers of Other Languages (ESOL) Populations: Students who are learning English may also be given picture cues to help them identify emotions. Furthermore, the counselor can prepare cards with emotions from the student's native language to use as cues.

Evaluation Plan: To measure effectiveness of the intervention, ask students to identify at least five emotions and represent those emotions with at least five pictures taken in nature. For example: A bright green leaf may represent happiness, a dead tree might represent depression, and a blue stream might represent sadness.

MY DOLLHOUSE

Shannon Halligan

In this activity, students are invited to make a dollhouse that includes everything one needs to feel safe and would enjoy living in.

Modality: Dollhouse sculpture

ASCA National Model Domain: Personal/Social

Deliver via: Individual; small groups may be possible with additional adult assistance

Age Level: Elementary, middle, and high school

Indications: A dollhouse is a symbol that is linked to the self, the home, and feelings about childhood, family, and experiences (Courtney, 2008). This can be an emotional activity, as often memories may arise and the therapist must be prepared to help a client process these feelings and experiences. Creating a dollhouse is an activity that works well with clients who need to be nurtured, increase self-care, and improve self-esteem. It works well with children who have difficulty verbally expressing their emotions and experiences. It also works well with clients who have experienced abuse and trauma, as it allows them to create an imaginary "safe place" to call home. In this activity, art therapy and play therapy are closely linked. A client can be encouraged to "play" with this dollhouse and the people/items inside.

Materials: Shoeboxes (for larger rooms), masking tape, wallpaper books, fabric swatch books, small carpet squares, magazines for images, markers, pencils, paper, glue sticks/glue gun/craft glue, scissors, wood pieces, popsicle sticks, found items, small boxes (for furniture), beads, wire, fabric, recycled items (paper towel tubes, caps, small bottles, foam, yarn, cotton, clothespins [to make people]), and clay (polymer clay, modeling clay, etc.); optional: books or magazines that show samples of dollhouses or use the Internet to search for dollhouses/how to make dollhouse furniture.

Preparation: Collect boxes, found objects, and recyclable items, and have them arranged in boxes so client(s) can choose desired items.

Instructions:
1. Ask the client to choose a shoebox that can be used as one room in the dollhouse. Invite the student to think about the decoration, furniture, items, and/or people that will go inside. Provide paper for the client to draw out the design first, if desired.
2. Invite the student to paint and decorate the walls first, to design the inside and outside of the house, and to cut windows/doors as desired.
3. Allow the student to make furniture and items to be placed inside.
4. Encourage the student to create people using clothespins or cut images of people from magazines.
5. Ask the student to place the items in the house. If needed, glue can be used to hold the items in place.
6. Create additional rooms, following steps 2 through 5, using shoeboxes and recyclables.

Rather than creating a two-dimensional version of a house, a client creates a three-dimensional house, which can enhance his or her understanding of the self, as well as express elements of details otherwise unable to be expressed.

This project is typically a long-term project that takes a number of sessions to be completed. This can be especially helpful with clients who struggle with planning, carrying out the steps necessary for problem solving, and those clients who quickly rush through activities without taking the time to work on details. There are many ways in which a dollhouse could be interpreted. A dollhouse can be representative of the self, so aspects of the client will be revealed in its creation process.

Suggested Modifications (for Special Needs Populations): Simplify the steps for a special needs population. Assist the client through each step with making choices, identifying items to include, and so on. Assist with assembling materials as needed.

Evaluation Plan: Evaluate the effectiveness of the activity through a debriefing discussion with the student addressing the finished product with the client. Ask them questions about their dollhouses; the following are examples of questions that may be asked:

Describe the inside of the house. Describe the outside of the house. How are these the same/different? What rooms are included? Who lives in this house? Are they alone, with family, or with friends? What rooms did they create? How are they decorated? What are the doors like? What are the windows like? What are the color schemes? Are the colors meaningful in some way? What rooms are excluded? Which rooms are eliminated? Are there any hidden parts of the dollhouse? Are there any unusual elements included?

In addition, you may want to consider the following: Did the client participate in the planning and execution process of making the dollhouse? Did the client work quickly or slowly? Did he or she focus on details? Is the client proud of their creation? Does he or she wish to share it with others? Or keep it hidden away?

REFERENCE

Courtney, J. (2008, June). The perfect dollhouse. *Play Therapy Magazine*, 6–7.

PERSONAL PIZZA PARTY

Tamara J. Hinojosa and Suzanne D. Mudge

*T*he purpose of this group activity is to foster reflective or academic discussion, team building, and/or it can be used as a wrap-up/ termination session. This is a multifaceted activity that includes creativity, movement, discussion, and culinary skills, so students are engaged from multiple perspectives. Afterward, to facilitate team building, group members have a meal together and then clean the eating and cooking area together.

Modality: Culinary

ASCA National Model Domain: Academic or Personal/Social

Deliver via: Group counseling

Age Level: Elementary, middle, or high school

Indications: This group activity is designed to help students develop/enhance self-awareness, interpersonal effectiveness, and communication skills.

Indications: Although pizza is a popular food choice, other food options could be used to accommodate different diets, nutritional needs, access to a kitchen, and so on.

Materials: Materials needed include cooking utensils (spatulas, knives, cutting boards, strainers, pans, etc.), kitchen timer, personal-sized premade pizza dough, pizza sauce, a variety of creative and fun ingredients (e.g., apples, pepperoni, jalapeños, bell peppers, olives, sardines, avocado, lemon zest, etc.) for topping the pizzas, and eating utensils (paper plates, forks, and napkins).

Preparation: Have the cooking area set up so that students can immediately begin preparing their pizzas.

Instructions:
1. Unlike traditional group sessions, this group will start in the kitchen/cooking area and group leaders and members will prepare ingredients together while group leaders facilitate team building/reflective discussions (e.g., *"So, how has this school year been? What is it like to know this is the last time we will meet?"*) or discussion about academic skills (e.g., measurements of ingredients, reading recipes, etc.).
2. Group members will be given their own personal premade pizza dough and make their own creative personal pizzas. As they prepare their pizzas, group leaders will facilitate discussion with prompts such as:
   a. *"How did you choose which ingredients to have on your pizza?"*
   b. *"What do your pizza ingredients say about you?"*
   c. *"If you could share your pizza with one person, who would that be and why?"*
3. Once students are ready to bake their pizzas, group leaders oversee the baking of the pizzas and will take precautions to ensure student safety. This may require leaders to place pizzas in ovens, setting timers, and so on.
4. Once pizzas are ready, students and group leaders will eat together and then clean the eating and cooking area together, with a focus on working together as a team to accomplish these tasks.

Suggested Modifications: If working with younger students, students can prepare their pizzas outside of the kitchen (and away from heating source) to decrease risks.

Evaluation Plan: Evaluation is built into this activity because students will eat together, and this is where the group leaders will be able to informally assess progress. At this point, students should be demonstrating a closer group bond. Also, they will then collaborate together to ensure the eating and cooking area gets cleaned and everyone plays an equal role in contributing to this task. If this is used as a termination session, the group leaders should be mindful about how they end the session.

POCKET PILLOWS

Shannon Halligan

In this activity, students create a transitional object that can be used to provide support during difficult transitions that they are experiencing.

Modality: Fabric Sculpture

ASCA National Model Domain: Personal

Deliver via: Classroom guidance

Age Level: K through 12th grade

Indications: Creating a transitional object (an item used to provide psychological comfort, especially in unusual or unique situations) is useful in a wide variety of situations. It can be especially helpful for children who are experiencing change, divorce, foster care/adoption, a new sibling, separation anxiety, nightmares, and so on.

Materials: Fabric, fabric markers, fabric paint, glue gun, cotton, needle/thread, ribbon, and so on.

Preparation: Have fabric choices and materials available at a table. Optional: precut squares to desired size.

Instructions: Provide the student with the following directions orally:
1. *"Choose two different fabrics: one to make into a small square pillow and the other for a pocket for the front of the pillow."*
2. *"Cut fabric to the desired size to make pillow."*
3. *"Use fabric markers and/or fabric paint to design the pillow."*
4. *"Cut a small square that will be used for a pocket on the front of the pillow."*
5. *"Sew together the pillow sides or use a hot glue gun to glue sides together."*
6. *"Glue the pocket on the front of the pillow on three sides, leaving the top side open so that it creates a pocket."*
7. *"Embellish the pillow and pocket with ribbon, buttons, sequins, and so on."*
8. *"Inside the pocket, place a sentimental object such as a photo, or a written item such as a poem, prayer, affirmation, letter, and so on. These items can be changed/rotated depending on the emotional need of the client."*

Suggested Modifications (for Special Needs Populations): Assist clients with assembly of materials as needed. In a special needs population, it is important to consider whether there are sensory needs, and creating a tactile and comforting object such as a pillow can provide a child with an opportunity to soothe, relax, or calm him- or herself. For older children/adolescents: Modify the pocket contents to contain a sentimental item for the client. For adolescents, it may be a poem, song lyrics, a letter, affirmations, and so on.

Evaluation Plan: The pillow is a transitional item that can be used to find comfort during change and a way to feel safe in an uncomfortable or unknown situation. It is important to encourage the child to use this pillow on a daily or ongoing basis as a form of comfort or as a coping tool. It may be important to share with caregivers the significance of this item so that it can be treated with importance for the child's sake.

The process of creating a pillow is multisensory, as it provides a tactile experience as well as a visual one. The final product is important, as it can be used as a coping tool, but the process of creating it can be the most therapeutic part. Processing with the client should not just be reserved for the final product, but during the artistic process.

REMEMBRANCE BEAD BRACELET

Mary G. Mayorga and Katrina Cook

*T*his activity is designed for use in small-group counseling for students experiencing grief or loss. By participating in this activity, group participants will create a bracelet that symbolizes their feelings about the person they are grieving, to keep as a transitional object for as long as they feel the need to have it.

Modality: Visual/Other—Jewelry Making

ASCA National Model Domain: Personal/Social

Deliver via: Group counseling

Age Level: Middle or high school (Appropriate for use with any age group— modify the processing questions to align with the students' developmental level.)

Indications: This activity is specifically designed for students experiencing grief or loss.

Materials: Leather cords and assorted beads large enough to fit on the leather cords, and scissors to cut the cords; select beads of different colors, textures, styles, materials, and so on, so there is a large assortment for the participants to choose from.

Preparation: Place the beads in open containers in the center of the table, where all the students have access to choose the beads they want. Have the leather cord and scissors available to either be cut by the leader (for younger children) or by group members (for older children).

Instructions:
1. Inform the participants that they will be able to create a bracelet using beads that symbolically represent the person (or pet) they lost.
2. Show the participants the assortment of beads in the center of the group.
3. Ask students to select beads that they feel may represent in some way the person they lost (e.g., this was her favorite color, choosing the wooden bead because he liked nature, or picking alphabet beads that spell out her name). The participants may choose as many beads as will fit on the bracelet, just a few, or even none if they prefer. Inform the participants that if they have something at home that they would like to add to their bracelets, they may do that as well.

4. After they have placed the beads on the cord, assist the students in cutting the cord to fit their wrists (or ankle if they prefer) with enough room left to tie a knot. Ask students to assist each other in tying their Remembrance Bead Bracelets on each other.

5. After each participant has constructed his or her bracelet, facilitate a discussion with the following questions: *"Explain why you chose those particular beads to represent the person you lost. What would you like us to know about this person? What was this activity like for you?"*

Suggested Modifications (for Special Needs Populations): Some students may not be developmentally able to grasp the concept of symbolically using beads to represent what a person meant to them. Have some alphabet beads available so students can use them to spell out the name of the person they lost.

Evaluation Plan: Informal observation of the activity occurs through the discussion the leader facilitates after the students complete their bracelets. The completed bracelets also serve as a part of the evaluation.

RESOLVING CONFLICT IN THE SAND

Charles E. Myers

School counselors can use this activity in dyadic or small-group conflict resolution. The activity provides a unique means to facilitate conflict resolution using the symbolism of miniatures in a co-contracted world. School counselors may start by asking students to consider their conflict and relationship, and what they may need to feel better about each other again.

Modality: Other—Sand Tray

ASCA National Model Domain: Personal/Social

Deliver via: Dyad or small group (two to four students)

Age Level: Late elementary, middle, or high school (Appropriate for use with any age group—modify the processing questions to align with the students' developmental level.)

Indications: This activity is useful in conflict resolution and relationship development, as well as an assessment of relationship dynamics. The use of sand tray and the symbolism students imbue to the miniatures provides them therapeutic distancing and allows them to talk about their concerns and feelings more easily.

Materials: Sand tray (ideally 20" wide, 30" long, and 3" deep, with inside bottom and walls painted a medium blue that can be used to represent water or sky); dustless sand to fill the tray about two-thirds deep; and a diverse collection of miniatures in prescribed categories (Homeyer & Sweeney, 2011; Myers, 2010).

Preparation: Set up on a table that is waist high, facilitating use of the sand tray from both a sitting and standing position. Display miniatures in categories to facilitate student selection.

Instructions:

1. Invite the students to become acquainted with the sand, *"Place your hands in the sand, notice how it feels, how it moves and responds to your touch."* Ask the students to share their sensations and observations; for example, *"How does the sand feel?"* and *"What do you notice about the sand?"* This process grounds the students and accustoms them to the medium.

2. Next, invite the students to *"Think about the conflict between you and your friend(s). Consider how you feel about what is going on."*

3. Say to the students, *"Now, keeping in mind the conflict and your relationship, select as few or as many miniatures as you like, and create a world (a picture) together without talking."*

4. As the students create their world together, the school counselor observes both the creation process and the nonverbal communications that reflect the relationship dynamics.

5. Once the students complete their sand tray, invite them to take in their creation, *"Take a few more moments in silence and look at what you created; walk around it and take it in from different angles."*

6. Invite the students to share, *"When you look at the world you created together, what do you notice? How do you feel?"*

7. Facilitate processing of the *product* (sand tray), starting from a global perspective, *"Tell me about your world,"* then focusing on specific areas of the tray. For example, the school counselor may ask, *"Tell me more about this circle of people,"* *"What is occurring in this section of the tray?"* or, *"If this _____ (miniature) could speak to this _____ (another miniature), what would it say? Or need?"*

8. Facilitate the processing of the *process* (school counselors' observations of the students in creating the sand tray) to help the students become more aware of their interactions and what they are communicating, moving from a global observation to more specific interactions. Questions/prompts may include: *"What was it like to create a world together without talking?"* *"I noticed that as you were building your world, the two of you avoided each other initially than began to build together";* *"What was it like when Toni placed the large alligator near your circle of kids?"* and *"How do you think she felt?"*

9. After exploring the students' conflict and relationship, as portrayed in the sand tray and in their nonverbal communications, move to conflict resolution using the symbolism of the tray.

10. Examples of conflict resolution using the sand trays are as follows. *"How was it for the dead tree in the corner when the birds all laughed at him?"* *"It sounds like the lion is angry because he feels hurt after the gorilla told the other animals her secret."* *"What does the boat need to stay afloat?"*

> *"How can the Batman help the alien remove all the road signs and barriers around it?"*

11. Close the counseling session by helping the students create goals.
12. Take a digital photo of the sand world that can be shared with the students and/or used in the future to remind students of their goals.

Suggested Modifications (for Special Needs Populations): School counselors need to keep in mind students' developmental level in the complexity of the language and level of processing they use and in the number of miniatures they provide. Younger students may need more concrete language and to be lead in the processing. Additionally, younger students may be overwhelmed with a large selection of miniatures; if necessary, reduce the number of miniatures available.

Evaluation Plan: To evaluate the effectiveness of this intervention, school counselors may ask students about their feelings regarding their conflict and relationship after the session, as compared to before. Additionally, school counselors could have the students develop and sign a conflict-resolution agreement.

REFERENCES

Homeyer, L. E., & Sweeney, D. S. (2011) *Sandtray: A practical manual* (2nd ed.). New York, NY: Routledge.

Myers, C. E. (2010). Discovering solutions in the sand. In S. Degges-White & N. L. Davis (Eds.), *Integrating the expressive arts into counseling practice: Theory-based interventions* (pp. 41–42). New York, NY: Springer Publishing Company.

Appendix

INTERVENTION CHART WITH SUGGESTED APPLICATIONS

INDICATIONS	MODALITY	TITLE	PAGE
Abuse/Trauma	Visual	My Dollhouse	309
	Visual	Creative Expression of Healing	60
	Visual, Writing	The Remembrance Tree	115
Academic-Related Concerns	Drama	Doing Something Different	265
	Movement/Dance	Being Atlas: Carrying the Weight of the World	190
	Music	Lyrics and My Life	153
	Music, Movement/Dance	Cakewalk Hip Hop: Dance Your Way to Academic Success	175
	Visual	Creating a Vision (Board) With Your Students	13
	Visual	Four Directions	15
	Visual	The Myth of the Phoenix	104
	Visual	Totem Activity	22
	Visual	Your True North: The Life You Learn From and the Life You Live	55
	Writing	Color-Coded Elements	215
	Writing	Imagining a Future Me	217
	Writing	My (Gritty) Collage	221
	Writing	The Playbook	222
Addiction	Visual	Culture Shock	62
Anger	Music, Movement/Dance	Pop Goes the Feeling	202
	Visual	Reflecting in Color	114
	Visual	Anger Switch	59
	Writing	Personalized Stress Ball	246
Anxiety	Drama	Albert Ellis's ABCs the Drama Way	259
	Music, Movement/Dance	Pop Goes the Feeling	202

(continued)

(continued)

(continued)

INDICATIONS	MODALITY	TITLE	PAGE
	Narrative	Elvis Blindfold Maze	273
	Narrative	The Collaborative Story	236
	Visual	Feeling Frustrated and Sad	80
	Visual	Freeze Frame	82
	Visual	The Many Feelings of Nature	307
	Visual	Reflecting in Color	114
	Visual	Self-Expression: Letting Your Worries Go	122
	Visual, Movement	Emotional Obstacle Course	192
Flexibility	Movement/Dance	Balloon Walk	187
Goal Setting	Visual	Imaginative Mind Mapping	20
	Visual	Creating a Vision (Board) With Your Students	13
	Visual	Success, Stones, Solutions	127
	Writing	The Playbook	222
Grief/Loss	Other (Jewelry)	Remembrance Bead Bracelet	314
	Visual	Friends and Family	84
	Visual	Creative Expression of Healing	60
	Visual Arts, Music	The Music of My Life	166
	Visual, Writing	Memory Making	100
	Visual, Writing	The Weight That I Carry	144
	Visual, Writing	The Remembrance Tree	115
	Writing	Expressing Grief Through Poetry Writing For Spanish-Speaking Students	237
Ice Breaker	Drama	I See Your True Colors	274
	Visual	I'm the School Counselor. What Do I Do?	36
	Visual	Mandalas and Mindfulness: Identifying the Real Me	96
Identity Issues	Visual	Recycled Reflections: A Visual Journal Project	112
	Visual	Self-Discovery Through Nature	120
	Writing	"I Love Being Me": Be the Author of Your Own Story	243
	Writing	Who Am I?	254
Interpersonal Relationships	Drama	Doing Something Different	265
	Drama	Imagine Yourself as a House	276
	Drama	My Superhero Strength	280
	Imaginary Play	Sand Tray for Special Needs Groups	287
	Movement/Dance	Scrambled Feelings	204
	Movement/Dance	Balloon Walk	187
	Movement/Dance	Strike a Pose: Expressing Emotions Through Body Postures	210
	Movement/Dance	The Banana Split	188

(continued)

(continued)

INDICATIONS	MODALITY	TITLE	PAGE
	Narrative	The Collaborative Story	236
	Visual	Can You Feel Your Personality?	232
	Visual	Our Multicultural Stars and Selves	106
	Visual	I Have "Two Eyes, a Nose, and a Mouth"	91
	Visual	Mandalas and Mindfulness: Identifying the Real Me	96
Physical Aggression	Music, Movement/ Dance	Pop Goes the Feeling	202
Problem Solving	Music	Musical Questions	169
Responsibility	Other (Experiential Counseling)	Stepping Stones	206
	Other (Horticulture)	A Cup of Community	302
	Visual	Conflict Garden: Using Expressive Arts to Address Conflict With Adolescents	297
	Writing	The Playbook	222
Self-Esteem	Drama	Imagine Yourself as a House	276
	Movement/Dance	Strike a Pose: Expressing Emotions Through Body Postures	210
	Other (Experiential Counseling)	Stepping Stones	206
	Visual	Puzzled	110
	Visual	What's in Your Locker?	148
	Visual	Culture Shock	62
	Visual	My Dollhouse	309
	Visual	Self-Discovery Through Nature	120
	Visual	Mandalas and Mindfulness: Identifying the Real Me	96
	Visual, Writing	The Weight That I Carry	144
	Writing	Imagining a Future Me	217
	Writing	Strengths Scrabble	248
	Writing	Who Am I?	254
Self-Exploration	Bibliotherapy	"I Love Being Me": Be the Author of Your Own Story	243
	Drama	Imagine Yourself as a House	276
	Movement/Dance	Balloon Walk	187
	Movement/Dance	Being Atlas: Carrying the Weight of the World	190
	Other (Culinary)	Personal Pizza Party	311
	Visual	Heroes: Identity and Adaptability in the World of Work	32
	Visual	If Animals Went to School: Making Connections	92
	Visual	Mandalas and Mindfulness: Identifying the Real Me	96
	Visual	Multimedia Timeline Life Map	164
	Visual	Progressive Paintings	109

(continued)